JOINING THE MISSION

Joining the Mission

A Guide for (Mainly) New College Faculty

Susan VanZanten

WILLIAM B. EERDMANS PUBLISHING COMPANY

GRAND RAPIDS, MICHIGAN / CAMBRIDGE, U.K.

© 2011 Susan VanZanten

Published 2011 by
Wm. B. Eerdmans Publishing Co.
2140 Oak Industrial Drive N.E., Grand Rapids, Michigan 49505 /
P.O. Box 163, Cambridge CB3 9PU U.K.

Printed in the United States of America

17 16 15 14 13 12 11   7 6 5 4 3 2 1

Library of Congress Cataloging-in-Publication Data

VanZanten, Susan, 1955-
Joining the mission: a guide for (mainly) new college faculty / Susan VanZanten.
p.   cm.
Includes index.
ISBN 978-0-8028-6263-1 (pbk.: alk. paper)
1. Christian universities and colleges — United States — Faculty.
2. Universities and colleges — United States — Religion.
3. College teaching — United States. 4. Education, Higher —
Aims and objectives — United States.   I. Title.

LC383.V36   2011

378′.071 — dc22

2010043282

www.eerdmans.com

Contents

Preface: The Beginning of a Vocation

This book is a guide for people who are moving into academic life as college professors, whether they are coming directly from graduate school or transitioning from a professional career. More specifically, it is directed toward those who are joining the faculty of one of the nine hundred religiously affiliated colleges or universities in the United States, which collectively enroll about 1.5 million students annually. Even more particularly, it is intended to assist new faculty members at "mission-driven" institutions — those schools that understand a religious connection as a significant component of their identity and practices. As we will see, such institutions define and perform their missions in a variety of ways, and individual faculty members can also participate in and contribute to that mission in diverse ways. This book will focus on those institutions that identify themselves with the Christian religious tradition — the largest category of religiously affiliated schools in North America — although some of its ideas may be applicable to other religiously affiliated institutions.

Like any profession, the academy has its own shaping history, distinctive culture, and quirky social practices. Furthermore, it is not monolithic; it has numerous subcultures, ranging from the Carnegie-classified Research Institution (familiarly known as the "R1") to the two-year community college, from the traditional Ivy League bastions of Harvard and Yale to the brash upstart for-profit institutions like the University of Phoenix and ITT Technical Institute. The huge differences among such institutions are matters that are seldom discussed in graduate education, which always prepares one to be a scholar but seldom prepares one to be a college professor, with the full range of responsibilities entailed by that position.

The shortcomings of American graduate education have been an increasing object of concern during the past two decades, giving rise to, among other initiatives, the national Preparing Future Faculty (PFF) program, which operated from 1993 to 2003 with support from The Pew Charitable Trusts, the National Science Foundation, and The Atlantic Philanthropies. The PFF program was intended to transform the way future faculty were prepared by providing graduate students "with opportunities to observe and experience faculty responsibilities at a variety of academic institutions with varying missions, diverse student bodies, and different expectations for faculty."[1] More than 45 doctoral institutions began PFF programs during this decade, working with nearly three hundred partner institutions. During the final years of the program, PFF joined forces with several professional organizations, such as the American Chemical Society, the National Communication Association, and the American Psychological Association, to concentrate on educating future faculty about pedagogical issues. To the extent that more attention is paid to the role of teaching in a faculty member's life, the PFF had a limited success, but even that focus narrowed to disciplinary concerns. For the most part, graduate schools today are still turning out candidates for the Research University of 1962 rather than for the Reality University of 2012.

Graduate education concentrates on the detailed assumptions, theories, and practices of a specialized academic discipline. During our graduate apprenticeship, we learn much about how to be a sociologist or literary scholar or biologist; some of us may be introduced to the art and science of teaching; and a few may even learn about the history and philosophical premises of our discipline. But during twenty years of working with new faculty across the country, I have met few who in their graduate studies learned about the history and philosophy of higher education, much less the specific role played by the mission-driven college or university. Commencing a career at such an institution, either directly from graduate school or after working as a business executive, nurse, consultant, elementary/secondary educator, or engineer, new faculty often feel as though they've been caught up by a tornado and rudely dumped in the brilliant but confusing world of Oz. This book attempts to provide an orientation to this new world both by providing fundamental information about aspects of academic life and by discussing the special demands of a mission-driven institution.

1. "Preparing Future Faculty," http://www.preparing-faculty.org/.

Learning about the broad contours of mission-driven institutions as well as exploring the particular geography of your own school will assist you in the important process of vocational discernment. In today's educational parlance, *vocation* often refers to a trade or occupation; "vocational training" prepares one to be an auto mechanic or a hair stylist. However, in the Christian tradition, *vocation* signifies something more than just a job. The Latin root, *vocare,* means "to call"; in the European medieval period, certain practices such as entering the priesthood or joining a religious order were deemed "vocations," or holy callings from God. During the Reformation, Luther and Calvin expanded the notion of vocation. Luther held that all Christians share a common "Vocation" to love and serve others, but that they carry it out through a variety of specific "vocations" that could range from being a missionary, to milking cows, to teaching grammar to recalcitrant college students. (The only occupations that the ever-irascible Luther ruled out were usury, prostitution, and being a monk.) Although some Catholics still understand vocation as referring soiely to a calling to the priesthood or a religious order, Vatican II endorsed a wider sense of vocation as including lay people participating in the creative work of God through a variety of efforts. In the fullest Christian sense of the word, a vocation includes occupation (as a college professor), but it also involves civic responsibilities, family life, church participation, leisure practices, and consumer habits.

Although American popular culture sometimes celebrates vocation as an individualistic impetus to live a moral, self-fulfilling life, a Christian understanding of vocation includes two key components: the transcendent and the community. Presbyterian pastor and novelist Frederick Buechner writes, "The place God calls you to is the place where your deep gladness and the world's deep hunger meet."[2] Vocational discernment involves identifying one's passions and abilities, but also distinguishing the needs of the world. The paramount goal is not self-fulfillment but service to one's neighbors as a way of participating "in the ongoing creative and redemptive activity of the Triune God," as one of my colleagues likes to describe the divine economy.[3] To receive a call means *someone* is calling; what I am to do in response to that call provides me with purpose; and this call and response occur within and are guided by community.

2. Frederick Buechner, *Wishful Thinking: A Seeker's ABC* (San Francisco: Harper, 1993), p. 95.

3. Doug Koskela, associate professor of Theology, Seattle Pacific University.

During your first years in an academic setting, your colleagues and administrators will be closely examining whether you "fit in," but it is important that you, too, consider whether an institution is the right fit for your abilities, gifts, and passions. This entails learning about the realities, expectations, structures, goals, and values of the community which you are joining. A vocationally attuned professor will strive to serve the institutional mission rather than be driven by professional standing, status, and salary. As you learn about the identity and commitments of the institution you are joining, you should ask yourself, "Do I believe in the mission? Can I enthusiastically participate in this identity and claim it as my own with integrity? Can I passionately embrace these commitments and dedicate myself to pursuing the college's goals? As I join the mission, what contributions can I make? How do the opportunities offered by the institutional context match up with my own vocational gifts and call? Can my strengths be put to use in my new academic home? How can I help my school to strengthen or improve its mission?" Establishing a Catholic institution of higher education, John Henry Newman stated in 1858, involved "arduous, pleasant, and hopeful toil."[4] You have embarked on a similar task, and I hope that this book will provide support for that difficult, enjoyable, and promising effort.

In the course of discussing academic life at mission-driven institutions, I will employ examples from my experiences, drawing on what I have learned little by little over my years as a college professor at mission-driven institutions. Like Henry David Thoreau, "I should not talk so much about myself if there were any body else whom I knew as well. Unfortunately, I am confined to this theme by the narrowness of my experience."[5] I will also give examples from the lives of some of the faculty with whom I have worked, changing names and identifying details. For simplicity's sake, this book will use *college* and *university* interchangeably to refer to any institution offering post-secondary education, whether undergraduate or graduate.[6]

Arthur Holmes, professor of philosophy at Wheaton College for many years, was fond of telling a story about a group of medieval craftsmen en-

4. John Henry Newman, *The Idea of a University*, ed. Martin J. Svaglic (Notre Dame: University of Notre Dame Press, 1982), p. 469.

5. Henry David Thoreau, *Walden and Resistance to Civil Government*, ed. William Rossi, 2d ed. (New York: Norton, 1992), p. 1.

6. In Chapter 7 I will consider why these terms have become virtually identical in American higher education today.

gaged in the decades-long, backbreaking job of constructing a colossal Gothic cathedral. Some were working on the soaring flying buttresses; others were piecing together a delicate, stained-glass rose window. The more menial laborers were putting up an unadorned but functional masonry wall. One day the bishop strolled around the construction site to visit with the laborers. "What are you doing?" he asked one workman. "I'm laying bricks," the man responded curtly. "And you?" the bishop asked a second laborer. "I'm building a wall," he said, leveling the mortar. The bishop turned to a third man who held a brick in his hand: "What are you doing?" "Your grace," the man responded with pride, "I'm building a great cathedral to the glory of God!"

As professors, we could understand our job as the teaching of statistics, or grammar, or genetic theory. Or we could view ourselves as helping to advance the field of statistics, or grammar, or genetic theory through our researching, writing, and teaching. But a vocational understanding of the task of the professor involves understanding our place in a larger endeavor, comprehending the ways in which our work in statistics, grammar, or genetic theory forms an integral part of the big picture, the cathedral of our institution's mission.

CHAPTER 1

What Is a Mission-Driven Institution?

In these days of public accountability and assessment, most institutions of higher education (along with businesses and nonprofit agencies) have an organizational mission statement articulating their reasons for existence and primary objectives. Regional accrediting bodies evaluate an institution's success in light of the degree to which it achieves the objectives established in this mission statement. Therefore, if an institution's goal is to provide a two-year general education that will allow its graduates to transfer into a four-year program, it would not be penalized in the accreditation process for failing to offer a B.A. One of the essential pre-conditions for accreditation by the Northwest Commission on Colleges and Universities, for example, is that "the institution's mission is clearly defined and adopted by its governing board(s)."

Such mission statements serve to establish the educational parameters within which a school will function and acknowledge that in American higher education, there is a range of higher education on offer. The mission statements of R1 institutions tend to concentrate on the production of knowledge, while those of comprehensive universities and liberal arts institutions are liable to be more centered on student learning. While the public probably recognizes the difference between research institutions and teaching institutions, I suspect that few students or faculty members at a major state institution could identify their school's mission statement. How many students at the University of Washington would be able to relate that "The primary mission of the University of Washington is the preservation, advancement, and dissemination of knowledge"? The Web sites of research universities seldom feature their mission; some, such as

1

Yale, even note that because they serve so many different functions, an overall mission would be impossible to define, opting instead for individual college, school, and department mission statements. Smaller private institutions pay more attention to mission. They have meticulously worded mission statements that establish their distinctive identities, unique values, and distinguishing cultures. While students and faculty at research institutions may be blithely unaware of their school's mission, at other kinds of institutions, mission statements are found on banners festooning the quad, engraved on classroom plaques, attached to electronic signatures, and featured in public relations materials. Mission statements may even become the target of student (and faculty) parodies because of their seeming ubiquity. But at mission-driven institutions, a prominent aspect of campus life includes an ongoing conversation about and continued exploration of mission.

Residual rhetoric from a religious past, the word *mission* originated with the denominational colleges of the early days of American higher education. We will consider that history in the next chapter. While all educational institutions have some kind of mission, with differing degrees of specificity, emphasis, and recognition, a "mission-driven institution," as I will define it here, has three characteristics.

First, it is a private institution, which allows it to hire its faculty and staff, define objectives and practices, and create programs and curricula in ways unheard of at public institutions. From one point of view, this may be seen as greater freedom — to talk about faith commitments in the classroom, for example — while from another point of view, this might be seen as restrictive — requiring all faculty to hold a certain theological position. Nonetheless, private institutions are able to define their mission in ways unavailable to public institutions, and this right is recognized in law, by accreditation agencies, and even by the American Association of University Professors.

Second, a mission-driven institution understands its mission as integrally related to religious belief. According to the U.S. Department of Education, nine hundred postsecondary institutions described themselves as "religiously affiliated" in 2005, which includes Baptist, Catholic, Jewish, Lutheran, Mennonite, Mormon, Orthodox, Presbyterian, Reformed, Wesleyan, and Quaker schools, as well as ecumenical, evangelical, and fundamentalist institutions. (See the diagram on p. 4.) Within this group, the strength of religious affiliation varies considerably, from a token historical connection to a strictly defined adherence to a particular religious order, church, or denomination. Mission-driven institutions connect their educational mission to religious beliefs in some way. Their central identity, values, and practices emerge from their religious identity, values, and practices. Consequently, mission-driven schools are committed to providing an education for the whole student — intellectual, emotional, spiritual, and ethical. Their expected graduation outcomes move beyond imparting knowledge and skills to assisting students to develop moral commitments and ethical practices. Such schools may strive to graduate involved citizens, people of good character, or humble servant-leaders, to name just a few of the more common values-related outcomes. This stands in sharp contrast to many contemporary educational institutions that have deliberately given up the idea of trying to form character and instill moral purpose in their graduates. Perhaps the most blunt spokesperson for this point of view is the abrasive Stanley Fish, whose "Tip to Professors: Just Do Your Job," first published in the *New York Times,* railed against the idea that colleges should attempt to develop virtues or "nurture such behavioral traits as good moral character." Fish provocatively asserts,

> I can't speak for every college teacher, but I'm neither trained nor paid to do any of those things, although I am aware of people who are: ministers, therapists, social workers, political activists, gurus, inspirational speakers and diversity consultants. I am trained and paid to do two things . . . : (1) to introduce students to materials they didn't know a whole lot about, and (2) to equip them with the skills that will enable them, first, to analyze and evaluate those materials and, second, to perform independent research, should they choose to do so, after the semester is over. That's it. That's the job.[1]

While many American educational leaders, including Derek Bok, the former president of Harvard and butt of Fish's attack, have lamented the "underachievement" of American colleges,[2] the mission-driven institution continues to hold ambitions other than solely imparting knowledge and intellectual skills.

Finally, the mission-driven institution purposefully keeps its mission

---

1. Stanley Fish, "Tip to Professors: Just Do Your Job," *New York Times,* 22 October 2006; http://fish.blogs.nytimes.com/2006/10/22/tip-to-professors-just-do-your-job/. Fish has elaborated on this position in *Save the World on Your Own Time* (New York: Oxford University Press, 2008).

2. Derek Bok, *Our Underachieving Colleges: A Candid Look at How Much Students Learn and Why They Should Be Learning More* (Princeton: Princeton University Press, 2005).

Profile of U.S. Postsecondary Education

By Bob Andringa, Council for Christian Colleges & Universities

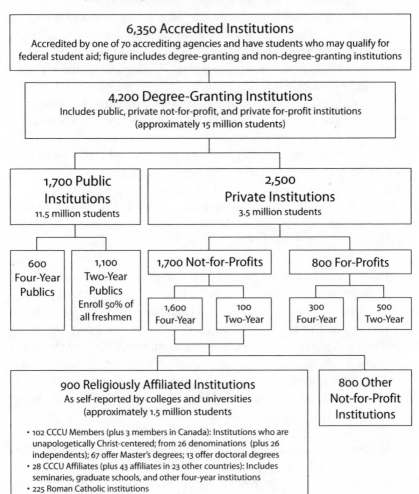

6,350 Accredited Institutions
Accredited by one of 70 accrediting agencies and have students who may qualify for federal student aid; figure includes degree-granting and non-degree-granting institutions

4,200 Degree-Granting Institutions
Includes public, private not-for-profit, and private for-profit institutions
(approximately 15 million students)

1,700 Public Institutions
11.5 million students

2,500 Private Institutions
3.5 million students

600 Four-Year Publics

1,100 Two-Year Publics
Enroll 50% of all freshmen

1,700 Not-for-Profits

800 For-Profits

1,600 Four-Year

100 Two-Year

300 Four-Year

500 Two-Year

900 Religiously Affiliated Institutions
As self-reported by colleges and universities
(approximately 1.5 million students

• 102 CCCU Members (plus 3 members in Canada): Institutions who are unapologetically Christ-centered; from 26 denominations (plus 26 independents); 67 offer Master's degrees; 13 offer doctoral degrees
• 28 CCCU Affiliates (plus 43 affiliates in 23 other countries): Includes seminaries, graduate schools, and other four-year institutions
• 225 Roman Catholic institutions
• 100+ Bible colleges
• 150+ Seminaries
• About 150 other institutions who are more or less intentional about integrating their faith with their mission
• About 150 other institutions who have pretty much neglected their faith tradition

800 Other Not-for-Profit Institutions

Sources: U.S. Department of Education; National Center for Education Statistics; Higher Education General Information Survey (HEGIS), "Fall Enrollments in Institutions of Higher Education" and "Institutional Characteristics" surveys; and "Integrated Postsecondary Education Data Systems (IPEDS)," "Fall Enrollment" and "Institutional Characteristics" surveys.

at the forefront of its efforts: initiating its new members into the mission's importance, exploring innovative and improved ways to implement the mission, and testing and revising the mission to meet new challenges and circumstances. Resisting "missional amnesia,"[3] such colleges and universities do not allow their founding mission to become merely an antique relic occasionally pulled out of a dusty storage closet for high academic ceremonies. Instead, that mission is employed daily as one of the most fundamental educational tools — a hammer or lever. Mission-driven colleges and universities repeatedly rehearse their story in a variety of venues, and they hope that all of their faculty will embrace this story as their own, will enthusiastically join the mission by identifying the particular ways in which they can contribute to its continuance and future.

Types of Mission-Driven Institutions

Mission-driven institutions come in all Carnegie-classified shapes and sizes, including research universities, comprehensive institutions, and liberal-arts colleges. Another key distinction among mission-driven institutions occurs in the way the relationship between a religious tradition and mission is embodied. The most significant way in which this occurs is in faculty-hiring practices. Many institutions require their faculty to embrace a Christian faith commitment and thus include questions of belief or theology along with more typical interview queries into pedagogical philosophy, scholarly goals, and contributions to campus life. Other kinds of mission-driven institutions opt to maintain connections with their religious tradition in ways other than faculty appointments. Institutions with restricted faculty hiring practices engage in additional ways of pursuing their mission, but a school's hiring practices are a central way of distinguishing several common types of institutions.

Schools with restricted hiring practices may either require 100 percent of their faculty to have a particular faith commitment or attempt to hire a "critical mass" of faculty with such a profession. Robert Benne terms these two different models the *orthodox* and the *critical-mass*.[4] What constitutes

---

3. Caroline J. Simon, *Mentoring for Mission: Nurturing New Faculty at Church-Related Colleges* (Grand Rapids: Wm. B. Eerdmans, 2003), p. 13.

4. Robert Benne, *Quality with Soul: How Six Premier Colleges and Universities Keep Faith with Their Religious Traditions* (Grand Rapids: Wm. B. Eerdmans, 2001), pp. 49-50.

a critical mass can vary from school to school, ranging from three-quarters of the faculty, to a bare majority of 50 percent, to a strong minority. Benne considers other practices beyond hiring in developing his typology, such as church support, public rhetoric, required courses, ethos, and governance, but since I am focusing on hiring practices, I will use the terms *100 percent* and *critical mass* to distinguish the two kinds of schools with restrictive hiring practices.

The kinds of faith commitments required at mission-driven schools with restrictive hiring practices also vary. Some schools want either all or a critical mass of their faculty to belong to a specific church, denomination, order, or theological perspective; others require all or most of their faculty to subscribe to a general statement of faith; still others are looking for committed members of any Christian church, whether Catholic or Orthodox or Protestant. I will call these the *exclusive college,* the *evangelical college,* and the *ecumenical college.* Benne calls a mission-driven institution without any religious hiring restrictions *pluralist.* Such colleges and universities deliberately cultivate a plurality of religious positions among their faculty, including non-Christian religions and nonbelief, but faculty typically are asked to agree "to support the mission" in some kind of fashion, whatever their own religious convictions might be. Such institutions may opt to maintain their missional identity by means of particular campus organizations or programs rather than through hiring. They might have a Vice President for Mission whose responsibility is to uphold the tradition and contributions of the founding religious body both programmatically as well as rhetorically, or a mission-related center that runs curricular or co-curricular programs. Institutions with either a critical mass or a pluralist hiring policy may require their students to take a certain number of religious or theological courses so that they learn about Lutheran liturgy, or Jesuit theology, or Mennonite missions. Chapel, spiritual formation programs, community service requirements, and residence hall rules are additional areas that may embody and reflect a college's mission.

The idea of exercising any kind of restriction on faculty hiring immediately raises red flags for some people. Of course, all colleges or universities have some kind of restrictions on whom they hire: particular graduate degrees, areas of specialization, teaching skills, scholarly promise, and so on — these rule out some candidates and advance others. However, we tend to think of these kinds of requirements as "qualifications," the kinds of preparation, skills, abilities, and interests necessary for performing one's job well. We also recognize that those qualifications that prepare someone to be a writer-in-residence in an MFA program, however, are going to be quite different from those possessed by a strong candidate for a molecular genetics position at an R1. Because the demands of the positions differ, so do the qualifications. Similarly, working as a faculty member at a mission-driven institution involves a different set of demands and expectations. We wouldn't think twice about the educational goals of an institution prompting it to hire all or a critical mass of Ph.D.s. So why does the idea of wanting to hire all or a critical mass of, say, Baptists cause us to pause?

Each type of mission-driven institution envisions its educational goals in slightly different ways, and each model has its strengths and weaknesses. The 100 percent exclusive college is able to form a closely knit community in which the common embrace of beliefs and values provides a narrative and vocabulary that can pervade campus life. There's a unity, coherence, and community possible in such an institution unthinkable in the pluralist college. Such an institution is in a strong position to support a "living tradition," one in which a religious heritage continues to be embraced and honored even while undergoing changes and refinements due to the intellectual work of the college. It can draw on and develop the unique strengths of that heritage across a whole variety of academic disciplines. Joining such a mission can be like moving into a friendly small town, pledging a convivial sorority or fraternity, or finding the hospitable church of your dreams. Small towns and sororities can have their downsides, though, and the longing for unity can have repressive aspects. Traditions are liable to stiffen, wither, and petrify without room for criticism or change. Too much consensus can lead to group thinking and stultify creativity and openness to new perspectives. All of these pitfalls are serious problems for any organization but especially so for educational institutions, which are committed to the search for truth and the critical assessment of ideas.

Strengths and weaknesses are reversed at the pluralist college. The variety of perspectives at such an institution can generate productive dialogue and disagreement, opening up innovative ways of understanding, prompting fresh interpretations. But the extent of the differences can also potentially produce a cacophony of sounds without any clear melody. What happens in one classroom or course may have little to do with what happens in another venue; students and faculty alike may find themselves talking past each other without a common story, history, or vocabulary to ground them. Faculty will have a wide latitude of ways in which they can engage with and provide general support for the mission, but that freedom may bring with it a high degree of uncertainty. How much support of the mission is enough? Does such missional adherence need to appear in a certain realm of faculty work, such as in one's teaching, one's scholarship, or one's advising? To what extent are faculty required or expected to participate in particular mission-related extra-curricular events?

In the critical mass colleges, another difficulty arises with the potential formation of an in-group and an out-group: those faculty who personally embrace the religious identity and those faculty who merely tolerate it. The rifts between the two can grow large, with feelings of marginalization occurring on either side. The issue of religious identity can create one more division in a culture that is already prone to division, whether by disciplines ("The business school is always treated better than the philosophy department"), tenure and rank ("She's only an assistant professor — what right does she have to voice an opinion on this curricular issue?"), or academic position ("His ideas are suspect because he's an administrator, and we know they are always trying to undermine the faculty"). Faculty outside the institutional religious tradition may feel marginalized ("They always give the best teaching assignments to the Catholics!"), but those faculty who identify with that religious tradition may feel exploited ("Why do I have to serve on almost every campus committee — just because I'm a Methodist?").

Communities of Mission-Driven Institutions

Mission-driven schools have joined common cause in several different kinds of associations. Perhaps the most widespread is the banding together of schools that share a theological or denominational heritage, such as the Association of Jesuit Colleges and Universities, the Association of Presbyterian Colleges and Universities, and the Lutheran Educational Conference of North America. Two other significant bodies to which your institution might belong are the Lilly National Network of Church-Related Colleges and Universities (LNN) and the Council for Christian Colleges and Universities (CCCU). Both sponsor a variety of faculty and student programs designed to support mission-driven institutions.

The Lilly National Network of Church-Related Colleges and Universities was founded in 1991 to address "issues of common interest to institutions in church-related higher education" and "to strengthen the religious nature of church-related institutions through a variety of activities and publications."[5] The ninety-one members represent a diversity of denominational traditions and institutional types, including Roman Catholic, Southern Baptist, United Methodist, Presbyterian, Church of God, and Lutheran. Lilly Network institutions fall into all three of our categories: critical mass, pluralist, and 100 percent. LNN does not require its member institutions to have a restricted faculty hiring practice. The network's activities include workshops for administrators, regional and national conferences, mentoring programs, summer faculty seminars, and two book award programs. A new effort as of 2007 is the Lilly Graduate Fellows Program in Humanities and the Arts, which supports and mentors small cohorts of graduate students who are interested in becoming teacher-scholars at mission-driven Protestant and Catholic institutions of higher education. With its focus on the arts and humanities, the LNN does not treat the social sciences, sciences, or professions and so addresses only part of the curriculum and academic structures of any college or university.

Founded in 1976, the CCCU's mission is "to advance the cause of Christ-centered higher education and to help our institutions transform lives by faithfully relating scholarship and service to biblical faith." In 2010, the CCCU had 184 members or affiliate institutions in 24 different countries. To become a full member of the CCCU, a school must be an accredited, four-year comprehensive institution with curricula rooted in the arts and sciences. It also must have an institutional mission statement that is "Christ-centered and rooted in the historical Christian faith," require all of its faculty members to be professing Christians, and have curricular and extra-curricular programs that "reflect the integration of scholarship, biblical faith, and service."[6] Within those common parameters, however, we find three different types of institutions: (1) the denominationally bound schools, such as Calvin College, which require their faculty to be members of a certain denomination or theological tradition *(exclusive)*, (2) the traditionally evangelical colleges, such as Wheaton and Westmont *(evangelical)*, and (3) the more ecumenical institutions, such as Seattle Pacific or North Park, which hire faculty representing a wide diversity of the Christian family, ranging from Greek Orthodox to Roman Catholic, Lutheran to Mennonite, Assemblies of God to nondenominational Bible churches *(ecumenical)*. The CCCU carries out public advocacy on behalf of Christian higher

5. "The Lilly Fellows Program in the Humanities and the Arts," www.lillyfellows.org.
6. "Council for Christian Colleges and Universities Profile," www.cccu.org/about/profile.

9

education, runs twelve student programs in locations such as Washington, D.C., Cairo, and Oxford; and sponsors a variety of faculty development activities including seminars, grants, and conferences. Some institutions — like Calvin, Gordon, and Westmont — are both CCCU and LNN members.

Changing Identities

A further complication in understanding the variety of ways that an institution can be mission-driven arises from the fact that institutional identities shift and evolve. The history of American higher education makes that fact very clear. Although most religious colleges were originally founded by a sponsoring denomination or order which provided the budget, the students, and (typically) a clergy-president or priest-president, only a few institutions today maintain an affiliation in which the school is legally owned by a church or an order, or in which a church or an order controls the majority of positions on the board of trustees. During the past fifteen years, for example, numerous Baptist colleges and universities have severed their legal and financial ties with their state Baptist conventions, while at the same time continuing to embrace a Baptist identity. At many schools, hiring practices have undergone similar changes, moving away from requiring that all faculty share a common confession or theological tradition toward critical mass or pluralism. Some historians see such moves as the first slide down the slippery slope of secularization, but others believe that a school can remain mission-driven without being church-controlled or restricting hiring on religious grounds.

A somewhat surprising development that has emerged during the past ten years in this narrative of change is the story of recovery, in which a college purposefully sets out to reclaim or retrieve its religious heritage and mission, often through instituting changes in faculty hiring and roles. Perhaps the best-known instance is Baylor University, where in 2000 President Robert B. Sloan launched an ambitious and controversial program called Baylor 2012, with the goal of moving Baylor into the "top tier of American universities while reaffirming and deepening its distinctive Christian mission."[7] There have been several similar initiatives at other church-related

7. "Baylor 2012," http://www.baylor.edu/vision/index.php?id=312. For an account of the controversy, see *The Baylor Project: Taking Christian Higher Education to the Next Level*, ed. Barry G. Hankins and Donald D. Schmeltekopf (South Bend, Ind.: St. Augustine's Press, 2007).

institutions, including renewed conversations about what it means to be a Catholic college or university. But when the story line of an institution begins unfolding in a new direction — whether toward a weaker religious affiliation or toward a stronger religious identity — additional strains can appear. Faculty hired under the old dispensation face off against faculty hired under the new. Some may have signed up to pursue one mission only to discover that the institution now has reconceived or re-articulated its mission in one way or another.

As you move into a new institution, it is important to learn about the history of the institution and its current trajectory in terms of mission-based hiring and job performance. Where, in this complex tapestry of mission-driven institutions, does your school locate itself? Is faculty hiring driven by the mission? What kind of formal ties to a founding denomination, order, or church remain? Must all or some of the members of the board of trustees belong to that founding group? Does part of the institution's budget come from a religious body? Are professors expected, or welcomed, or encouraged, or required to draw on the religious tradition in their teaching and scholarship? One aspect of vocational discernment involves more fully understanding the ways in which your university is mission-driven before examining what it means for you, personally, to join that mission. In thinking through these issues, you should recognize that at most institutions, there is not one strictly defined way in which a faculty member is expected to support the school's mission; rather, there is a diversity of ways in which one can play a part. Mission-driven institutions, as part of the body of Christ, esteem the hands and the eyes, the ears and the feet, the history professor and the business professor, the dynamic personality and the quiet mentor. One's vocation as a professor at a mission-driven institution can follow many different narratives. While there are many common responsibilities and tasks, your unique gifts and history allow you to make a distinctive contribution to your institution's mission. By considering the various shapes that professorial responsibilities can take at a mission-driven institution, you will be able to do a better job of deciding whether you are called to join the mission and how you might do so.

CHAPTER 2

A Very Brief History of Western Higher Education

Walk onto any college campus in North America or Europe, and you will probably enter a green world of lawns, flowers, trees, fountains, and courtyards at the heart of the campus. Often laid out in four straight lines with accompanying walkways and affectionately referred to as "the quad," the physical center of most colleges resembles nothing so much as a garden. (My own university has a garden-like "loop" in the lower campus and a more formal garden square — which, ironically, is a geometric circle — at the heart of the upper campus.) Robert Harrison writes, "Institutions of higher learning . . . have a long history of association with the garden, be it the parks and groves of the famous Greek schools, the Roman villa, the bowers of Sainte-Genevieve in medieval Paris, the Italian garden academies of the Renaissance, the British 'college garden,' or the idyll of the traditional American campus."[1] With the arrival of spring, many a professor is subjected to a choral plea to "hold class outside" on the sunlit grass rather than in a stuffy room. My spring-term American literature students habitually argue that it is at least an aesthetic if not an intellectual crime to talk about Thoreau's *Walden* within the white walls and fetid fluorescents of a classroom. The verdant expanses of college campuses inspire games of Frisbee, discussions of Freud, and arguments over Feuerbach, not to mention the odd juxtaposition of bikinis and computers, sunscreen and academic tomes.

The associations between the academy and the garden go back to the

---

1. Robert Pogue Harrison, *Gardens: An Essay on the Human Condition* (Chicago: University of Chicago Press, 2008), p. 60.

ancient Greeks and entail more than just an accidental matter of setting, as we will see. Cultivation and growth are essential parts of both. In order to understand your new academic garden, a short history of higher education may be helpful. Our origins affect where we are, establish the issues that underlie contemporary debates, and provide models to draw on for potential change. Until fairly recently, the history of higher education in the West generally and in the United States in particular has primarily been a story of Christian higher education. Faith-informed education is not a historical anomaly; rather, it is the norm. The echo of medieval cloister gardens reverberates within today's ivy-covered walls in more ways than one.

This chapter considers the broad story of Western higher education, with attention to ideas that contribute to our current practices. Many of today's debates about a university's identity and mission, as well as about what and how we should teach — content and pedagogy — are longstanding issues in the academy. This chapter will explain the origins of some common terms and introduce some influential thinkers in the philosophy of higher education. As a survey, it is inherently simplistic and unrealistically tidy, but its broad brush strokes are designed to prepare the canvas on which you can paint your own portrait of a faithful teacher-scholar.

Classical Education; or, It's All Greek to Me

Our story begins with the ancient Greeks, for the debates among toga-clad philosophers of fifth-century Athens established concerns that have been recurrent issues in higher education ever since. Greek education was premised on the state's need for good citizens, and its primary objective was character education for civic virtue. Both citizenship and thus education were available only to free-born males. "Liberal" (*eleutheros*) means "free," so "liberal education" originally meant "education for free-born men." The Athenians, however, disagreed over the most effective way to produce virtuous citizens and political leaders, with the two primary schools of thought made up of "the orators" and "the philosophers."[2] We might also call them "the pragmatists" and "the idealists."

The orators, or pragmatists, contended that the basic goal of educa-

2. Bruce A. Kimball, *Orators and Philosophers: A History of the Idea of Liberal Education* (New York: Teachers College Press, 1990).

tion was to pass on traditional beliefs and to convince others by means of skillful rhetoric. With the rise of democracy in the aftermath of the Persian Wars, Athenian society was transformed as the right of citizenship was opened to former outsiders, such as naval men and wealthy tradesmen.[3] These newcomers needed to learn how to act as citizens, so traveling scholars called *sophists* ("wise men") provided such training in short, intensive courses. The sophists' goals were practical: they prepared their students to win debates and influence public policy by teaching them how to use written and oral language clearly, eloquently, and persuasively. The sophists focused on winning arguments, endorsing "the triumph of rhetoric over reason, of skill in debate over truth."[4] Good citizens, the orators held, were produced by learning oratorical techniques.

The opposing school of philosophers, which included Socrates, Plato, and Aristotle, held that the basic goal of education was "to improve the soul." Such soul formation eventually would lead to the exercise of civic virtue and was accomplished through the pursuit of truth. Socrates argued that the way to find truth, and hence virtue, was through speculative reason and dialectic — inductive conversations that came to be known as the Socratic method. The philosophers feared that the sophists were neglecting the more important goal of moral virtue by emphasizing oratorical skill; after all, one could be a powerful orator but a moral failure, possess competency without character. Socrates' most famous student, Plato, founded the Athens Academy to prepare aristocrats for their role as political leaders. While Socrates had conducted his educational discourses in the Agora — the public marketplace and civic center — Plato established his school outside the city walls in an enclosed garden grove sacred to the hero Academos, the origin of both the word *academic* and the tradition of a garden setting. Plato believed that knowledge precedes action, that one must *know* what virtue is before one can *choose* to act virtuously. Improving the soul took time and discipline; a good character could not be produced simply in a brief oratorical course. Education at the Academy was based on close teacher-student relationships that involved extended conversations over time. In the *Phaedrus,* Plato articulates an educational philosophy that links gardening and pedagogy: "To the degree that life animates them both, soil and soul both lend themselves to cultivation, or to the gardener's

---

3. Edward J. Power, *A Legacy of Learning: A History of Western Education* (Albany: State University of New York Press, 1991), p. 19.

4. Power, *A Legacy of Learning,* p. 23.

caretaking activity. The soul is not only like soil, in other words, it is itself a kind of soil — call it an organic-spiritual substance — in which the teacher, like the gardener, can sow his most valuable seeds and nurture their growth to full maturity."[5] The virtuous citizen can thus be formed only in a face-to-face, interactive endeavor: "To write on the soul of a living person is altogether different from writing on papyrus. Genuine teaching does the former and is more like an act of planting than of inscribing."[6]

Aristotle studied at the Academy for twenty years before opening the Lyceum, another Athenian school. Discarding the more abstract dialectical method, Aristotle endorsed scientific empiricism as the best route to truth. Instruction at the Lyceum took place by means of lectures,[7] and Aristotle's students practiced close observation of nature, persons, and institutions. When information had been compiled, they used deductive reasoning to reach conclusions. While Plato was an idealist, believing in the existence of universal truths that could be discerned through dialectic, logical reasoning and critical thinking, Aristotle pursued truth through concrete particulars, which would then point to the ideal world. Moral virtue, Aristotle held, would develop from force of habit as well as direct instruction.

Perhaps the most influential Athenian educator, however, is the less-familiar Isocrates, sometimes identified as a philosopher and other times called an orator. Isocrates believed that men (not women) were naturally inclined to be virtuous and that education's primary function was to cultivate that natural virtue through teaching practical knowledge and cultural values. Practical knowledge would provide the information and skills (such as oratory and composition) that were necessary to be a good citizen. The transmission of cultural values took place through close reading of Greek literature. But moral formation was beyond the purview of the teacher: "Boys who come to school without virtue leave the same way, and nothing that teachers do matters. But naturally virtuous boys might become effective teachers and superior political leaders if learning cultivates their virtue."[8]

In the debates between the orators and the philosophers, as well as the different approaches of Plato, Aristotle, and Isocrates, we find the origins of many current educational issues: Should education transmit cultural

---

5. Plato, quoted in Harrison, *Gardens,* pp. 63-64.
6. Harrison, *Gardens,* pp. 61-62.
7. Power, *A Legacy of Learning,* p. 45.
8. Power, *A Legacy of Learning,* p. 39.

norms or encourage one to question? Form moral character or practical abilities? Seek mastery or truth? Proceed inductively or deductively? Rely on discussion or lecture or observation? Take place face-to-face or online? However, with the rise of the Macedonian Empire under Alexander the Great in the fourth century B.C.E., Isocrates' educational model of cultural transmission proved the most influential. Alexander, who had been tutored for seven years by Aristotle, believed that Greek culture represented the highest civilized norm and set about Hellenizing his vast empire by introducing Greek thought, art, music, and literature into the newly conquered territories. Although Greek city-states had been defeated politically, Greek culture triumphed. The Empire relied on a strong centralized political system, so education in the many dispersed urban centers was directed not toward training citizens but rather toward producing cultured people. Even the study of rhetoric and oratory became less concerned with practical persuasion and more focused on elegance, verbal flourishes, and learned allusions. One became cultured — absorbing the ideals of the Greeks — by studying classical literature, but since Greek was a second language for most imperial subjects, schooling began to focus on language study and grammar. Hellenic education included some geometry, arithmetic, music, and astronomy, but the scientific curriculum was secondary to the study of literature. Former schools of rhetoric and philosophy were incorporated in Antioch, Athens, Alexandria, Beirut, Constantinople, Delphi, and Rhodes, and for the first time called *universities.*

One of the jewels in Alexander's crown was the city of Alexandria, which he founded in the Nile delta in 332 B.C.E., named after himself, and established as a center of Greek learning. With the largest library in the ancient world, a "museum" in which to conduct scientific study, and extensive botanical and zoological gardens, Alexandria became the intellectual center of the world in the centuries immediately before and after Christ, for when Rome conquered and expanded Alexander's empire, the cultural force of Hellenism continued. Alexandrian scholarship emphasized an Aristotelian empirical approach to both literature and science. The library's vast collection — some estimates are that it held 700,000 manuscripts by the first century B.C.E. — prompted numerous translations, compilations, and commentaries, including the Septuagint translation of the Old Testament. The University of Alexandria also was the site of the development of many early scientific theories, such as those of Archimedes, Euclid, and Ptolemy.

This was the intellectual world into which Christianity emerged. As the new faith spread through the Roman Empire, questions about the appropriateness of an education based upon pagan Greek writers arose. "What has Athens to do with Jerusalem?" famously inquired the church father Tertullian in 203, ruling that Christians could not teach at Hellenic schools but could attend them, since students would be free to disagree with pagan ideas. But when the church began founding its own schools, it began to incorporate Greek learning. Arthur Holmes suggests that "Christianity's engagement in higher education began in third-century Alexandria,"[9] at this point more of an intellectual center than either Athens or Jerusalem, when Origen added studies in mathematics, astronomy, grammar, literature, rhetoric, and Greek philosophy to the Alexandrian catechetical school. Origen argued that since God created human reason and established natural law, pre-Christians like the Greeks were able to discover truth that could serve the church. For example, it was the duty of the Bishop of Alexandria to consult with the Alexandrian astronomers — the best in the world — to determine the correct date for Easter.

Origen was the first church father to employ what soon became a popular analogy, referring to "the spoils of the Egyptians." When the Israelites fled Egypt in the Exodus, they took the gold and jewels of their wealthy oppressors with them. Later, these riches were put to new use in constructing the tabernacle. In a similar way, Origin argued, when Christians are liberated from paganism through salvation, they can use the riches of Greek learning in the service of God. Other church fathers were more wary of the pagan classic texts, with St. Jerome advising a pragmatic approach: Christians should use these works to learn the basic rules governing good speaking and writing (rhetoric) but should ignore their content. They could gain skill but not virtue from a classical education.

One hundred years after Origen's death, Augustine of Hippo was born in A.D. 354 in North Africa. He received a typical Roman education, which had become strongly influenced by the school of the orators, focusing on the effective use of formal rhetoric, with little attention given to moral formation. Although he became a skillful rhetorician, Augustine began to read widely, searching restlessly for something that he never fully grasped until he began studying the Scriptures and became a Christian. Augustine's subsequent writings on theological and educational issues laid significant foundations for Christian learning. Drawing heavily on Plato, Au-

9. Arthur F. Holmes, *Building the Christian Academy* (Grand Rapids: Wm. B. Eerdmans, 2001), p. 8.

gustine argued that education should move beyond the useful to embrace the ideal, for what human beings most deeply desire to know is God. For the Romans, the goal of learning was practical wisdom, but for Augustine, the goal of learning was the wisdom of God. He believed that education should form better Christians rather than better citizens.

Education begins with faith and then proceeds to understanding, or, as Augustine wrote, *Crede, ut intelligas* ("Believe in order that you may understand"). We first believe in a God with attributes of truth, goodness, beauty, and order; we then study God's creation (which reflects God's nature) to gain knowledge. That knowledge leads to an expanded faith, a richer comprehension of God's reality, even though that reality will never be totally grasped by limited humanity. Our study of creation ultimately helps us to know God better. The final result is doxological: "Liberal learning leads to the contemplation of God, and, for Augustine and the medievals who followed his lead, it elicited an ongoing commentary of prayer and praise. . . . The liberal arts develop the mind's ability to see nature's laws and so to enjoy its order and beauty."[10]

The Monastery Schools;
or, Thanks to the Irish for Saving Civilization!

Augustine died during the death throes of the Roman Empire in 430. From the Sack of Rome in 410 to the rule of the last Western emperor in 476, the light of learning dimmed as libraries were looted, books were burned, and Roman order was destroyed under the barbarian onslaught. As chaos swept the European continent, educational systems collapsed, the great continental libraries were sacked, and few manuscript copyists survived. At some point during these Dark Ages, the Great Library at Alexandria was destroyed, and much of Aristotle's writings lost. But, as Thomas Cahill recounts in his gripping *How the Irish Saved Civilization,* "As Rome went from peace to chaos, Ireland went from chaos to peace."[11] After the British-born Roman Patricius (St. Patrick) evangelized Ireland in the fifth century, the flourishing Irish monasteries "enshrined literacy as their central religious act."[12] Irish monks spent hours copying and decorating

---

10. Holmes, *Building the Christian Academy,* pp. 26-27.

11. Thomas Cahill, *How the Irish Saved Civilization* (New York: Anchor, 1996), p. 122.

12. Cahill, *How the Irish Saved Civilization,* p. 163.

parchment manuscripts, preserving much of classical literature in the process. Beginning in the sixth century, Irish monks journeyed to ravaged Europe to establish monasteries and bring the fruits of their literary labor to the now benighted continent. "Wherever they went the Irish brought with them their books," Cahill writes, "many unseen in Europe for centuries and tied to their waists as signs of triumph, just as Irish heroes had once tied to their waists their enemies' heads."[13]

A handful of catechetical and monastery schools were the sole remaining educational institutions. The studies they offered came to be known as *the seven liberal arts,* a phrase coined by Cassiodorus, a former Roman senator and Christian who had been educated in a classical Hellenic school. In 550 Cassiodorus founded a monastery school devoted to the teaching of Christian doctrine and the liberal arts. Although the Greeks had never specifically identified seven liberal arts, Cassiodorus named and divided the seven liberal arts into two areas: the Trivium — grammar, rhetoric, and dialectic — and the Quadrivium — arithmetic, geometry, astronomy, and music. In a move typical of medieval symbolism, he suggested that these seven areas of study were the seven pillars of wisdom mentioned in Proverbs 9:1 and the seven lamps of the Hebrew tabernacle.

With the ascension of Charlemagne in 800, learning found a new champion. Charlemagne ordered each diocese and monastery to open a school. The monastery schools prepared monks for the contemplative life, but the cathedral schools trained men for the active life of priests, church administrators, and civil servants. Both institutions emphasized moral formation through the study of the liberal arts. Monastic education relied heavily on symbolic reasoning, using biblical symbolism to explain natural phenomena: "Using a tree as a symbol of the cross and of God's purposes in salvation history was much more important than trying to understand what a tree was, naturally speaking, and how it thrived."[14] Monastery education, with the assistance of the Irish Christians, had saved the classical educational legacy.

---

13. Cahill, *How the Irish Saved Civilization,* p. 196.

14. Norman Klassen and Jens Zimmermann, *The Passionate Intellect: Incarnational Humanism and the Future of University Education* (Grand Rapids: Baker, 2006), p. 48.

The Dawn of the Universities;
or, The Medieval Recovery of Logic

What we now call the university first appeared in Europe during the eleventh century in England, France, and Germany. The growing wealth and population of Europe, the classical learning preserved in the monasteries, and the re-introduction of Aristotelian writings saved by Islamic scholars but lost in the collapse of Rome contributed to this development. Institutions to educate the leaders required by the expanding commercial order both grew out of monastery schools and were established by secular authorities. The university colleges were modeled after monastic orders, but also were influenced by the medieval guild system of masters and apprentices, with the establishment of faculties and students. Most offered studies in four faculties: a preparatory course in arts, and advanced specialized study in law, medicine, and — the anointed queen of the sciences — theology.[15] The faculty rather than the church governed these universities, and degrees were awarded for the first time. By 1500, there were seventy-nine universities in Europe.[16]

The medieval European university stressed meticulous analysis rather than symbolic interpretation and affirmed the role of reason in supporting religion and faith. This religious and philosophical tradition became known as *scholasticism*. The most significant Christian educator in this period was Thomas Aquinas, who advocated for the central role of logic based upon study of the recently recovered work of Aristotle. The previous focus on the Trivium, with detailed exposition of classical texts and the writings of the church fathers, began to fade in favor of the empirical studies of the Quadrivium. Holmes explains,

> Dialectic (later to be known as the "old logic") had been a helpful tool for analyzing and interpreting texts, but Aristotle's "new logic" of the syllogism made it possible to demonstrate the truth or falsity of propositions. Knowing the truth was even more important to Aquinas than simply understanding a text. . . . Education, according to Aquinas, should develop the God-given capacity to know what is true and good.[17]

15. Francesco Cordasco, *A Brief History of Education* (Totowa, N.J.: Littlefield, Adams, 1967), p. 32.

16. William Boyd and Edmund J. King, *The History of Western Education*, 12th ed. (Lanham, Md.: Barnes & Noble, 1995), p. 129.

17. Holmes, *Building the Christian Academy*, p. 50.

Aquinas believed that God created humanity with innate capacities for observation and logical thinking that, together with natural revelation, allowed them to know many things. While natural revelation can prove the existence of God (Aquinas provided five rational proofs for God's existence), specific Christian doctrines such as the Trinity or the Incarnation are revealed only in the special revelation of the Scripture and in the person of Jesus Christ. The scholastic universities "emphasized the intrinsic value of God's creation and human nature. Things were interesting in their own right, not merely as signposts for a narrowly theological interpretation of reality. Christians realized that reason and the ability to understand nature were gifts from God that deserved to be explored and celebrated."[18] Rigorous systematization, logical thought, and empirical observation replaced medieval mysticism and symbolism, paving the way for the rise of modern science. At the same time, however, the universities paid less attention to grammar, rhetoric, and literary studies in order to emphasize logical propositions and classification schemas, well suited for the study of law, medicine, and theology.

Renaissance and Reformation; or, The Revival of Classical Letters

While any major historical period is indebted to a confluence of events, the Western renaissance of the fifteenth and sixteenth centuries is especially beholden. The rising power of the French and British monarchies and the declining power of the papacy were accompanied by the economic expansion stemming from exploration and colonization, all orchestrated by the new merchant class. Gutenberg's magnificent invention of 1450 completely transformed learning and literacy, giving rise to the forces that led to the Protestant Reformation. Intellectuals and university professors rejected medieval scholasticism as arid and irrelevant, advocating a "rebirth" of the classical approach.

The language and literature of ancient Greece and Rome formed the primary area of renaissance study. With the goal of developing exemplary human beings, such education became known as *humanism*. "The word *humanist* either implied or confirmed the meaning of a teacher of the good, human, and liberal arts. What the Greeks had called 'paideia,' these

18. Klassen and Zimmermann, *The Passionate Intellect*, p. 49.

teachers called 'humanities.'"[19] Classical works of literature, philosophy, and history provided models of the good life that could be imitated. Humanism's "main goal was self-knowledge and character formation through the reading of edifying texts from the past."[20] Literary humanism embraced the study of rhetoric and style and paid new attention to the subjective world of the emotions. The scholastic emphasis on formal logic, which had grown mechanical and rote, gave way to a new enthusiasm for "the power of rhetoric in extolling virtue and of poetry in charming the emotions. Eloquent wisdom — rather than the logical training with which scholasticism prepared students for theology or law — was again the focus of education."[21] Studying the classical texts was also seen as being more valuable in an expanding age. While today we may think of the sciences rather than the humanities as being more pragmatically useful, during the renaissance an education in rhetoric, languages, and law laid a surer path to social and economic success. Furthermore, studying Greek and Latin, along with other ancient languages and literature, was more useful for the study of Scripture, unlike scholastic logic.

Renaissance humanism was primarily a Christian movement with the goal of developing Christian character and virtue. Its leading figure was the Dutch scholar Erasmus, who believed, along with Augustine and Aquinas, that God in his providence had given pagan authors great insight into truth. At this point, humanistic education and religious education were one and the same thing; there was not yet any such thing as "secular humanism." Erasmus believed that the study of classical languages and literature would cultivate moral virtue and a Christian character, not because knowledge necessarily leads to virtue but rather because doing challenging intellectual work, reading carefully, taking detailed notes, analyzing texts, and so on was a moral discipline and thus formed virtue.[22] As a Christian humanist, Erasmus also advocated that the Bible should be presented in the common language of the people.

Biblical access for the laity was a crucial part of the Reformation movements of the sixteenth century led by Luther and Calvin. Martin Luther had received a scholastic education at the University of Erfurt, but his revolt against the Roman Catholic Church included an assault on scholas-

19. Power, *A Legacy of Learning*, p. 159.
20. Klassen and Zimmermann, *The Passionate Intellect*, p. 69.
21. Holmes, *Building the Christian Academy*, p. 57.
22. Power, *A Legacy of Learning*, pp. 179-80.

tic philosophy: God's existence, for Luther, was a matter of faith, not reason. Luther valued the study of Latin and Greek not so students could read ancient classical literature, which he considered heathenish, but rather because such linguistic abilities facilitated studying the Scriptures.[23] He was thus neither a scholastic nor a humanist. Luther held that reason was useful for earthly affairs such as commerce and politics, rather than for apprehending transcendental truth. A man fond of paradoxes, Luther argued that the Christian simultaneously lives in two kingdoms — the world of nature and the world of God — and participates in both. Rather than transforming the secular world into the kingdom of God, Christian education should bring both into conversation with each other. This two-kingdom theology resulted in a division between faith and learning, which were seen as complementary in nature.

The other great Reformer, John Calvin, was more of a humanist. Calvin was educated at the University of Paris, studying Aristotelian logic and science like Luther, but he later embraced classical learning while studying law at Orleans and Bruges. The Academy that he founded in Geneva in 1559 emphasized classical languages and rhetoric, for as he writes in *The Institutes,*

> We cannot read the writings of the ancients on these subjects [politics, philosophy, science, rhetoric, medicine, mathematics] without great admiration. We marvel at them because we are compelled to recognize how pre-eminent they are. But shall we count anything praiseworthy or noble without recognizing at the same time that it comes from God? Let us be ashamed of such ingratitude, into which not even the pagan poets fell, for they confessed that the gods had invented philosophy, laws, and all useful arts. Those men whom Scripture calls "natural men" were, indeed, sharp and penetrating in their investigation of inferior things. Let us, accordingly, learn by their example how many gifts the Lord left to human nature even after it was despoiled of its true good.[24]

Theologically, Calvin's endorsement of humanism came from his view of God's sovereignty, the rule of Christ over all of creation, and the presence

---

23. Frederick Eby, *Early Protestant Educators: The Educational Writings of Martin Luther, John Calvin, and Other Leaders of Protestant Thought* (New York: AMS Press, 1931), pp. 19-20.

24. John Calvin, *Institutes of the Christian Religion,* Library of Christian Classics, vols. 20-21, ed. John T. McNeill, trans. Ford Lewis Battles (Philadelphia: Westminster Press, 1960), II, ii, 15, pp. 274-75.

of common grace. He argued that God created human beings with reason and the capacity to learn. Like Augustine, Calvin emphasized the unity of truth, learning as an act of praise, and the need for learning to begin with Christian commitment. The primary goal of higher education, Calvin argued with reference to the new understanding of vocation articulated by all the Reformers, was not knowledge (like the medieval scholasticism) nor cultured character (like humanism) but rather to train people to serve God in every area of the world, to equip them to take action to transform human culture and society. Yet because human reason has been affected by sin and the Fall, intellectual processes are fallible.

By the middle of the sixteenth century, the Reformation spirit had spread to the Catholic Church with the establishment of new religious societies "whose main endeavor, unlike the medieval monastic establishments, was the direct involvement in practical affairs, principally education."[25] The Society of Jesus, founded by Ignatius of Loyola in 1540, was the primary instrument of counter reformation through education. The Jesuits tried to hold on to the best elements of medieval education while, at the same time, employing the new literary humanism. They founded numerous universities whose curriculum was rooted in the study of Latin and Greek, and then added the humanities, philosophy, and theology — with a heavy dose of Aquinas. These institutions paid less attention to science and mathematics. Much like St. Jerome, the Jesuit study of the classics emphasized their use for developing the art of composition.[26] Jesuit institutions held high academic standards and enforced rigorous study habits, banking on "superior educational training as an effective religious weapon against Protestantism."[27]

The great humanistic ideals of the Renaissance and Reformation thus led to a newly awakened interest in classical art and literature. But studying ancient texts as a means of forming Christian character was only "a nominal reality" by the end of the sixteenth century. An education in the humanities soon came to mean learning Greek and Latin grammar (hence "grammar schools") through rote drills and repetition, as well as developing an elegant rhetorical style in speech and composition. Much of humanistic education became narrow and lifeless, just like scholasticism before it.[28]

---

25. Cordasco, *A Brief History of Education*, p. 55.
26. Power, *A Legacy of Learning*, p. 193.
27. Cordasco, *A Brief History of Education*, p. 57.
28. Cordasco, *A Brief History of Education*, p. 44.

The Rise of Modern Science; or, Just the Facts, Ma'am

While European education continued to be informed by humanism in the seventeenth century, new forces emerged that led to a significant educational revolution. Francis Bacon led the charge with *The Advancement of Learning* (1605), criticizing classical education's lack of attention to science, and *Novum Organum* (1620), which proposed a new empirical methodology. The scholastics never experimented with the stuff of nature; they merely studied Aristotle's observations. The humanists, on the other hand, often seemed more interested in words than facts, rhetorical elegance than useful knowledge, style over substance. Bacon argued that the way to discover truth was not through studying the classics but rather through an empirical process of gathering data through observing, performing an analysis, and reaching a conclusion. The modern scientific method stems from Bacon's notion of objective observation, followed by secondary confirmation or replication of results, and his optimism that knowledge will lead to progress became the hallmark of modern Enlightenment thought.[29] Knowledge, Bacon famously claimed, is power.

Bacon's motivation and presuppositions were thoroughly Christian. He believed that God's orderly design of creation made the study of science possible, and that human beings needed to use human reason to study that creation in order to help others. "The medievals could be content to contemplate," Holmes writes, "but for a Reformed believer like Bacon contemplation brought a call to work. His view of work as a creation mandate undergirded his vision of science 'for the glory of the Creator and the relief of man's estate.'"[30] Identifying fixed natural laws through observation and inductive reasoning would allow humanity to identify universal truths and to reform natural processes to promote human flourishing. For example, when we learn through empirical observation how germs cause illnesses, we can develop ways to control their spread and mute their destruction. In emphasizing usefulness, Bacon echoes the pragmatism of the orators, although the discipline extolled as the most useful is now the sciences rather than the arts of rhetoric. Grounded in scientific empiricism, education became concerned with the discovery and compilation of facts rather than the formation of character or the transmission of the past. Furthermore, Bacon insisted that "the book of God's works" and "the

---

29. Klassen and Zimmermann, *The Passionate Intellect*, p. 76.
30. Holmes, *Building the Christian Academy*, p. 73.

book of God's word" be studied separately: "Faith and learning could not therefore be integrated as they had been in the medieval university. The unity of truth (truths of revelation and truths of reason) no longer promised an integrated worldview; thanks to God's gift of reason and the order of his creation, science could do perfectly well alone. Religion was not relevant in doing science as such, but only in addressing conditions which make it possible and the ends to which it is devoted."[31]

While Bacon based the foundations of objective truth on empirical observation and experience, another major Enlightenment thinker, René Descartes (1596-1650), turned to the power of the mind to discover truth. Descartes was aware that the senses could be deceptive, but he believed that the one indisputable reality was "I am thinking." Therefore, all human knowledge, learning, and education rest on the foundation of human rationality. Norman Klassen and Jens Zimmermann point out that "In his quest for certainty, Descartes made emotions, language, and external reality separate from thought. Reason was now defined as thought without connection to the world of the senses."[32] In his devotion to the power of reason and the value of objectivity, Descartes was attempting to find a way through the violent chaos that had once again erupted on the European continent. Language and textual interpretation provided complex, ambiguous, subjective roads to truth, and the bloody aftermath of the Reformation in the Thirty Years' War suggested the danger in having such diverging paths. When faith resulted in such radically different perspectives, with Catholics and Protestants slaughtering each other, European princes battling the Holy Roman Empire, Puritans hanging Quakers, and Calvinists burning Anabaptists, it was clearly time for a more rational, objective approach. The rise of national identities also played a central role in these struggles, which were not solely motivated by religion; nonetheless, the new objectivity was intended to heal the social fragmentation and quell the violence that subjectivity seemed to have spawned.[33] If humans acted more rationally, they would become more virtuous.

For generations, educators had assumed that the study of the classics would impart both knowledge and moral character, but Bacon's empiricism contended that we learn best through observation and experience,

31. Holmes, *Building the Christian Academy,* p. 76.

32. Klassen and Zimmermann, *The Passionate Intellect,* p. 78.

33. Stephen Toulmin, *Cosmopolis: The Hidden Agenda of Modernity* (New York: Free Press, 1990), p. 70.

and Cartesian foundationalism promised to produce greater human virtue. The rise of modern science and scientific rationalism thus introduced a new way of knowing that affects education to this day. But it also unwittingly reinforced a dualism already implicit in literary humanism's neglect of science, which "implied a split between moral truths found in the study of texts and in the study of nature."[34] That division became even more pronounced with the rise of science. Language and literature were subjective and unreliable; scientific observation and reason were objective and consistent. Consequently, for some Enlightenment thinkers, all shackles of the past needed to be cast off. Civic virtue, moral behavior, genuine humanism, beneficent actions — all could be achieved without the assistance of the church, Scripture, or the Christian tradition. The French Revolution promised much based on these principles.

Enlightenment philosophy and the rising prominence of the New Science, along with the debacle of the Napoleonic Wars, prompted the development of new, state-run university systems with the primary educational objective of citizenship rather than faith. Thomas Albert Howard explains, "In the eyes of many late eighteenth-century intellectuals, universities had come to be regarded as antiquated hold-overs from the Middle Ages, confessionally rigid, pedagogically retrograde, socially useless, and fiercely protective of their ancient corporate privileges."[35] New national systems of higher education were established across the continent, and under the leadership of Friedrich Wilhelm von Humbolt, the University of Berlin was established with a focus on scientific research rather than teaching, as a way to more effectively meet the needs of contemporary society. It soon became the model for all Continental and, eventually, American higher education.[36]

Education Comes to America; or, The Old-Time College

American higher education began as Christian education with the founding of Harvard College in 1636, six years after the Puritans arrived in the New World. Harvard's original mission was to educate future ministers,

34. Klassen and Zimmermann, *The Passionate Intellect*, p. 72.

35. Thomas Albert Howard, *Protestant Theology and the Making of the Modern Germany University* (Oxford: Oxford University Press, 2006), pp. 1-2.

36. Power, *A Legacy of Learning*, p. 208. Howard's book examines the theological path of the emerging modern scholarly ethos, a point that is often overlooked in accounts of the rise of the modern university.

lest the first colonists were to leave "an illiterate ministry to the churches when our present ministers shall lie in the dust."[37] The ardent reforming spirit that the Puritans brought to church and society was also applied to education, as they attempted to create a new kind of college. In this, the Puritans were following in the same steps as their seventeenth-century Continental counterparts. Mark Noll elaborates: "The most ambitious efforts to shape a distinctly Christian worldview came in the Puritans' attempts to restrict or even supersede the philosophy of Aristotle. Not surprisingly, Puritans were never entirely successful in this attempt. Aristotelian structures had guided university instruction in Europe since the thirteenth century and had continued to be the basis for instruction in the Protestant academies and universities, in spite of fulminations by Luther and Calvin against the authority of Aristotle."[38] Although they endorsed the study of the classics, the Puritans questioned the premise of Aristotelian ethics that knowledge would lead to virtue. Against such a rational approach, the Puritans argued that "morality was at bottom volitional and affectional. Behavior arises from, and reflects, the dispositions of the heart — and the state of the heart depends on the free exercise of God's grace."[39] Ethical practice was not merely a matter of intellectual knowledge; the will and emotions also played a significant role, and these fallible human qualities needed spiritual regeneration.

Puritan education, then, was designed to be holistic, including the classical curriculum of grammar, rhetoric, and dialectic (understood as "the distillation of the common grace which God had given the ancients"); scriptural literacy; and a concern for conversion.[40] Only minimal amounts of science and mathematics were taught.[41] The curriculum reflected the mission: New England churches expected their clergy to be able to read the Scriptures in the original Hebrew and Greek, to study theology in Latin, to be conversant with classical literature; and to develop skills in public speaking and reasoning. Daily chapel services and periodic revivals reflected the educational philosophy that "the maine end of [a student's] life

37. William C. Ringenberg, *The Christian College: A History of Protestant Higher Education in America,* 2d ed. (Grand Rapids: Baker, 2006), p. 38.

38. Mark A. Noll, "Introduction: The Christian Colleges and American Intellectual Traditions," *The Christian College: A History of Protestant Higher Education in America,* 2d ed., pp. 5-6.

39. Noll, "Introduction," p. 6.

40. Noll, "Introduction," pp. 8-9.

41. Ringenberg, *The Christian College,* pp. 46-47.

and studies is, *to know God and Jesus Christ which is eternall life* . . . and therefore to lay Christ in the bottome, as the only foundation of all sound knowledge and Learning."[42] With the Puritans, as with Augustine, faith was the basis for understanding.

By 1770, nine colleges had been founded in North America, and with the exception of the University of Pennsylvania, all had strong ties to an established church, whether Congregationalist, Anglican, Presbyterian, Baptist, or Dutch Reformed. All produced ministers, lawyers, and civic leaders and offered a traditional classical education, but to a very small number of students. But in the first half of the nineteenth century, American higher education began expanding exponentially: at the beginning of the century, there were twenty colleges; within a decade there were forty; and by midcentury, two hundred. By way of comparison, during this same period in England, only one new institution was founded.[43] The loosening of state control and good old American competition facilitated the tremendous growth in the number of educational institutions. The new nation needed homegrown educated leaders, and what William Ringenberg calls "the old-time college" prepared these leaders to be good Christian citizens. Fueled by the fervor of the Great Awakening, mushrooming Methodist and Baptist groups founded many colleges, but the growing number of state schools also operated primarily as religious institutions, as George Marsden explains:

> Until the Civil War, the vast majority of American colleges were founded by churches, often with state or community tax support. Since higher education was usually thought of as a religious enterprise as well as a public service, it seemed natural for church and state to work hand in hand, even after the formal disestablishment of the churches. Protestant colleges were not only church colleges but also public institutions. Even the state colleges or universities that were founded after the American Revolution . . . had to assure their constituents that they would care for the religious welfare of their students. Almost all were or became broadly Protestant institutions, replete with required chapel and often with required church attendance on Sunday.[44]

42. Harvard's "Rules and Precepts," quoted in Noll, "Introduction," p. 9.

43. Michael S. Pak, "The Yale Report of 1828: A New Reading and New Implications," *History of Education Quarterly* 48, no. 1 (2008): 36-37.

44. George M. Marsden, "The Soul of the American University: A Historical Overview," in *The Secularization of the Academy*, ed. George M. Marsden and Bradley J. Longfield (New York: Oxford University Press, 1992), p. 11.

This cozy relationship originated from an educational philosophy that, Noll suggests, attempted to combine the best of Enlightenment thought with traditional Christian values. The American political revolution had been premised on Enlightenment ideas of freedom, democracy, and natural rights, embracing egalitarianism and innovation over hierarchy and tradition, a democratic New World of free individuals instead of the Old World of authoritative institutions. Yet the Protestants that made up the vast majority of the newly formed state did not want to endorse the skeptical Enlightenment of a Hume or a Voltaire, abandoning the truthfulness of historic Christianity. Nor did they want to embrace the freedom without limits threatened by the chaos of the French Revolution.

During the initial years of the great American democratic experiment, especially between 1795 and 1820, Americans turned instead to an Enlightenment philosophy descended from Descartes called Scottish Common Sense Realism, which claimed that our innate intuitive sense (aka common sense) grasps the existence of the external world and moral principles. Just as empirical observation reveals the workings of nature, intuition will disclose moral law. For nineteenth-century realists, "intuition" was a rational faculty, not a touchy-feely sentiment. Noll comments, "What the Scottish philosophers and the American educators had done was to restate Christian morality in a scientific form without having to appeal to the special revelation of Scripture or to the authoritative traditions of the church."[45] He explains the significance of the shift: "Puritans had grounded their thinking in special revelation and had worked to turn specific revelation into a framework for all of learning. The educators of the new United States grounded their thinking in the Enlightenment and worked to give special revelation a place within that framework."[46]

By the mid-nineteenth century, American education had become thoroughly permeated by this new way of thinking, as the country basked in what Noll calls "the Christian-Cultural Synthesis." The curriculum combined traditional classical education with the assumptions of Scottish Common Sense Realism. All students followed exactly the same course of study, with few, if any, electives. In 1828 at Yale, for example, students in the first three years focused on Greek, Latin, and mathematics, but also studied some geography, history, science, astronomy, English grammar, and

45. Noll, "Introduction," p. 13.
46. Noll, "Introduction," p. 14.

rhetoric.[47] Instruction was done by means of rote memorization, drills, and recitation in languages and mathematics, as students took information in and spit it back out in a pedagogy of regurgitation. According to the faculty psychology prevalent at the time, reminiscent of Erasmus's theories, such exercises served as mental calisthenics, tuning and training the mind for the rigors of future thought. The study of classical literature was concerned with grammatical and linguistic skills; it was only in the extracurricular literary societies that Homer's ideas of courage and nobility were discussed, or Shakespeare and Milton read. Jon Roberts and James Turner explain the uniformity of the old-time college: "The classical college did not wish to equip one student differently from another. Rather, it intended to discipline each student's mental faculties through the same general studies and to furnish every brain with the same broad smattering of information."[48]

Collegiate life improved in the senior year, when students enrolled in a yearlong capstone course in moral philosophy, usually taught by the college president, who was typically a clergyman. The course "applied Christian principles to a wide variety of practical subjects and also was an apology for Christianity, typically based on Scottish common sense philosophy. It was also preparation for citizenship."[49] The capstone course represented a radical shift in that it engaged students in thought about real-world problems. Students debated a variety of issues. Is a lie ever justifiable? Should the United States change its immigration policies? Can wars be beneficial? What are the social impacts of the (then-popular) phenomena of singing schools?[50] The subject matter of moral philosophy courses ranged widely, including economics, law, government, history, politics, animal rights, ethics, psychology, aesthetics, and fine arts — most of which were later to evolve into distinct disciplines. There was also a heavy dose of theology and apologetics. The topical relevance and the often dynamic disputes among professors and students made the capstone course a popular change from the first three years of study and also served to provide a transition from training in "mental discipline" to the thorny work of actually maneuvering through a particular issue. Students were encouraged to debate, question, and think.

47. Frederick Rudolph, *Curriculum: A History of the American Undergraduate Course of Study since 1936* (San Francisco: Jossey-Bass, 1977), pp. 65-66.
48. Jon H. Roberts and James Turner, *The Sacred and the Secular University* (Princeton: Princeton University Press, 2000), p. 84.
49. Marsden, "The Soul of the American University," p. 14.
50. Rudolph, *Curriculum*, pp. 91-92.

The primary goal of the moral philosophy capstone was to place knowledge within the framework of the Christian worldview and thus to provide unity and coherence to the college curriculum. Douglas Sloan explains:

> The very centrality of moral philosophy as the most important course of the senior year derived from the promise it held out of checking, ordering, and directing an otherwise mounting intellectual chaos. In summarizing and synthesizing the four years of college study, moral philosophy attempted three crucial tasks: to connect the students' general education with a large range of new subject matter, to provide guides and inspiration for the ethical application of knowledge, and, by relating all subjects to higher general laws of nature, to furnish an integrating principle for the entire curriculum.[51]

The unity created by the moral philosophy course rested in a crucial theological premise. Because God created everything, all human knowledge and discovery is an encounter with God's creation and forms a cohesive whole. This theological conviction was then supported with an epistemological confidence bestowed by the Scottish Enlightenment that human reason could read God's creation correctly, could uncover the underlying meaning and inherent connections. Rather than rhetorical skills and mental discipline, the moral philosophy course was designed to demonstrate the big picture of education.

The apologetics in these courses was typically based on natural theology, for science was gaining an authoritative role. Emily Dickinson, for example, was an astute student of botany, geology, and astronomy at the Mount Holyoke Female Seminary in the 1830s, which was the closest a woman could come to attending college in this period. Her often-precise scientific knowledge is reflected in many of her poems. Ringenberg reports that schools added laboratory equipment, expanded the science curriculum, and hired permanent staff to replace the more transitory tutors: "Consequently, the number of science professors in America grew from twenty-five in 1800 to sixty in 1828 to more than three hundred by 1850."[52] This growth was closely allied with religious instruction, because the study of natural phenomena was understood to be spiritually edifying. Little at-

---

51. Douglas Sloan, "Harmony, Chaos, and Consensus: The American College Curriculum," *Teachers College Record* 73 (1971): 246-47.

52. Ringenberg, *The Christian College*, p. 68.

tention was paid to practical applications. Scientific study was apologetic and doxological, first serving to prove God's existence and then functioning as a stimulus to praise. Christian faith both prompted scientific exploration and grew as a result of that exploration.

Take, for example, Edward Hitchcock, the president of Amherst College (in Dickinson's hometown). In his 1845 inaugural address, he argued that the study of science provided evidence of God's goodness:

> [Chemistry] abounds with the most beautiful exhibitions of the Divine wisdom and benevolence. . . . The wide dominations of natural history, embracing zoology, botany, and mineralogy, the theologist [sic] has even found crowded with demonstrations of the Divine Existence and of God's Providential care and government; and every new province that has been explored by the naturalist only serves to enlarge our conceptions of the Creator's works, and to impress us more deeply with their unity and perfection.[53]

The metamorphosis of the caterpillar into the butterfly and the tadpole into the frog taught the lesson of the resurrection; the lengthy geological history of the earth demonstrated God's hand in wind and rain and rock formations. Most nineteenth-century Christians did not believe that the Bible provided a scientific account of the natural world; instead, they reveled in the way that scientific discoveries helped them to learn more about God through God's world.

Roberts and Turner point out that "although moral philosophers and natural theologians did not in principle deny the value of faith, they tended in practice to minimize its role and to glorify instead *proof* and *argument.*" Similarly, because "empirical knowledge supported theistic convictions," American colleges increasingly emphasized "the value of the acquisition and transmission of knowledge."[54] Education thus became more empirical and rational, and less directed toward ethical virtue. Noll perceptively sums up the consequences:

> Antebellum Christian educators, thus, possessed divided minds. They seemed to be saying intellectually that their faith rested on an ability to

---

53. Edward Hitchcock, *The Highest Use of Learning: An Address Delivered at His Inauguration to the Presidency of Amherst College* (Amherst, Mass.: J. S. Adams, 1845), pp. 25, 28-29.

54. Roberts and Turner, *The Sacred and the Secular University*, pp. 26-27.

demonstrate its validity to the satisfaction of modern science and modern philosophy. At the same time they often acted as if revelation and God's activity provided its own best explanations. The difficulties in holding these contrasting convictions were not readily apparent in the years before the Civil War. Later, in the last third of the nineteenth century, however, they became the occasion of the greatest crisis in the American history of Christian higher education, when a series of major changes transformed the character of both public values and collegiate instruction.[55]

Only a scattering of Catholic colleges were founded before the Civil War, as Catholicism initially was illegal in many of the English colonies and later severely repressed in the newly formed United States. Catholic institutions most often arose as part of the mission of a religious community, such as the Augustinians, the Benedictines, the Dominicans, the Franciscans, the Congregation of the Holy Cross, or the Jesuits. The first Catholic college, Georgetown, was established in 1789 on the Jesuit Continental model, followed by Fordham (1841), Notre Dame (1843), and Holy Cross (1843). These institutions were distinguished by both their organizational structure and their classical-rhetorical curricula. Like their Continental counterparts, the early American Catholic colleges were secondary collegiate institutions with a six-year curriculum in grammar, humanities, and rhetoric: "The goal was *eloquentia perfecta,* the ability to speak Latin fluently and with persuasive power."[56] Extensive coursework in Bible studies and theology were also required. By 1830, a capstone class called Philosophy had been added at Georgetown; Philip Gleason speculates that the goal was probably to match the Moral Philosophy course common in the old-time Protestant colleges.[57] The early Catholic college, like its Protestant counterparts, was primarily devoted to "preparatory work for the seminary, missionary activities, and moral development."[58]

55. Noll, "Introduction," p. 20.

56. Philip Gleason, *Contending with Modernity: Catholic Higher Education in the Twentieth Century* (New York: Oxford University Press, 1995), p. 5.

57. Gleason, *Contending with Modernity,* p. 5.

58. Power, *A Legacy of Learning,* p. 37.

The Modern Research University;
or, What Happened to the Uni-?

Historians of higher education unanimously agree that the years following the Civil War witnessed a sea change in American education, a tsunami that transformed the Christian old-time college into today's modern research university. In the process, the regnant religious identity of American higher education seeped away. Private institutions loosened their ties with their founding denominations or orders, and public institutions drifted away from overt Christian goals. The history of Christian higher education's diminishing role in American culture has been told several times, with differing degrees of emphasis put on the influence of the German research university, the escalating importance of science, the growth of industry and business, and the increasing religious pluralism of America. All of these elements are important to the story, but I will focus on three factors with significant ramifications for today's mission-driven institutions: educational growth and diversification, the development of disciplinary specialization, and the restructuring of the college curriculum. There never was a nefarious anti-Christian conspiracy to rid American higher education of religious ideas and ideals, but a conjunction of events and the law of unintended consequences unwittingly led to the secularization of American higher education, with serious effects for our work today.

College attendance grew at a phenomenal rate after the Civil War. Between 1870 and 1900, the U.S. population nearly doubled, but the number of college students grew fivefold. In 1870, 1.7 percent of 18- to 21-year-olds were attending college; in 1930, 12.4 percent were college students.[59] Accommodating these growing enrollments were a variety of new kinds of institutions, both public and private, with strikingly different missions than the old-time college. Of particular note was the new research university, inspired by the Continental model epitomized by the University of Berlin. The old-time American college had been primarily an undergraduate institution, but after years of debate, graduate study was formally organized at Yale and the first Ph.D. was granted in 1861.[60] In 1876, Johns Hopkins University was founded as an exclusively graduate institution, and The Catholic University of America was established in 1889 to promote advanced study and research. In the last quarter of the century, many

---

59. Noll, "Introduction," p. 25.
60. Cordasco, *A Brief History of Education*, p. 132.

venerable colleges — such as Harvard, Columbia, and Princeton — fell under the influence of the European model and morphed into research universities, adding extensive graduate programs and a new emphasis on faculty research and scholarship.

The modern university was primarily concerned with the production of knowledge rather than the transmission of knowledge or the development of character. The search for truth through research became "a crusading cause," Richard Storr says, "[resembling] religion in zeal and even in terminology. In 1905, the sociologist Albion Small asserted — indeed preached: 'The prime duty of everyone connected with our graduate schools is daily to renew the vow of allegiance to research ideals. The first commandment with promise for graduate schools is: Remember the research ideal, to keep it holy!'"[61] Graduate programs expanded rapidly, with institutions offering the doctorate more than tripling between 1900 and 1940.[62] The existence and prestige of today's R1 institutions stems from this origin, and today most four-year colleges offer at least a few graduate programs, usually in the professions. The exclusively undergraduate, liberal-arts old-time college is a rare breed.

A second kind of institution created as an alternative to the traditional liberal arts college was the land-grant state college, which answered the demands of manufacturing, mechanization, urbanization, and continued Western expansion. The Morrell Land Grant Act of 1862 provided land and funding for the establishment of at least one college in each state that would offer affordable education in agriculture, engineering, and mechanic arts. If the old-time college's goal was to produce more gentlemen-citizens, and the research university's goal was to produce knowledge, the land-grant institution existed to produce workers with the necessary skills to advance America's economic and industrial growth. Growth in college attendance also resulted from the establishment of specialized colleges for new populations: women, African-Americans, and European immigrants, both Catholic and Protestant. The Congregationalists, Presbyterians, Methodists, and Baptists continued to work their way across the continent, leaving colleges in their wake. Immigrants from religious traditions outside the American Protestant mainstream also founded their own schools: the Dutch (Calvin College, 1876), the Mennonites (Bethel, 1893), the Swed-

61. Richard J. Storr, *The Beginning of the Future: A Historical Approach to Graduate Education in the Arts and Sciences* (New York: McGraw-Hill, 1973), pp. 48-49.

62. Storr, *The Beginning of the Future*, p. 58.

ish Lutherans (Gustavus Adolphus, 1862), the Swedish Covenant (North Park, 1891), and the Norwegian Lutherans (Pacific Lutheran, 1894). Because political, social, and economic conditions were allowing American Catholics more freedom, approximately 150 new Catholic colleges were founded between 1850 and 1900.[63] Other expansion came when multimillionaire industrialists such as Cornelius Vanderbilt, Washington Duke, Asa Candler, and John D. Rockefeller gave huge sums either to transform an existing small college or to found a new private institution, producing Vanderbilt, Duke, Emory, and the University of Chicago.

Meanwhile, the old-time colleges themselves were undergoing momentous changes. The old classical curriculum topped off with the cherry of moral philosophy uniformly followed by every student gave way to today's most common curricular structure: a major field of study, general education, and electives. Charles Eliot, inaugurated as the president of Harvard in 1869, led this move by establishing the elective system in order to allow for concentrated course work in a specific discipline. The old-time college, Eliot claimed, had "no practical lessons." The "young men" at Harvard needed both "an accurate general knowledge of all the main subjects of human interest" and "a minute and thorough knowledge of the one subject which each may select as his principal occupation in life."[64] Different students could major in different subjects, according to their interests and abilities.

This development of academic specialization, Roberts and Turner argue, was the most significant factor in the transformation of American education in the nineteenth century. The growing complexity of science fed this phenomenon. Information was exponentially exploding to the degree that a scholar could only hope to till a small corner of the knowledge garden, but this pragmatic focusing was often accompanied with a new philosophical perspective on knowledge. Earlier scholars had conducted indepth research and become experts in an area, but "the decisive distinction of the new specialization . . . was not narrowness of range but acknowledgment of disciplinary isolation." Knowledge was no longer seen as part of a single God-created universe: "Disciplinary specialists thus began to snip apart the previously undivided map of knowledge into separate territories. Between these 'disciplines' they started to erect methodological fences

63. Power, *A Legacy of Learning*, p. 32.

64. Charles Eliot, quoted in Roberts and Turner, *The Sacred and the Secular University*, p. 84.

hard for nonspecialists to scale. They declared . . . that knowledge does not form a whole but, on the contrary, properly divides itself into distinct compartments." Because "unique methodological principles and scholarly traditions govern life within each of these [disciplinary] boxes," competent scholars would restrict themselves to their own discipline.[65] Knowledge came to be seen as self-contained, with each discipline possessing its own epistemology, methodology, and tradition.

The physical sciences were divided into discrete fields of study — geology, biology, chemistry — and the human sciences (sociology, economics, psychology) emerged as distinct disciplines, aligning themselves with the scientific method rather than being addressed as part of the topical approach of moral philosophy. The rise of the academic disciplines as specialized and isolated pursuits is reflected in the formation of professional associations. The American Chemical Society was founded in 1876, the American Society of Mechanical Engineers in 1880, the Modern Language Association in 1883, the American Psychological Association in 1892, the American Physical Society in 1899, the American Philosophical Association in 1900, the American Anthropological Association in 1902, and the American Sociological Association in 1905. The role of college professor became detached from that of clergy, and higher education became a distinct profession, with its own set of membership criteria (including a Ph.D.). Such professionalization included specialization, becoming an expert in one's field, and conducting original research or interpretation.

In the transformation of professors into professionals, the curricula, identity, and mission of higher education were affected. With the increased emphasis on disciplinary thought, a kind of isolation ensued. As Roberts and Turner comment, "specialization could prove toxic to a coherent education. If one field of knowledge had no essential connection with another, how could the curriculum hold together?"[66] Cross-curricular connections were sacrificed, and the traditional senior capstone course fell away like an unnecessary appendage. Specialists in English and physics, sociology and chemistry could have little to say to each other. College professors began identifying themselves in terms of their disciplines rather than by their institutional homes, seeing their primary allegiance to the pursuit of truth in their field rather than to the mission of their institution.

Given disciplinary specialization and increasing professionalism, it

---

65. Roberts and Turner, *The Sacred and the Secular University*, pp. 86-87.
66. Roberts and Turner, *The Sacred and the Secular University*, p. 89.

only made sense to separate one's religious beliefs from one's academic specialty, and a growing number of Christian professors did just that. Specialization was inherent to the new research university, but it also transformed college faculty and curriculum. Structurally, religious belief was confined to chapel attendance, extracurricular activities, and a required course in the Bible — a specialized study that was first introduced in the 1870s and then proliferated by the end of the nineteenth century.[67] With greater religious pluralism due to immigration waves of European Catholics and Jews, a new judicial emphasis on church/state separation, and a fading Protestant consensus, the religious aspects of many institutions simply disappeared, although looming Gothic chapels continued physically to dominate the landscape of many institutions. At some of the oldest institutions, such as Harvard, Yale, and Princeton, religious education was allotted solely to the divinity school, in another case of specialization. Smaller, church-related institutions often maintained their historic roots in the form of a college chaplain or campus ministry, but many faculties and curricula became thoroughly secular. Ringenberg charts the course of change in this way: major state universities and a few elite private institutions began the secularization process in the late nineteenth century, followed by the secondary state institutions and more of the elite privates at the turn of the century; during the 1920s, the major denominational colleges followed.[68] In most of American higher education, faith and learning had become completely separated from each other. Modernism had prevailed in what historians call "the University Revolution."

Marsden insists that this history is not necessarily the loss of an educational Golden Age. The old-time Christian college provided limited, if any, access to anyone who was not white, male, or Protestant. Much of its curriculum was outdated and irrelevant, and its pedagogy was ineffective. Noll similarly comments, "Throughout the nineteenth century, a bachelor's degree in the liberal arts remained more an ornament of the upper middle class than a doorway to intellectual growth or economic success."[69] But others, such as James Burtchaell in *The Dying of the Light: The Disengagement of Colleges and Universities from Their Christian Churches,* tell the story of the secularization of American education in more negative terms.

The two major exceptions to this pattern were the more conservative

---

67. Roberts and Turner, *The Sacred and the Secular University,* p. 92.
68. Ringenberg, *The Christian College,* p. 114.
69. Noll, "Introduction," p. 17.

Protestant denominational or nondenominational colleges and the Catholic colleges, which, at least until the 1960s, intentionally rejected modernism, following Pius X's 1907 encyclical *Pascendi Dominici Gregi,* and mounted "a strenuous campaign to promote the work of Thomas Aquinas as an intellectual anchor for Catholic intellectual life."[70] This "Catholic Renaissance" or Scholastic Revival was based upon an "intimate linkage . . . between intellectual understanding, moral commitment, and longing for spiritual fulfillment."[71] Catholic higher education embraced a Neo-Thomistic synthesis of faith and reason, in which properly exercised logic would bring the scholar to the same truth taught by the church. Noll elaborates: "What made this neo-Scholasticism so profoundly important . . . was not just its sense of intellectual depth and adventure, but also its many links to social action, missionary service, and liturgical renewal."[72] Although Catholic education thus maintained a strong sense of unity, coherence, and transcendence, it remained isolated from the broader American intellectual culture both because of its own wariness of American mores and because of its slow transformation from an immigrant church into an indigenous body.

During the twentieth century, the major shift in American educational practices inaugurated by the University Revolution continued, aided both by internal battles within Protestant denominations over fundamentalism and/or liberalism and by a new national infusion of support for higher education. At the turn of the century, church-related colleges still enrolled about half of all college students,[73] but by 2005, of the approximately 15 million postsecondary students in the U.S., only about 1.5 million were attending self-reported "religiously affiliated institutions." Private institutions enrolled 48 percent of students in four-year programs in 1954, but that figure had dropped to 30 percent by 1978.[74] By the end of the twentieth century, the most prestigious American educational institutions were the flagship state universities and a few of the former old-time colleges, such as Harvard and Yale, which had radically revised their mission and vision.

Post–World War II nationalistic pride and a prosperous economy ex-

70. Mark Noll, "The Future of the Religious College: Looking Ahead by Looking Back," in *The Future of Religious Colleges,* ed. Paul J. Dovre (Grand Rapids: Wm. B. Eerdmans, 2002), p. 81.

71. Gleason, *Contending with Modernity,* p. 122.

72. Noll, "The Future of the Religious College," p. 82.

73. Ringenberg, *The Christian College,* p. 129.

74. Ringenberg, *The Christian College,* p. 138.

tended the nineteenth-century education revolution even further. While Europeans confined postsecondary educational opportunities to a select few, Americans began to view access to higher education as a right, while national rhetoric, like that of the classical Greeks, connected education with the duties of citizenship. The 1947 President's Commission on Higher Education recommended, "If education is to make the attainment of a more perfect democracy one of its major goals, it is imperative that it extend its benefits to all on equal terms."[75] Subsequently, the federal government adopted a series of policies to expand opportunities for higher education to a much greater segment of the American population. The G.I. Bill provided funding for almost eight million veterans to receive an education. Citing the "social and economic benefits to the nation from having better educated citizens," President Harry Truman's "New Deal" promoted the development of two-year junior colleges and began massive federal subsidies to support both public and private four-year colleges.[76] Higher education thus enjoyed a period of unprecedented prosperity and became increasingly accessible to women, ethnic minorities, and economically underprivileged students. The new financial opportunities, coupled with the broader patterns of professionalization and secularization in higher education and the post–Vatican II shift to lay governance, transformed the American Catholic educational system in the sixties, shattering its former intellectual unity.[77] Catholic institutions no longer shared a common definition of what entailed a Catholic identity. Gleason points to "a lack of consensus as to the substantive content of the ensemble of religious beliefs, moral commitments, and academic assumptions that supposedly constitute Catholic identity, and a consequent inability to specify what that identity entails for the practical functioning of Catholic colleges and universities."[78]

Yet the financial and enrollment success in the decades following the war came at some cost. In a memorable phrase coined in 1963 by Clark Kerr, then Chancellor at the University of California, the "uni-versity" had become a "multi-versity." Kerr wrote, "The multiversity is an inconsistent institution. It is not one community, but several. . . . A community, like the medieval communities of masters and students, should have common in-

---

75. Power, *A Legacy of Learning*, p. 307.

76. Power, *A Legacy of Learning*, p. 306.

77. Noll, "The Future of the Religious College," p. 83; Monika K. Hellwig, "Emerging Patterns among Roman Catholic Colleges and Universities," in *The Future of Religious Colleges*, p. 105.

78. Gleason, *Contending with Modernity*, p. 320.

terests; in the multiversity, they are quite varied, even conflicting. A community should have a soul, a single animating principle; the multiversity has several. . . ."[79] Kerr's condemnation prompted what Mark Schwehn has called "the loss of soul discourse" that entangles the jungle of complaints regarding American higher education today.[80] The metaphor of soul encompasses a cluster of related concerns: character education, discussion of moral and ethical values, affirmation of spirituality, respect for and education about religious institutions and traditions, and the precedence of student learning over the production of knowledge. The social prestige and financial strength of the modern research university have prompted many institutions to abandon their own missions to emulate that of another. During the past three decades, complaints about higher education's lack of intellectual coherence, moral direction, and academic quality range from Allan Bloom's *The Closing of the American Mind: How Higher Education Has Failed Democracy and Impoverished the Soul of Today's Students* (1987), to Bill Reading's *The University in Ruins* (1996), to Derek Bok's *Our Underachieving College: A Candid Look at How Much Students Learn and Why They Should Be Learning More* (2006). The growing national interest in defining institutional mission and assessing whether that mission is being accomplished stems, in part, from a persisting lack of clarity about what a college or university should hope to accomplish.

In a swing of the pendulum, the twenty-first century has subsequently witnessed an increased concern for civic virtue, character formation, and spirituality among both public and private institutions. In 2005, the Association of American Colleges and Universities (AAC&U) launched a decade-long initiative called Liberal Education and America's Promise (LEAP): Excellence for Everyone as a Nation Goes to College, which published *College Learning for the New Global Century* in 2007, claiming that "the academy stands at a crossroads. Millions of students today seek a college education, and record numbers are actually enrolling. Without a seri-

79. Clark Kerr, *The Uses of the University*, 4th ed. (Cambridge: Harvard University Press, 1995), pp. 14-15.

80. The "loss of soul" discourse began with George Marsden, *The Soul of the American University: From Protestant Establishment to Established Nonbelief* (Oxford: Oxford University Press, 1994); and includes Robert Benne, *Quality with Soul* (Grand Rapids: Wm. B. Eerdmans, 2001); *Christianity and the Soul of the University: Faith as a Foundation for Intellectual Community*, ed. Douglas V. Henry and Michael D. Beaty (Grand Rapids: Baker, 2006); and *The Soul of a Christian University: A Field Guide for Educators*, ed. Stephen T. Beers (Abilene, Tex.: Abilene Christian University Press, 2008).

ous national effort to recalibrate college learning to the needs of the new global century, however, too few of these students will reap the full benefits of college."[81] The fourth "Principle of Excellence" identified in the LEAP report is "Engage the Big Questions," and the Spring 2007 issue of *Liberal Education* has a series of articles examining how both contemporary big questions (poverty, HIV-AIDS, global warming) and enduring big questions (meaning, value, and purpose) can be addressed in a liberal education. The AAC&U — like its ancient Greek forebears — advocates that liberal education should instill "personal and social responsibility," but such goals continue to be contested in the academy, with serious questions about how to define civic virtue, not to mention how to inculcate it.

Spirituality is currently a hot topic in the academy, thanks to the ongoing study of Spirituality in Higher Education, conducted by the Higher Education Research Institute (HERI) at UCLA. In 2003, HERI began surveying undergraduates and faculty in a multi-institutional, longitudinal study designed to identify patterns of spirituality and religiousness among college students. Initial results reveal a high level of student interest in spiritual values but also show that most colleges and universities are "doing little either to help students explore such issues or to support their search in the sphere of values and beliefs." Most college juniors, for example, report that their professors have never encouraged discussion of spiritual or religious matters or provided opportunities for discussing the meaning or purpose of life.[82]

Faculty responses confirm the student data. Despite often describing themselves as religious (64 percent) or spiritual (81 percent), few faculty (30 percent) agree that "colleges should be concerned with facilitating students' spiritual development." Institutional context clearly plays a role, as 18 percent of faculty in public universities and 23 percent in public colleges agree with this statement, compared to 62 percent of faculty in Catholic colleges and 68 percent of faculty in "other religious" colleges.[83] In addition to the high value that college students put on integrating spirituality into their lives, the study of spirituality is gaining greater prominence in research and theorizing in fields such as health care, psychology, social

---

81. *College Learning for the New Global Century: A Report from the National Leadership Conference for Liberal Education and America's Promise* (Washington, D.C.: AAC&U, 2007), p. vii.

82. "Spirituality in Higher Education: A National Study of College Students' Search for Meaning and Purpose," http://www.spirituality.ucla.edu/.

83. "Spirituality in Higher Education."

work, and business. The LEAP initiative, HERI findings, and new research trends have prompted a great deal of soul searching about how best to deal with spirituality, values, and life purpose in higher education.

One way that some in higher education have been engaging the question of spirituality with their students, encouraging them to think "outside themselves," is through the concept of vocation. From 2000 to 2007, the Lilly Endowment, Inc., awarded a total of $218 million to eighty-eight four-year, church-related, accredited institutions in the United States to establish Programs for the Theological Exploration of Vocation (PTEV) on their respective campuses. By locating spirituality within Christian theology and focusing on vocation, the PTEV initiative provided a guided yet far-from-uniform strategy to help students examine the purpose of life. The eighty-eight PTEV schools devised a wide variety of programs to assist students in understanding and exploring their vocation. With each school receiving almost $2 million to establish a five-year program, PTEV activities appeared in every imaginable part of campuses: classrooms and residence halls, academic advising and career counseling, volunteer work and community service. Most colleges housed from ten to twenty initiatives under their PTEV umbrella, with various programs for students, faculty, staff, alumni, parents, and even high school students. After completing a successful initial five-year program, most of these institutions were awarded an additional three-year sustaining grant of $500,000, for which they had to generate matching funds.[84] In 2009, the Lilly Endowment, Inc., awarded the Council of Independent Colleges (CIC) a grant totaling nearly $2.4 million for a program to continue the focus on theological exploration of vocation in independent higher education. As part of this initiative, the CIC established NetVUE (Network for Vocation in Undergraduate Education), a nationwide campus-supported network facilitating conversation about vocational exploration. By 2010, 125 private colleges and universities had joined NetVUE.[85]

Mission-driven institutions in the twenty-first century, then, find themselves at the forefront of a broad genuine educational concern for character, meaning, values, and spirituality that is nonetheless often difficult to implement in many of today's secular colleges and universities

84. "Programs for the Theological Exploration of Vocation," http://www.ptev.org/schools.aspx?iid=4.

85. "Network for Vocation in Undergraduate Education," http://www.cic.org/netvue/netvue_website/index.html.

without a clear center of meanings and values. In addition, the multi-university continues to experience ongoing tensions between the production of knowledge and the transmission of knowledge, the goal of producing skills and the goal of developing character, and the relationship of knowledge and action. The mission-driven institution is not immune to these pressures, but it provides a different environment in which to address them.

CHAPTER 3

Teaching: Call and Response

At most mission-driven institutions, the primary responsibility of a faculty member is teaching. If you have been hired by a research university or comprehensive institution — offering both graduate and undergraduate programs — the emphasis on and expectations for teaching may be less, especially if you are a graduate-level professor. But for most professors at mission-driven institutions, teaching takes up a majority of their time and is considered to be their most important duty. Liberal-arts colleges and undergraduate programs at comprehensive universities define themselves primarily as teaching bodies. They position themselves in the market on the strength of this identity, and their promotional material proclaims pedagogical dedication. Their operational procedures emphasize teaching, as their comparatively heavy course-loads imply and their formal requirements for promotion and tenure attest. At Seattle Pacific, for example, the faculty handbook states, "Since teaching is the paramount responsibility of faculty at SPU, effectiveness in this area will be weighted most heavily in evaluation of faculty competence and contribution." In the great cathedral of learning, the daily work of teaching represents the basic job of putting brick on top of brick to construct the humble yet essential walls that make up the entire structure: flying buttresses, rose windows, gargoyles, and all.

It is ironic, then, that so few of us begin our careers with much of a clue about how to teach. Our graduate education and professional experience have made us experts in one field or another, and we are subsequently expected to be able, almost by osmosis, to help our students master that knowledge, skill, or technique. When I began teaching American literature thirty years ago, no one had taught me how to teach. I had worked as a graduate assistant in two large lecture courses, grading quizzes and papers, and leading discussion groups, and I had taught three sections of freshman composition, following a prescribed syllabus, but I had never organized and taught any course completely on my own. Therefore, I resorted to a common practice of novice professors: I taught the way that my best teachers had taught me. I gave lengthy reading assignments, delivered high-powered lectures, and occasionally paused to engage in sharp *Paper Chase*-esque questioning — spontaneously calling on students to answer thought-provoking questions. As a student, I had loved the intellectual challenge of wrestling with difficult texts, tracking a complicated lecture, and remaining at high alert in case I was required to contribute a gem of wisdom. This, of course, was because I was an academic nerd. Unfortunately, only a handful of the more than two thousand students I have taught over the years have also been academic nerds, and it didn't take me long to learn that this way of teaching was not the most effective.

In his wonderful book *The Courage to Teach: Exploring the Inner Landscape of a Teacher's Life,* Parker Palmer claims, "Good teaching cannot be reduced to technique; good teaching comes from the identity and integrity of the teacher."[1] While Palmer rightly calls us to recognize the importance of our own identity as teachers, I have also come to believe that knowing something about how to teach is also crucial. In my first feeble teaching attempts, I was being true to my personal identity; my problem was that I wasn't being sensitive to my students' identity, and I didn't know anything about how people learn. Good teaching techniques mechanically employed without the heart of a teacher are inadequate, but knowing your "inner landscape" often is not enough to facilitate learning. Good teachers know *who* they are and are true to themselves, but they also know something about *how* to teach as well as *what* to teach. Some people believe that good teachers are born, not taught; you either have the teaching gene or you don't. There's a certain irony in believing that you can teach anything but how to teach. But as Maryellen Weimer insists, "The assertion that nobody knows what makes teaching good is a myth."[2] Good teaching is both an art and a science. That's not to say that every once in a while — about once in a hundred cases, I'd say — you won't stumble across someone who instinctively knows exactly how to teach.

1. Parker J. Palmer, *The Courage to Teach: Exploring the Inner Landscape of a Teacher's Life* (San Francisco: Jossey-Bass, 1998), p. 10.

2. Maryellen Weimer, "It's a Myth: Nobody Knows What Makes Teaching Good," in *Teaching College: Collected Readings for the New Instructor,* ed. Maryellen Weimer and Rose Ann Neff (Madison, Wis.: Magna Publications, 1990), p. 13.

Still, very few teachers are born; most of us have been called and have to learn how to answer that call. During the past three decades, a huge amount of research has documented what makes up effective college-level teaching, and this chapter and the next will draw on this research.

The Mountains and Valleys of the Inner Landscape

As Palmer explores so eloquently in his book, our personal gifts, deepest commitments, and self-understanding should inform our roles as teachers. Bad teachers, he claims, distance themselves from their teaching and split their "personhood from practice." The key is to discover "the teacher within."[3] While I am reluctant to criticize *The Courage to Teach* too severely, because it has had an important impact both on me and on many other people that I know, the idea of "the teacher within" strikes me as being overly romantic. First, our identity as teachers is constantly evolving and growing — or should be — as we encounter different contexts, challenges, and students. I'm a much different teacher now that I'm older, a mother, a cancer survivor, a faculty developer, and so on. Second, a good instructor needs a teaching identity that is distinct from her or his identity as a parent, or a friend, or a tri-athlete. During your first years of teaching, one of your most important tasks will be to find that teaching persona and voice, discerning which of many different but effective teaching styles best suits your strengths. Some of us are loud, dramatic, and flamboyant teachers; others are clear, calm, and measured. Some of us are warm and fuzzy; others are brisk and business-like. Some are introverts; some are extroverts. Our teaching persona needs to be authentic, not forced or artificial, but it will be a persona. Teachers are not simply "themselves" in front of a class or when working with a student; we create a stance, a vocabulary, and boundaries in every interpersonal relationship. And it's not appropriate for us to treat our students as our best friends, our lovers, or our children. Professors need a "teacher face" that comfortably fits with their other faces. Exploring your inner landscape means realizing what your personal traits, strengths, and weaknesses are, so that you can better develop that "teacher face."

Recognizing the many possible pedagogical personalities, Peter Filene tells beginning teachers to ask themselves "What kind of teacher do you want to be?" However, he also notes that many studies have identified five

3. Palmer, *The Courage to Teach*, pp. 17, 29.

personal characteristics that any good teacher needs: (1) enthusiasm about both the subject and the process of teaching, (2) clear communication skills, (3) organization, (4) the ability to stimulate students to learn, and (5) genuine care and respect for students.[4] If you find yourself gravely deficient in any of these areas, you should reconsider whether you have a genuine vocation to teach. If you don't like most college students, being a professor is not a good career choice. Ultimately, the two most important vocational questions for the would-be professor are "Am I willing and able to meet the needs of my students?" and "Does teaching provide me with moments of joy?" As Palmer describes it, teaching should be "a life-giving choice."[5] Good teaching, Ken Bain asserts, revolves not around exercising power or displaying brilliance at the cost of the students, but rather centers on care and concern for students and their learning.[6]

Nonetheless, even for skillful, confident, and successful teachers, there will be many days of pain, and in your first years of teaching, you will descend into deep emotional valleys. Palmer tells an amusing anecdote about his encounter with "the student from hell," to which anyone who has taught for any amount of time can relate.[7] If we truly care about our subject, our students, and learning, teaching will sometimes be agonizing. And if our teaching persona is authentic, when a class session or course assignment goes dreadfully wrong, we will feel as if we have failed. We will take it personally. I think it is a good sign when teachers worry about a class that has gone poorly, as it demonstrates that they care about and are attuned to their students. I'm more concerned about those faculty members who think that every one of their class sessions is brilliant. While we need to analyze why a class failed, we also need to realize that sometimes it isn't our fault. The group chemistry is wrong, or there was a fire alarm that emptied out the freshman residence hall from three A.M. to six A.M. And when we do encounter the student from hell, Stephen Brookfield cautions us not to fall into "the trap of conversional obsession," focusing all our attention on a handful of misbehaving students at the cost of the rest of the class.[8]

4. Peter Filene, *The Joy of Teaching: A Practical Guide for New College Instructors* (Chapel Hill: University of North Carolina Press, 2005), p. 7.

5. Palmer, *The Courage to Teach*, p. 16.

6. Ken Bain, *What the Best College Teachers Do* (Cambridge: Harvard University Press, 2004), p. 139.

7. Palmer, *The Courage to Teach*, pp. 40-47.

8. Stephen D. Brookfield, *The Skillful Teacher: On Technique, Trust, and Responsiveness in the Classroom,* 2d ed. (San Francisco: Jossey-Bass, 2006), p. 213.

Teaching can be one of the most painful emotional activities, but also one of the most exhilarating. All it takes to affirm a teaching vocation are those occasional times when everything "clicks" in a classroom, or you receive a brilliant student essay, or a group of students makes a creative but clear presentation that teaches you something, or a graduate comes back for homecoming and tells you what a difference your history class made in his or her life, or one of your students is admitted to an outstanding graduate school. When students have grown intellectually, emotionally, socially, and spiritually because of your work, teaching is the best job in the world.

Mistaken Teaching and Teaching Mistakes

In my work with new faculty, I have discovered that the many mistakes I made during my first years as a college teacher are all-too-common errors. Although there is a certain amount of misguided behavior that everyone must stumble through in order to learn something, here are some common mistakes made by novice professors, mistakes that can be watched for and guarded against during those first difficult years.

The major error, one that is produced and reinforced by our entire higher educational system, is to equate good teaching with knowing your stuff. If you have a Ph.D. in sociology, we assume that you are able to teach an introduction to sociology; if you are an attorney, you should be able to teach business law; if you are a pediatric nurse, you should be able to teach family health theory. When we operationalize this mistake in preparing for teaching, we direct all of our efforts toward mastering the material. My first teaching position was at a very small college where I made up half of the English department. That meant that despite my graduate work in American literature, I had to teach all kinds of other courses in English literature. One of the greatest challenges came when I was assigned sixteenth- and seventeenth-century British literature, in which I had to teach Edmund Spenser's *The Faerie Queen,* a long, dense, allegorical Renaissance epic in verse, which I had never even read in graduate school. I spent hours deciphering the text and poring over the secondary material, convinced that my students would show me up, ask me a question that I couldn't answer, or otherwise embarrass me.[9]

9. Find yourself in a similar situation? Check out Therese Huston, *Teaching What You Don't Know* (Cambridge: Harvard University Press, 2009).

---

5 Most Common Teaching Mistakes

1. Focusing on knowing the material yourself
2. Preparing too much
3. Emphasizing content-delivery
4. Teaching the way your favorite professors taught
5. Lecturing too much

This leads to a second mistake often made by beginning teachers: over-preparing for class. Since there is no clear sign that one is finished preparing, as there is when one, say, weeds a garden, over-preparation is easy to do. You can always read one more article, add one more section to your lecture, design a few more discussion questions, or figure out one more thing that might go wrong in a lab assignment. And when you are new and insecure, you probably will. Robert Boice, who has extensively researched the performance of early-career faculty, identifies the over-preparation of teaching materials as one of the "three most dangerous pitfalls" of the novice faculty member.[10] His research found that excessive amounts of preparation seldom bore fruits of learning: typical results included unengaged and ungrateful students, poor comprehension and performance, and mediocre course evaluations. To top it all off, Boice discovered by tracking new teachers that those who spent the most time preparing to teach "most often suffered from influenza, headaches, and dysphorias."[11] Boice's *Advice for New Faculty Members* provides a superb discussion of how to counter the temptation of over-preparation by working in brief, regular sessions that are timed. The key concept is to decide upon a reasonable amount of time needed to prepare for any specific class period and then to limit yourself to that amount of time. I'm not talking about the work of initially designing the course, which we will address below, or even of grading papers, tests, or projects, but rather of the amount of time needed each week to prepare for a class period. I think a good general rule of thumb is two to three hours for each class hour for a new class, and one to two hours for each class hour for a repeated class. Schedule class preparation periods in your Daytimer or Outlook, and

10. Robert Boice, *Advice for New Faculty Members: Nihil Nimus* (Boston: Allyn & Bacon, 2000), p. 6.

11. Boice, *Advice for New Faculty Members*, p. 13.

then do your best to stick to that schedule. As Boice recommends, "Stop, in a timely fashion."[12]

These first two mistakes lead us to the third common error: thinking that good teaching consists of extensive content-delivery. We assume that if we know everything there is to know about a topic and are able to efficiently condense and competently deliver all that information during a class period through a lecture, perhaps accompanied by PowerPoint, we are good teachers. Or if a course covers all the material in the microbiology text, it must be a good course. However, content and coverage do not necessarily add up to good teaching. We can define good teaching simply: "Good teaching takes place when student learning occurs." Unfortunately, an extensive amount of course material can be presented and "covered" without *any* student learning taking place. It may be tempting to blame the students for this lack of success, but the professor bears a large part of the responsibility. We'll come back to the importance of student learning shortly, but first let's identify a few more common mistakes of novice teachers.

As I've already noted, we tend to teach the way that we have been taught, or at least the way that we've been taught that we liked the best. As a student, I absolutely loathed small-group work, so when I began teaching, I never used small groups in my classroom. I, like many professorial types, am an "abstract reflective" learner. That means that I tend to be thoughtful, introspective, introverted, scholarly, creative, and interested in knowledge for knowledge's own sake. No wonder I became a college professor. But only about 10 percent of the American population are abstract reflective learners, and even fewer become college professors. Few of the students in my classroom were Mini-Me's. I needed to learn how to teach the students that I had, not the student that I was.

Teaching the way that we were taught, teaching to ourselves, preparing with an obsession with coverage and content — these lead to an over-reliance on lecturing. After all, if there is so much material to be covered, we need to use the most efficient way in which to cover it, which is the lecture, especially if one can talk rapidly. Although faculty are beginning to use more student-centered activities, the most commonly employed teaching technique across the United States is the lecture. According to the 2007-2008 HERI Faculty Survey, 51.8 percent of full professors and 43.3 percent of assistant professors report using extensive lecturing in teach-

12. Boice, *Advice for New Faculty Members*, p. 51.

ing.[13] And yet numerous peer-reviewed studies have repeatedly proven that lecturing is one of the least effective ways to teach, producing comparatively low levels of learning for most students. In *How College Affects Students,* Ernest T. Pascarella and Patrick T. Terenzini state, "With striking consistency, studies show that innovative, active, collaborative, cooperative, and constructivist instructional approaches shape learning more powerfully, in some forms by substantial margins, than do conventional lecture-discussion and text-based approaches."[14] Why do so many professors continue to lecture in the face of the evidence? I suspect that lecturing is popular because it is the traditional means of college instruction, and it is a comparatively easy way to teach. Yet the secret to successful teaching — defined as student learning — is not complicated and has been extensively documented. Let's begin exploring this by talking about how people learn things and who our students are.

Learning and the Brain

There is one fundamental question all would-be teachers need to honestly face: Do you believe that people can learn? This may seem to be painfully obvious, and yet we often act as if some people are innately "smart" and other people are "not so smart." According to Robert Leamnson, "Teachers . . . have no choice but to believe that people can get smart by learning. Students in Europe, and particularly Asia, tend to believe the same. In the United States, however, smartness is widely believed to be something one simply has, or has to some degree." For students, this belief means "that what they can learn has been delimited in advance by their level of smartness — something fixed and immutable."[15] And for professors, this assumption suggests that their sole responsibility is to present and explain the material; students will either "get it" or not.

But learning can be studied and understood as a physical process. Much recent research has probed the physical operations of brains, and

13. Linda De Angelo et al., *The American College Teacher: National Norms for the 2007-2008 HERI Faculty Survey* (Los Angeles: HERI, 2009), p. 135.

14. Ernest T. Pascarella and Patrick T. Terenzini, *How College Affects Students, Volume 2: A Third Decade of Research* (San Francisco: Jossey-Bass, 2005), p. 646.

15. Robert Leamnson, *Thinking about Teaching and Learning: Developing Habits of Learning with First-Year College and University Students* (Sterling, Va.: Stylus, 1999), p. 90.

this rapidly expanding field has important implications for teaching and learning. I will describe some of these findings in simple terms, based on the work of Leamnson and the sage counsel of John Medina.[16] Essentially what happens when we learn something is that a connection is established between one and another of the hundred billion neurons that make up our brain. This occurs when a "teacher" neuron prompts a "learner" neuron to move from a dormant to an active state. Such movement "places" the new information in immediate memory, which has the limited capacity to hold about seven pieces of declarative information for about thirty seconds. But after one repetition, the information is moved into working memory, which has a much larger capacity and can retain information for sixty to ninety minutes. With continual and varied repetition, the information eventually will move into long-term memory.

Imagine that in a lecture, a professor defines *ecology* as "the study of the relationships and interactions between living organisms and their natural or developed environment." When Joe Student hears these words, the definition goes into his immediate memory. Joe quickly scribbles a shorthand version of the definition in his notes, and the definition moves into his working memory. But unless he repeats the information several times and in several ways, it will not move into his long-term memory. This description is painfully oversimplified, as neural connections form a vast, intricate system of feedback loops, multiple connections, expansions and convergences. Leamnson explains, "There are two points of significance here for teachers. First, it is the multiple connections between neurons that allow perception and thought, and not just the existence or the number of neurons. Second, it is experience and sensory interaction with the environment that promotes and stabilizes neural connections."[17]

Neuroscience thus provides nine "brain rules" with potential implications for teaching:[18]

1. *People are natural explorers:* The ability to learn appears to be genetically programmed into us, part of the way in which God created human beings. As Anatole France wrote, "The whole art of teaching is

16. John Medina, *Brain Rules: Twelve Principles for Surviving and Thriving at Work, Home, and School* (Seattle, Wash.: Pear, 2008).

17. Leamnson, *Thinking about Teaching and Learning*, p. 13.

18. Medina identifies twelve "brain rules," but I discuss the nine most relevant for college teaching.

only the art of awakening the natural curiosity of young minds for the purpose of satisfying it afterwards."[19]

2. *Every brain is different:* Since each life experience has been unique, our neural "wiring" is also unique, so individuals have different ways of processing and connecting information.

3. *Attention facilitates learning:* If we find information interesting in some way, it is more likely to move into our long-term memory. That's why advertising uses sex to sell mundane products such as cars.

4. *Meaning registers before details:* People remember meaning before they remember detail. Meaning occurs when someone can connect a new piece of information to an old one. I think of my students' brains as pegboards; my task is to find the right hole into which to insert the peg of new information.

5. *Humans are visual learners:* We use a majority of our brains to process visual stimuli, and there is good evidence that most people prefer visual over other sensory information. We pay more attention to something that moves than something that stands still — the tiger rather than the tree.

6. *Repetition is crucial for memory:* Timed repetition and rehearsal are critical for the successful creation of long-term memory.

7. *Stressed brains don't learn well:* Your own experiences no doubt confirm this one.

8. *Sleep helps the learning process:* This is not only because the lack of sleep causes stress; neuroscience has recently identified the ways in which the brain moves information into long-term memory through the process of sleep. We need sleep in order for learning to sink in.

9. *Exercise aids learning:* Moderate, regular exercise facilitates learning and rebuffs the negative effects of stress.

For young people, college is often a time of high stress, little physical exercise, and even less sleep, yet these are crucial components in the learning process. While we can encourage our students to attend to these parts of their lives, the first six brain rules have particular pertinence for us in our roles as teachers.

19. Anatole France, *The Crime of Sylvestre Bonnard*, trans. Lafcadio Hearn (New York: John Lane, 1920), p. 198.

Who Are Your Students?

Writers and speakers know the importance of considering one's audience, and teaching is no different. To help students learn, we need to think about their identities, abilities, characteristics, needs, and inclinations. Their cognitive development, generational identity, and individual ways of learning provide important contextual considerations for effective teaching.

First developed in 1968, William Perry's "Model of College Student Cognitive Development" remains a useful tool for understanding patterns of thought and behavior characteristic of traditionally aged college students (eighteen to twenty-two years old). Developmental psychology assumes that people grow by passing through a number of identifiable stages, and many different developmental models have been proposed. All such models raise questions. Is it descriptive or prescriptive? How much does environment affect development? Are developmental stages neat and tidy, or are there overlaps? Does everyone move sequentially through each step, or do people sometimes move backward or skip a stage? But despite their tentative nature, such models are useful ways of identifying what may occur when a college-aged student enters your classroom. According to a simplified version of Perry's model, a typical undergraduate moves through three levels of cognitive understanding. Each level is more complex and has qualitatively different assumptions about how to know and evaluate anything, including school, teachers, and learning. Recognizing these stages may help explain some of your students' puzzling behavior and responses to class activities and assignments.

Stage one is that of *Dualism*, in which "the student sees the world in polar terms of we-right-good vs. other-wrong-bad."[20] Simple, easily identifiable, correct answers exist for every question, and the teacher's job is to convey those answers. There are good guys and bad guys, clearly identified by the color of their hats. Learning involves taking detailed notes, memorizing the professor's pronouncements, and repeating them on the exam. If the student follows the rules — i.e., does the reading, writes the papers, and attends class — he or she will inevitably be rewarded with good grades. When a diversity of opinion arises, as in a class discussion, a dualistic student might think that this is an arbitrary exercise set by the teacher and will be frustrated that the professor doesn't just close down the discussion and

20. William G. Perry Jr., *Forms of Intellectual and Ethical Development in the College Years* (New York: Holt, Rinehart & Winston, 1970), p. 9.

give *the* answer. Dualistic students are more interested in facts than opinions. Near the end of this stage, a student may realize that some answers have not yet been found, but will think that more study will turn up plain answers.

In stage two, *Multiplicity,* a student comes to realize that in some areas there are no clear right answers. Because of conflicting facts, differences in opinions, inadequate information, differing presuppositions, and non-identical contexts, a number of legitimate views might exist. As a consequence, "the student perceives all knowledge and values, including authority's, as contextual and relativistic and subordinates dualistic right-wrong functions to the status of a special case, in context."[21] In stage two, students may go through phases such as embracing ambiguity out of deference to the teacher ("This murky yes-and-no is the answer she wants"), rebelling against any kind of judgment ("No one can tell me that I'm wrong"), or embracing complete relativism ("That's your opinion; I have my own"). Perry says that "a drastic revolution" has occurred.[22] Students re-examine decisions that they have made earlier, such as in what to major, what they think about evolution or homosexuality, and what they believe about religion. This can be a period of crisis, as students question and test previously unexamined assumptions. In this stage, students no longer expect the professor to have "the right answer," but they do see the professor as a source of expertise and information. They are highly suspicious of grading as being completely arbitrary. Facts are questionable; opinions rule.

The dream of all teachers is that students, with our assistance and the further physical development of their brains, are eventually able to reach the third stage of *Commitment,* in which students find a place in a relativistic world by embracing some form of personal commitment. In this stage, students can discriminate among facts, opinions, and interpretations, and they understand that learning involves taking in multiple pieces of information and critically examining and comparing them before deciding upon an approximate truth or solution, one that may well be revised in the future with additional information. With critical commitment, students are not paralyzed by the seeming abundance of information and conflicting opinions, but are courageous enough to make choices and to act thoughtfully. They are willing to examine a fact or belief,

21. Perry, *Forms of Intellectual and Ethical Development in the College Years,* pp. 9-10.
22. Perry, *Forms of Intellectual and Ethical Development in the College Years,* p. 109.

bring a variety of information to bear upon it, question it, and ultimately embrace a tentative answer. Personal confidence and intellectual humility dwell together.

Perry's work reveals that many students, perhaps up to 75 percent, move through all three developmental stages during their four or five years in college, and he identifies the transition from dualism to multiplicity as the most crucial in terms of its emotional impact and sense of crisis. It's the period of loss of faith — in facts, in authority, in certainty. While Perry's model focuses on cognitive and moral development, other developmental psychologists such as Lawrence Kohlberg and Carol Gilligan have examined similar frameworks in moral development, with James Fowler applying the same kind of model to stages of faith development.[23] Fowler posits that college-aged students often enter college non-critically accepting the faith, if any, in which they have been raised. Their personal religious expression is correct; others are wrong. Students' educational experience and encounters with people unlike themselves often provoke a period of crisis in which they reject all faiths, embracing relativity and multiplicity. They learn to question, criticize, and analyze. Eventually, we hope, students move to commitment, choosing what they believe for themselves after critically examining the options. They may return to the faith of their parents and their church, now critically chosen as their own, or they may embrace a different faith.

Levels of cognitive development may differ within one classroom, although it will be more common to find a first-year course dominated by dualistic students, and a senior or graduate seminar with more students at the committed level. If your student population includes "non-traditional students," or adult learners, they may be at more advanced levels of cognitive development, in Perry's terms. Recognizing cognitive development may sensitize you to what is happening when a precocious sixteen-year-old freshman objects strenuously to the idea that *Heart of Darkness* may be simultaneously both racist and anti-racist or is stunned to hear — apparently for the first time — that Genesis includes two different creation accounts.

Besides being aware of levels of cognitive development, teachers

23. Lawrence Kohlberg, *The Philosophy of Moral Development* (San Francisco: Harper, 1980); Carol Gilligan, *In a Different Voice: Psychological Theory and Women's Development* (Cambridge: Harvard University Press, 1982); James Fowler, *Stages of Faith* (New York: Harper, 1981).

should be aware of a second important aspect of student identity: the "peer personality" of their generation. Because of shared social, historical, and cultural experiences, coupled with being parented by a previous generation, today's students, often called Millennials, have some distinctive characteristics, just like the Baby Boomers. Like any meta-model, generational theory can lead to overgeneralizations and stereotyping, but as a sociological "ideal type," Millennials are readily recognizable. Defined as those who were born after 1982, Millennial students will be the largest, most diverse, and "most educationally ambitious generation ever, with more than three out of four college freshmen projecting they will earn a graduate degree."[24] Neil Howe and William Strauss identify the key characteristics of Millennials as including feeling "special," being protected, having had their lives structured, exuding confidence and optimism, aspiring to high achievement, and feeling pressured.[25] In addition, as we have seen, this generation is more spiritual and open to a search for deep meaning.

Perhaps the most important trait for learning purposes, however, is their extreme sociability. Millennials are sheep, not cats. They work together, play together, date together, and stay constantly connected by means of cell phones, laptops, BlackBerries, iPods, Facebook, and Twitter. Their social nature means that group activities prompt their attention and provide meaning; thus they prefer cooperative learning and collaboration rather than sitting alone in a library carrel reading a book. Robert DeBard points out that faculty who are Baby Boomers (born between 1943 and 1962) and Generation Xers (1963-1981) teaching Millennial students (along with sprinklings of other generations with adult learners) produce "a very complex environmental equation." He has compiled a comparative list of different traits that "can depict some of the flash points of potential conflict between Boomers, Gen Xers, and Millennials as well as give some indication as to how these conflicts can be reconciled in order to better serve the current generation of students."[26]

24. Michael D. Coomes and Robert DeBard, "A Generational Approach to Understanding Students," in *Serving the Millennial Generation*, ed. Michael D. Coomes and Robert DeBard, New Directions for Student Services, No. 106 (San Francisco: Jossey-Bass, 2004), p. 12.

25. Neil Howe and William Strauss, *Millennials Rising: The Next Great Generation* (New York: Vintage, 2000).

26. Robert DeBard, "Millennials Coming to College," in *Serving the Millennial Generation*, p. 39.

Comparing Generational Differences

	Boomers	*Gen Xers*	*Millennials*
Trust	Confident of self, not authority	Low toward authority	High toward authority
Response to institutions	Cynical	Considered naive	Committed
What they most admire	Taking charge	Creating enterprise	Following a hero of integrity
Career goals	Build a stellar career	Build a portable career	Build parallel careers
Desired career rewards	Title and the corner office	Freedom not to do	Meaningful work
Parent-child involvement	Receding	Distant	Intruding
Feelings about having children	Quantity control important	Doubtful	Definite
Childhood experience	Indulged as children	Alienated as children	Protected as children
Paramount in education	Freedom of expression	Pragmatic approach	Structure of accountability
Preferred kind of evaluation	Once a year with documentation	"Sorry, but how am I doing?"	Feedback whenever I want it
Political approach	Against oppression	Apathetic, individualistic	Pro-community
The big question	What does it mean?	Does it work?	How do we build it?

This is a slightly reworked version of Table 3.1 in Robert DeBard, "Millennials Coming to College," in *Serving the Millennial Generation*, ed. Michael D. Coomes and Robert DeBard, New Directions for Student Services, No. 106 (San Francisco: Jossey-Bass, 2004), p. 38.

The complexity of human identity noted in Medina's second "brain rule" becomes apparent as we attempt to make generalizations about "who your students are." Unique brain development as a function of biology and environment also results in different kinds of strengths in learning styles. While many different models of learning styles have been developed, I find the *Index of Learning Styles* formulated by Richard M. Felder and Linda K. Silverman to be useful. They propose that learners range in preferences in four dimensions: active/reflective, sensing/intuitive, visual/verbal, and sequential/global.[27] As we noted earlier, only a few of today's students are the

27. For descriptions of the Index, the learning styles, and a free online learning style

60

kind of reflective, solitary, abstract thinkers that professors tend to be. Most college students are "concrete active" or "sensing perceiving" learners. Coupled with their generational tendencies, it is not surprising that "most undergraduates prefer to learn in groups rather than on their own. As a result, they are more comfortable and effective in discussions than in lectures. Moreover, they tend to grasp concrete facts more readily than abstract concepts or theories."[28] These students need high degrees of structure and lucid, sequential steps spelled out for them in assignments. They tend to be tangible and practical, wanting to know why they are doing something and requiring specific examples to grasp theoretical concepts. Uncomfortable with ambiguity — often because of the double whammy of their cognitive developmental level and their learning style — they need immediate feedback on the progress of their learning. They need different kinds of input — tactile, aural, visual — in order to grasp concepts.

Gender, class, and ethnicity also affect the ways in which people learn. The authors of *Women's Ways of Knowing*, for example, note that many women are "connected knowers," attempting to connect and reconcile different points of view, trying to mediate among oppositions, and paying special attention to context. This is contrasted to "separate knowers," more typically men, who are adversarial, eager to analyze and argue, ready to pursue principles at the cost of relationships.[29] And working-class students, Peter Filene notes, may use more informal discourse in the classroom, be comfortable with heated and loud debate with many interruptions, and exhibit more skepticism toward academic standing and authority.[30] Finally, the ever-increasing number of cultures and ethnicities found in American college classrooms further complicates matters. Different cultures manifest different attitudes toward such salient issues as authority, collaboration, self-disclosure, and personal forcefulness.

Obviously, individual students should never be stereotyped by their generation, gender, class, or ethnicity; it's entirely possible to encounter a fifty-year-old dualistic thinker, an articulate, argumentative young woman, or a self-assertive Asian-American student. But these generaliza-

---

profile, see the following Web site: http://www4.ncsu.edu/unity/lockers/users/f/felder/public/ILSpage.html.

28. Filene, *The Joy of Teaching*, p. 15.

29. Mary Field Belenky, Blythe McVicker Clinchy, Nancy Rule Goldberger, and Jill Mattuck Tarule, *Women's Ways of Knowing: The Development of Self, Voice, and Mind* (New York: Basic Books, 1986).

30. Filene, *The Joy of Teaching*, p. 19.

tions are useful in at least three ways. First, because they are commonly true, they can help you anticipate some of the dynamics of different situations, such as a class full of white, middle-class eighteen-year-olds, or one primarily comprised of working adults. Second, when a class has a dominant group (such as the white, middle-class eighteen-year-old), you may be able to better anticipate and meet the needs of the two African-American students, or the divorced adult learner with three kids. Third, recognizing both the broad patterns and the possible diversity within a class helps you understand the significance of respecting students' differences by using a variety of teaching methods, one of the seven best practices of effective teachers.

Seven Practices of Effective Teachers

There is no standard formula for good teaching, since your teaching persona and your students' identity, along with your subject area or discipline, all play decisive roles. But in a seminal study published in 1987, Arthur Chickering and Zelda Gamson identified seven teaching practices that have had consistent success in generating student learning. Numerous studies have confirmed Chickering and Gamson's findings, which provide a straightforward and helpful way to begin to think about good teaching. Effective teachers do the following:

1. Respect students' differences, using a variety of teaching methods that take into account various ways of learning and knowing.
2. Focus on active rather than passive learning.
3. Provide opportunities for cooperative learning and collaboration among students in the pursuit of clearly defined tasks.
4. Evince high academic expectations, clearly conveyed and periodically repeated.
5. Provide timely and frequent feedback on student performance.
6. Pay consistent attention to time on task.
7. Develop a rapport with students that encourages and facilitates student-faculty interaction, both during class and outside of it.[31]

31. Arthur Chickering and Zelda Gamson, "Seven Principles for Good Practice in Undergraduate Education," *American Association for Higher Education Bulletin*, no. 29 (1987): 3-7.

If professors understand and respect the ways in which their students differ from them and also differ among themselves — their cognitive levels, generational identity, and learning strengths — one of the most effective ways to teach is to employ a variety of strategies. Stephen Brookfield wisely suggests that "every class . . . contain at least three different learning modalities. This will raise the chances that at some point . . . most students will find their particular learning style or preference has been addressed, which will be reassuring and energizing for them. It will also broaden their repertoire of engagement with various learning styles, thus allowing them to flourish in the future in a greater range of situations than would otherwise have been the case."[32] College teachers should balance the fact that everyone has preferred ways of learning with the fact that part of a college education is learning to learn in a variety of ways.

Some of the rest of the seven practices resonate with common sense (paying attention to time on task seems like a no-brainer); others are more surprising, such as the fact that students learn better when a teacher has high academic expectations and continually reminds the class about those expectations. The seven practices do not guarantee that an instructor will receive high course evaluations from students (a topic that will be addressed later), but they are strategies that have been consistently demonstrated to produce higher levels of student learning. Together, they can be simply summed up in three words: *involved students learn.* Another way that educational researchers have talked about this fact is with the language of "engagement." The work of George D. Kuh and others at the Center for Postsecondary Research at Indiana University has demonstrated that the time and energy students devote to educationally purposeful activities is the single best predictor of their learning and personal development. It's not *who* students are (their IQ, or their SAT score, or their high-school GPA), but *what* they do that most affects whether or not they learn something. The National Survey of Student Engagement (NSSE, pronounced "Nessie") and the Faculty Survey of Student Engagement ("Fessie") are administered at hundreds of colleges and universities to assess the extent to which students engage in educational practices associated with high levels of learning. The five top indicators of effective educational practices are a supportive campus environment, student/faculty interaction, levels of academic challenge, enriching educational experiences, and active and collaborative learn-

32. Brookfield, *The Skillful Teacher*, pp. 267-68.

ing.[33] Although NSEE and FSEE examine the larger college learning environment beyond the laboratory or classroom, they clearly complement the Seven Practices of Effective Teachers, which identify the best ways in which we can prompt, encourage, and even cajole student involvement and engagement — from use of time, to personal connection, to demanding expectations, to active learning.

What Is Active Learning?

The physical "brain rules" associated with attention, meaning, visual learning, and repetition reveal why the principles of active learning are so decisive. As Confucius pithily put it, "What I hear, I forget; what I see, I remember; what I do, I understand." Very few people (except for college professors, who already have lots of peg holes in their brains) retain information for any length of time merely by reading or hearing. Most people need to do something with that information, whether physically or mentally. In active learning, the teacher's focus is less on transmitting or delivering a body of information and more on prompting students to process and assimilate that material. That's not to say that information doesn't need to be delivered in the first place. Without delivery, there's no processing to be done. L. Dee Fink identifies three basic components in active learning: (1) the initial acquisition of the necessary information and ideas, (2) a process of visual observation or physical action, and (3) a means of reflecting on the meaning of the information or experience.[34]

Barbara Walvoord and Virginia Johnson Anderson describe the process whereby students initially encounter material with the phrase *first exposure*.[35] In many courses, first exposure takes place through either reading or lectures, or a combination of the two. Unfortunately, it is not uncommon for students to arrive in class without having completed the

33. See Pascarella and Terenzini, *How College Affects Students;* George D. Kuh et al., *Student Success in College: Creating Conditions That Matter* (San Francisco: Jossey-Bass, 2005); and George D. Kuh et al., *Assessing Conditions to Enhance Educational Effectiveness: The Inventory for Student Success* (San Francisco: Jossey-Bass, 2005).

34. L. Dee Fink, "The Power of Course Design to Increase Student Engagement and Learning," *Peer Review: Emerging Trends and Key Debates in Undergraduate Education* 9, no. 1 (2007): 15.

35. Barbara E. Walvoord and Virginia Johnson Anderson, *Effective Grading: A Tool for Learning and Assessment* (San Francisco: Jossey-Bass, 1998), p. 53.

reading, or having completed the reading, but remembering absolutely nothing about it. How often have you heard a student testify that she has read the entire assignment, but is unable to report on anything that it says? Poor reading comprehension and retention result when students fail to move information out of immediate memory into short-term memory.

For the highest degree of active learning to occur, students must come to class prepared, having already had their first exposure to and at least one repetition of the material. There are a variety of ways to prompt this: give students daily in-class quizzes, require them to write a regular journal entry or blog on the reading, give them online quizzes that must be completed before the class period, or have them turn in an outline or a summary of the reading. While these may seem like Mickey-Mouse activities to many of us, they are actually important strategies to help students become more responsible and engaged learners. However, it is also important that an instructor not spend a lot of time grading this kind of work. Online instructional systems such as Blackboard are able to grade a quiz automatically; a student assistant, if you are so fortunate as to have one, can check off whether a journal entry or an online post has been completed. Walvoord and Anderson have developed a brilliant, non-time-consuming system for encouraging out-of-class first exposure. With each reading assignment, students are given a question or two that they must answer in writing before the class begins. Students bring two copies of their responses to class and put one on the instructor's desk as they enter. They retain the other copy to use during the class activities. The instructor might begin by asking a number of students to read their responses, by posing a general discussion question, or by asking small groups to share and compare their answers. As the class continues, students actively work with the material in any one of a number of ways, which we will discuss below. By the end of the class period, the students will hopefully have changed, refined, expanded, or better understood the answers to the questions. This means that "grading" the initial response would not be a useful exercise. Instead, the instructor need only check off that the exercise was completed.[36] Some instructors find it useful to skim through the responses to get a sense of the degree of understanding and the areas of confusion among students.

After the first exposure, students need actively to process or work with the material in order to truly learn it, gaining comprehension and long-

36. Walvoord and Anderson, *Effective Grading*, pp. 53-57.

term retention, forming and reinforcing multiple neural connections. Robert Leamnson describes the significance of repetition:

> Relationships of considerable complexity can become familiar through repeated experiences. In terms of brain circuitry, this would mean that a mental process had been repeated until multiple synapses had made one network of paths, or a mental state, the preferred one. To say that a mental process has been repeated does not mean that it is repeated exactly, the way one might repeat a long number to memorize it. More often mental circuitry gets "burned in," so to speak, when a circuit, possibly quite complex, is used repeatedly in a large variety of situations.[37]

A vast variety of strategies and techniques for active learning exists. Teachers need to consider their teaching persona and style, specific course objectives, and student population to determine which active learning strategies would be most effective. Students vehemently arguing about an issue in a small group may (or may not) be actively learning, but a solitary student silently thinking by means of an exploratory writing exercise is also actively learning. Even we academic types are active learners; we just tend toward less showy actions: reading critically, taking notes, thinking carefully and wrestling with issues. Most of our students, however, are less self-motivated and inwardly directed; they do better with collaborative, physically lively, multi-sensory activities. Designing a variety of active learning strategies for any class offers a fertile opportunity for creativity, but there is also a cornucopia of resources describing potentially useful activities. Regularly reading teaching journals in your discipline, attending pedagogical conferences, and talking with your colleagues are all effective ways to garner good ideas. You will find that some activities work better than others depending on the exact topic, class make-up, and point in the term. Some activities won't work for you, but you need to experiment a bit. Over a couple of years, you will develop an effective package of active learning practices that work for you, your course, and your students.

Here's an illustrative list of some active learning possibilities: Student presentations, panel discussions, symposia, group exercises, debates, dramatizations, role-playing, simulations, problem-solving, case studies, guided journal writing, independent study projects, game-playing, open-ended and closed small-group discussions, "fish-bowl" discussions, puz-

---

37. Leamnson, *Thinking about Teaching and Learning*, p. 15.

zles, interactive games, roundtables, mini-lectures, brainstorming, partnering, computer software development, polls and surveys, field trips, multimedia presentations, service-learning projects, video productions, Web site constructions, Wiki constructions, peer teaching, interviews, impromptu speeches, one-minute quizzes/papers, concept mapping, and writing test questions. In the next chapter we'll look in greater detail at two of the most commonly used active teaching techniques: small-group activities and — yes — lecturing.

CHAPTER 4

Teaching: Brick by Brick

The previous chapter considered broad pedagogical issues — how people and their brains learn, the importance of developing a genuine teaching persona, thinking about students' identities and learning styles, and the seven best practices of effective teachers, with special emphasis on active learning. Now we will become more practical, looking in greater detail at pedagogical processes of laying brick upon brick. Given space restraints, there is much that we will not be able to discuss here, such as teaching with technology, test construction, and cheating and plagiarism. But this chapter will cover the fundamental nuts and bolts — Teaching 101, if you will. We will begin with the basic steps of designing and planning a course and then consider in more detail a few of the learning activities most commonly employed in college-level courses.

Designing and Planning a Course

Planning a college-level course is an exacting task because for most courses, the possibilities are endless. Furthermore, it is easy to go about planning a course poorly — deciding what you want students to read and then plugging into a calendar a few papers or projects, a midterm, and a final. Good course planning that produces effective learning, however, involves a different sequence of acts. This section will outline a simple but effective way to design a course, drawing on the work of Barbara E. Walvoord, Virginia Johnson Anderson, and L. Dee Fink. Imagine that you have just been given a typical beginner's assignment of teaching an introductory course in your discipline. Here's how you might proceed.

Stage 1: Scouting the Territory

Find out everything that you can about the course: read the catalog description, talk with the department chair, and ask to see syllabi of previous iterations. Are there specific departmental goals the course needs to meet? Does it have prerequisites, and does it serve as a prerequisite for other courses? How often does it meet and for how long? Is it a face-to-face, blended, or online course? Determine the likely size of the class — twenty, forty, eighty students. If a classroom has already been assigned, visit it to familiarize yourself with the layout and the available instructional technology. Check into the institutional policies regarding such things as class attendance, final examinations, and plagiarism. For example, may students ask to change the time of their final exam if they have more than three scheduled for one day? May they ask to take an exam early to catch a plane home? Locate your school's master calendar to identify the first and last day of class, and scheduled holidays and reading days. This scouting provides the initial lay of the land on which you will then begin to construct your own class map.

Stage 2: Envisioning the Celestial City

In John Bunyan's *Pilgrim's Progress,* early on in his journey Pilgrim is granted a brief glimpse of his final goal, the Celestial City of Heaven. Similarly, you should begin your work by considering your ultimate vision for the class: what you want your students to learn. This is a crucial step but one that many professors omit. It will provide the foundation for the rest of your work of designing assignments, class activities, and evaluation procedures. Fink notes that in planning a course, faculty too often "simply develop a list of topics and then provide students with lots of information about each topic."[1] Instead, begin by identifying and writing down the

---

1. L. Dee Fink, "The Power of Course Design to Increase Student Engagement and Learning," *Peer Review: Emerging Trends and Key Debates in Undergraduate Education* 9, no. 1 (2007): 14.

most important purpose for the course. What is its thesis or ultimate destination? This account should be short, and it doesn't need to be confined to measurable goals. Walvoord and Anderson give these two quite different examples:

> At the end of the Introduction to Economics, I want my students
> - To use economic theory to explain government politics and their effects.

> At the end of Dental Hygiene, I want my students
> - To pass the state and federal boards which deal with my area;
> - To demonstrate habits of critical thinking and problem-solving;
> - To establish trust and cooperation with their patients.[2]

Here's my vision for one of my courses, a lower-division course that is typically one of the first courses that students take in the English major:

> By the end of Survey of American Literature, I want my students
> - To be skillful interpreters of American literature;
> - To be able to identify and compare major American authors, works, and literary movements;
> - To apply questions about faith and identity generated by American literature to their lives.

In identifying your vision, take into consideration your university's mission; after all, this course doesn't exist in isolation from the rest of the educational enterprise. Seattle Pacific's mission includes "producing graduates of character and competence," and my first two goals for the American literature survey are discipline-specific markers of competence, while the final item on my list is the way in which I have decided to focus on character issues in this class. It's tempting to include too many goals at this stage; it's better to keep your focus on two or three.

Stage Three: The Details of the City

Working from this big-picture vision, now write detailed concrete statements of what you want students to be able to do when they've finished the

2. Barbara E. Walvoord and Virginia Johnson Anderson, *Effective Grading: A Tool for Learning and Assessment* (San Francisco: Jossey-Bass, 1998), pp. 18-19.

course. While previously you identified a few general goals from your point of view, you will now flesh these out in more detail from the student's point of view. In educational or assessment lingo, such statements are variously called *learning goals, performance outcomes,* or *learning objectives,* and they will eventually show up on your course syllabus. Write as many of these as you need, using verbs. Don't merely describe what students will do ("Students will read works by Hawthorne, Melville, Emerson, and Dickinson"); describe exactly what students should be able to do once they've completed the course ("Students will be able to identify passages from Hawthorne, Melville, Emerson, and Dickinson and explain their thematic significance"). One way to write learning goals is to use Bloom's taxonomy,[3] a familiar tool for those in education but one which few college professors in other disciplines have ever encountered. (I had been teaching for seven years before I stumbled across it.) Bloom's taxonomy is a list of potential learning objectives arranged from lower to higher according to their scale of difficulty. Their progression mirrors William Perry's work in cognitive development.

Bloom's categories can be used both for course learning objectives and for writing test questions or essay prompts. Here are Bloom's six standard categories, along with examples of the kinds of test questions that would assess the mastery of each objective:

1. *Knowledge:* Students demonstrate a grasp of factual information. Verbs: annotate, compile, define, list, match, name, record, recall, recognize.

    Who wrote *Moby-Dick?*

2. *Comprehension:* Students show an ability to grasp the meaning of material and reframe it. Verbs: describe, summarize, discuss, explain, restate, identify.

    Summarize the plot of *Moby-Dick.*

3. *Application:* Students apply the material learned to new or concrete situations. They can use abstract ideas in concrete situations or solve simple problems within the discipline. Verbs: solve, apply, compute, calculate, illustrate, demonstrate.

    Illustrate how Melville employs metaphors in chapter 41.

3. *Taxonomy of Educational Objectives: The Classification of Educational Goals,* ed. Benjamin S. Bloom (New York: Longman, 1956).

4. *Analysis:* Students break information into its component parts to understand its organization and structure. Critical thinking or problem-solving is often involved. Verbs: compare, criticize, differentiate, estimate, discriminate.

   Compare Melville's and Emerson's views of the possibility of transcendent experiences.

5. *Synthesis:* Students put together the parts of something to form a new whole. Verbs: arrange, assemble, enumerate, extrapolate, formulate, generate, design, plan.

   Define and describe transcendentalism by using material from Melville, Emerson, and Thoreau.

6. *Evaluation:* Students make a judgment about a solution, thesis, paper, process. That judgment may include internal and external evidence and values. Verbs: defend, evaluate, appraise, assess, judge, revise.

   In your opinion, is Melville's understanding of God's power adequate? Why or why not?

L. Dee Fink has proposed a helpful modification of Bloom's taxonomy with the six general categories of learning organized interactively rather than hierarchically. He expands the definition of learning beyond knowledge and skills to include attitudes and beliefs, cautioning, "We need to go beyond wanting [students to] learn everything about the major topics; we need to formulate more exciting and challenging learning goals."[4] I don't want my students to learn about American literature just to learn about American literature; I want them to appreciate how language and narrative work, and I want the ideas in the literature to mean something to them. Fink's categories allow for these broader areas of concern. What he terms "significant learning" includes the following:

1. *Foundational knowledge:* the set of facts, principles, relationships, and so on that constitute the content of a course. It's what we want students to understand and remember.
2. *Application:* the ability to do something with the foundational knowl-

---

4. Fink, "The Power of Course Design to Increase Student Engagement and Learning," p. 14.

edge. This might involve physical skills, problem-solving, decision-making, or creative thinking.

3. *Integration:* the ability to identify the similarities or interactions between one subject and another, or between different theories, historical trends, beliefs, and so forth.

4. *Human dimension:* students' learning something in a course about themselves or about how to interact with others in life.

5. *Caring:* students' changing their feelings, interests, values, or beliefs in relation to a subject.

6. *Learning how to learn:* the ability to continue learning about the subject after the course is over.[5]

Fink believes that any course is capable of addressing — and probably should address — all six kinds of learning: "the more of all six the course can promote, the more significant will be the overall learning experience for the student."[6] By moving beyond information and application to learning or changing something about themselves, students will learn more as this attaches knowledge to a major peg hole in their brains — their concern with themselves and their identity.

Stage Four: Drawing the Map

You are now ready to begin working on a more specific outline for the course, a map for the journey. At this point the map will only identify the major stops along the way, the nature and sequence of the major tests and assignments, not supply a day-by-day description of the expedition. Walvoord and Anderson call this the "course skeleton," and it helps you to put together an "assignment-centered course" as opposed to a "coverage-centered course."[7] According to Walvoord and Anderson, "Coverage does not disappear under the assignment-centered model: basic facts, concepts, and procedures are still important; lectures may be used as a pedagogical device; textbooks may be assigned and read. However, the course planning

5. Fink, "The Power of Course Design to Increase Student Engagement and Learning," pp. 13-14. See also L. Dee Fink, *Creating Significant Learning Experiences: An Integrated Approach to Designing College Courses* (San Francisco: Jossey-Bass, 2003).

6. Fink, "The Power of Course Design to Increase Student Engagement and Learning," p. 14.

7. Walvoord and Anderson, *Effective Grading*, p. 26.

process begins by focusing on the assignments, tests, and exams that will both teach and test what the teacher most wants students to know."[8]

When I worked with the coverage model, I began designing my course by dividing the body of American literature (which I must "cover") into the weeks of the instructional term. Survey courses of any kind are especially liable to this kind of thought as the tyranny of coverage perpetually looms. Similarly, for an introductory course in the sciences or social sciences, the instructor might identify the number of chapters in the textbook and divide them up among the weeks of the term. My course skeleton for a ten-week class in the quarter system might look like this:

Week 1: Pre-Encounter literature
Week 2: Colonial literature
Week 3: Literature of the Republic
Week 4: American Renaissance
Week 5: American Renaissance
Week 6: Age of Realism
Week 7: Age of Realism
Week 8: Modern poetry
Week 9: Modern fiction
Week 10: Postmodernism

Once I had listed all the major periods that I needed to cover, I would add the tests and papers. In my early years of teaching, this always involved a midterm, a final, a short paper, and a long paper. All were intended to assess whether students had read, understood, and could interpret the works we had covered in class lectures and discussions.

The assignment-based course, in contrast, is constructed by taking what you want your students to learn (the learning objectives) and determining the specific ways in which they will learn those things (the learning activities) and the ways in which you will test whether they have learned these things (the assessment processes). Although I instinctively assumed that writing a paper or taking a test was "a learning experience," I had not carefully thought through how a particular assignment might teach and/or test; nor had I structured the assignments in such a way as to use them as learning activities. Constructing my course skeleton for American literature beginning with the learning objectives meant that I needed to develop

8. Walvoord and Anderson, *Effective Grading*, p. 26.

activities that would teach students how to interpret American literature; how to identify and compare major authors, works, and literary movements; and how to apply questions about faith and identity generated by the literature to their own lives, as well as assess the degree to which students had learned all these things. My assignment-based course skeleton might look like this:

Week 1:
Week 2: Essay #1: Short interpretive essay
Week 3: Test #1: Identify and compare
Week 4: Revision of essay #1
Week 5:
Week 6: Test #2: Identify and compare
Week 7:
Week 8: Essay #2: Short personal essay
Week 9: Test #3: Identify and compare
Week 10: Revision of essay #2
Final: Comprehensive exam with identification and comparison questions, a short interpretive essay, and a personal essay

The tests and assignments are specifically designed to fit the kind of learning that I most want for the course, and they also give students the opportunity to learn by means of practicing, revising, and repeating activities.

After developing a skeleton outline, you should check for potential mismatches between the desired learning objectives, methods of instruction, and means of assessment. Faculty often claim that they want to teach students how to synthesize, make ethical judgments, or think critically, but then they give exams that only ask students to repeat foundational knowledge. Or, if instructors do include test questions that require analysis or synthesis, they may not have given their students any practice in such thought processes. For example, the first couple of years that I taught American literature, one of my specific learning goals was for students to be able to *evaluate* transcendentalism from their own religious or ethical perspective. The final exam included what I modestly considered a brilliant essay question to that effect. Unfortunately, however, I had spent the class periods on this topic *defining* transcendentalism and dispensing *information* about transcendental authors and their works. I had given the students no specific instruction in or opportunity to practice the kind of higher-level cognitive processes that my brilliant question required. With-

75

out preparation in and practice of critical thinking skills, students' responses to questions that demanded these skills too often were merely a jumbled list of all the relevant (and sometimes irrelevant) facts or pieces of information that they could remember.

A second reality check in course planning involves considering the feasibility of the assignments in terms of your own workload. While it might be optimal in a literature, philosophy, or history course for every student to write a weekly five-page essay which is then discussed in an individual conference (in the manner of the British tutorial system), few of us have the time and teaching load that would permit this. Walvoord and Anderson give the example of a course skeleton for a business management course that required eight five- to eight-page written case analyses, one due every other week. The professor's primary course objective was to have his students be able to make business decisions using management tools, so the assignments fit the objective well. But this skeleton was a recipe for an exhausted professor and one mediocre case study after another. Walvoord and Anderson explained what happened: "The papers were coming at him so fast, and there were so many of them, that he didn't have time to give these students the guidance they needed to improve, so next time they repeated their mistakes."[9] All eight units in the course were mandated by accreditation standards, so reducing coverage was not an option. Instead, the instructor devised a series of short, sequenced assignments that gradually taught students how to write a good case study, section by section. By helping students learn how to think and write about one section at a time, he eventually received better case studies. Students were required to write and think about each case, but at the end of the semester, they had produced three good case studies instead of completing eight mediocre ones.

Stage Five: Driving Instructions

The final stage of course planning involves providing students with detailed and explicit instructions for each assignment. What may seem painfully obvious to you is often a complete mystery to them. Millennials, sequential learners, and Perry's dualistic thinkers are in special need of clear sequencing of tasks. As Walvoord and Anderson say, "Students will complete the assignment they think you made, not the assignment you actually

---

9. Walvoord and Anderson, *Effective Grading*, p. 36.

made."[10] The communication skills and organizational savvy of the effective college teacher come into play here. Assignments should always be given in writing, so students can consult them as they work on the paper, problem, or project, and you should check with students while they are working to see if any questions or misunderstandings have arisen. My assignments always spell out a recommended process that should be followed. Listing and explaining the standards and criteria that will be used in grading the assignment is also a key step. Some instructors prefer to provide a checklist for students to use to judge whether their work is complete; others may provide a grading sheet or rubric. Several examples of detailed written assignments are included in the following sections, which consider some of the most common and effective ways to help students engage in active learning.

Using Small Groups to Facilitate Learning

Item number three on the list of the seven best practices of effective teachers is to provide opportunities for cooperative learning and collaboration among students in the pursuit of clearly defined tasks. Collaborative learning requires groups of students to work together to solve a problem, complete a task, or create a product. Its effectiveness has been repeatedly demonstrated. In 1996 Karl A. Smith noted that nearly six hundred experimental studies and one hundred correlation studies had been conducted comparing the effectiveness of cooperative, competitive, and individualistic efforts. The results? "The more students work in cooperative learning groups, the more they will learn, the better they will understand what they are learning, the easier it will be to remember what they learn, and the better they will feel about themselves, the class, and their classmates."[11] Not only is collaborative work one of the most effective ways to learn anything, it also is especially apt for Millennials' ways of thinking and operating. Furthermore, the ability to work with a team to accomplish a task is one of the most frequently requested skills by employers. The ability to move beyond individual performance to collaborate on a task has become a central part of operating in to-

10. Walvoord and Anderson, *Effective Grading*, p. 38.

11. Karl A. Smith, "Cooperative Learning: Making 'Groupwork' Work," in *Using Active Learning in College Classes: A Range of Options for Faculty*, ed. Tracey E. Sutherland and Charles C. Bonwell, New Directions for Teaching and Learning, no. 67 (San Francisco: Jossey-Bass, 1996), p. 72.

day's complex, specialized, and global world, as anyone who works at Boeing, Microsoft, Starbucks, or Google can attest.

Yet many college professors resist using small groups. This is especially true in the sciences, despite considerable evidence from research conducted under the auspices of the National Science Foundation that "inquiry-based" or "problem-based" learning in which teams of students work to apply scientific principles and reasoning to real-world problems produces much higher levels of learning and comprehension than traditional lecture-based introductory courses.[12] In an article in the *Chronicle of Higher Education*, Jeffrey Brainard notes that liberal-arts colleges have been quicker to use these new pedagogical approaches than research institutions, where teaching effectiveness is not as highly prized and senior professors are reluctant to make changes.[13] I suspect one reason why so many professors may dread participating in small-group activities (beyond their preferred learning styles) is because such activities are so seldom well-designed. Although I've occasionally heard senior faculty with a penchant for lecturing criticize group activities as "busy work" for the students and "the lazy person's way out" for the instructor, structuring, facilitating, and evaluating group work is every bit as demanding as writing and delivering a good lecture. Group work can take place in class or outside of class. This section will focus on using groups within class, although many of the same principles will apply to groups working independently outside of class.

Begin by defining the objectives for the group work. What can students accomplish together that can't be done by your telling the class something in a lecture or by a single student working alone on a problem or a question? For example, one skill that I often teach is how to conduct a poetry explication. I can, and do, model this by unpacking a poem in a lecture, but the most effective way for students to learn how to do an explication — before I assign an explication essay — is for them to practice it together. Many eyes examining a poem always see more than two, as we also discover during class discussion. Weaknesses in assertions and lack of evidence quickly emerge during small-group exchanges. My goal in this group assignment is essentially to give my students problem-solving practice. Any group assignment needs to be clearly related to the course, so that

12. For more on problem-based learning in the sciences, see "Just-in-Time Teaching," http://134.68.135.1/jitt; "Peer-Led Team Learning," http://www.sci.ccny.cuny.edu/~chemwksp/index.html; and "Problem-Based Learning," http://www.udel.edu/pbl.

13. Jeffrey Brainard, "The Tough Road to Better Science Teaching," *The Chronicle of Higher Education*, 3 August 2007, p. A17.

Gospels ~ 2 to 3
Acts 2

Paul's letter
Pauline letter
NT Pauline

students see the value in the activity; knowing that a paper assignment is coming up that will require explication skills, for example, serves as a great motivator. The activity also needs to be interesting and challenging, but accomplishable in the given amount of time.

Although some instructors allow students to form their own groups, I advise instructors to create the groups themselves, deliberately thinking about the group structure in a way that is pertinent to the assignment. That may mean creating a certain mix of majors/nonmajors, stronger students/ weaker students, men/women, extraverts/introverts, and so on. In a general education course, I tend to attempt to balance gender and disciplinary interests; in a course in the major, I will pay more attention to academic performance and verbal assertiveness. If groups self-identify, friends will cluster together, and marginal students will feel more marginalized. A good small group will have an odd number — three, five, or seven — depending on the overall size of the class. Use a PowerPoint slide, overhead, or handout to indicate each group's number (or name, if you are creative) and membership. This eases the movement into group work during class time and helps students to learn each other's names. I tend to use the same groups for an entire term, but you can also create different groups for different tasks.

Two crucial elements of effective group work are a clear, deliverable goal and an established method of assessment. Consider the difference between telling a group to "talk about the reading" and asking them to identify the reading's three central points, the most significant question they still have about the topic, and one example of an application of the theory. Group work assignments must include a concrete outcome that the group will be responsible to deliver and a specific amount of time in which to conduct the work. Deliverables might be a paper, a presentation, a paragraph, an oral report, a design, a lab report, a Web site, a PowerPoint slide, and so forth. Wikis provide a new technological strategy for collaboration with a deliverable product. A brief handout or overhead outlining the question(s), with specific instructions regarding the deliverable, both provides a focus and demonstrates that you have carefully thought through the assignment; it is meaningful. For an in-class deliverable, I typically require each group to produce a written paragraph or short report that all participants sign before submitting. Sometimes I will ask selected groups for oral reports on their deliverable; this is especially useful when the groups are debating a controversial issue, as different groups may reach different conclusions. In a typical ninety-minute class, I might use some form of lecture and discussion for the first thirty-five minutes; ask small groups to work on a problem or

Revelation   CFR
                    W. View   79

question for fifteen minutes; and then spend the remainder of the class hearing the reports and the ensuing questions, discussions, and debates that will arise. Group objectives and deliverables need to be highly structured for first-year and second-year students; more advanced students can be given more latitude in how they proceed.

The first time you use groups in a class, it's useful to talk briefly about group dynamics: everyone's responsibility to contribute, the need to respect differing opinions but without fear of voicing disagreement, the need to stay on topic (time on task!). Students also may need an introduction to the idea of group roles. Some instructors assign roles; others let the students decide for themselves. Common group roles include the group leader, a timekeeper, a recorder, a checker, a summarizer, and an elaborator.[14] I most often use groups of five students, who are assigned to work together for the entire term. Each time there is an in-class group task, students are required to rotate roles: the leader, who is responsible for seeing that everyone talks and that the group stays on task; the timekeeper, who watches the clock to make sure that the deliverable is ready at the conclusion of the assigned time; the scribe, who writes the paragraph or short answer to be turned in; and the reporter, who must be ready to give an oral report if requested. Because one member of each group is without a prescribed role, absences won't wreak havoc. It's important to me that different students take on the role of leader, reporter, and so on, and I keep track of this (by means of the written report turned in by the group which identifies the roles).

Group interactions can be richer if individual students have the chance to reflect on a question or a problem and write down their ideas before the group discussion begins. This is especially helpful for more introverted students, and the group leader can initiate the discussion by having everyone in the group read his or her initial response. As the groups are working, your role as a facilitator and resource person should continue. Don't just sit at your desk and read the *New York Times*. Walk around the classroom and listen to the discussions. Tell your students that you are available as a resource — if they don't understand something, need additional information, have a disagreement, etcetera — so that they can call you over to their circle if they wish. Otherwise, I tend not to say much unless I notice that a group is sitting in silence or has moved completely off task, although the fact that I will walk up, stand near a group, and listen to their discussion, while disconcerting at

---

14. See "Doing Collaborative Learning," http://www.wcer.wisc.edu/archive/cl1/cl/doingcl/grproles.htm.

first, does tend to keep them focused. The time deadline and need for a deliverable also helps. After two or three group meetings, it sometimes becomes clear that one (it is seldom more than one) group isn't functioning, hasn't clicked or learned to work together. At this point, I might make a few strategic transfers of membership based on my observations.

When it comes to assessment, instructors need to evaluate both the deliverable and the group interactions. I return the written deliverables to the group during the next group assignment period, with brief comments, corrections, and a plus/check/minus grade that all members who were present receive. Individual students are accountable to be in class for the group work and to assume each designated role at some point during the term. I also require that each student turn in a one-paragraph written evaluation of their group's dynamics near the end of the term. I've found that students are not shy about identifying group troublemakers or slackers. Another strategy is to hold periodic group-processing sessions, asking each group to list three things it is doing well and one or more ways in which it could improve.[15]

Here's an example of a longer, complex group assignment that's been successful in a course for first-year honors students. This is a demanding assignment that weaves together many different learning activities and requires both individual and group responsibility. Beginning honors students can handle it, and I've also used a variation in upper-division courses, but it's not the kind of thing you could ask most first-year students to do. Here's the assignment sheet the students receive:

Your Name
Instructor's Name
USCH 1000
Due Date

Presentation and Paper #1:
Teaching and Analyzing a Chapter of *Guns, Germs, and Steel*

Let's plunge into college work. This assignment asks you to read and analyze a text, work in a collaborative group, make an oral presentation, write an argumentative essay, and employ effective revision skills — all in one fell

15. Smith, "Cooperative Learning," p. 76.

swoop. Your mission is twofold: (1) to teach, as a group of scholars, one chapter from *Guns, Germs, and Steel* to the rest of the class, and (2) to write, as an individual scholar, a paper describing and critiquing that chapter.

In *Guns, Germs, and Steel*, Jared Diamond first presents his argument in broad strokes and then devotes a number of chapters to particular manifestations of those broader ideas. The entire class will read, study, and discuss Chapters 1-6, but then six small groups will be responsible for respectively reading and teaching Chapters 8, 9, 11, 12, 13, and 14. You need not read the chapters presented by the other groups, and you should not assume, in your presentation, that the other members of the class have read them. (Of course, everyone is *welcome* to read all the chapters!)

After you read the chapter assigned to your group, you collectively should discuss its major points, the way in which those points fit in with Diamond's broader argument, and your responses. Make sure you understand Diamond's argument and supporting evidence before you begin to critique it. Then discuss if he convinces you. What are some flaws in his reasoning or evidence that you perceive? What examples do you find especially convincing? Are there parallels that either persuade or dissuade you from agreeing with him? How does your faith enter into your response? Be open to the fact that the members of your group might not agree on these issues, and try to discuss these disagreements openly and with charity. Group consensus is not necessary, and different perspectives could be included in the class presentation.

After you are sure that you understand Diamond's point and have thought about its strengths and weaknesses, your group should strategize about the best way to present the material. Your classroom presentation should be ten-fifteen minutes, and all the members of your group must verbally participate in that presentation. It is up to you to decide how best to organize and communicate the material. What central concept do you want the class to grasp? What particular example or examples do you want them to retain? You will find that Diamond's chapters are full of facts, details, and examples, and you won't be able to cover everything. What words, sights, tastes, or sounds would best help the class grasp the central idea? And finally, what differing points of view might be held in response to these ideas? The group presentation will be evaluated on three criteria: (1) content (accurate identification of Diamond's central points, representative examples, and logical critique), (2) clarity (of presentation), and (3) creativity (capturing your audience's interest), with three points possible for each criterion and a total of nine class participation points.

Following the group presentation, you will write a paper with the purpose of evaluating the argument of the chapter assigned to you. In order to do this, you will need to give a summary and description of that argument, as well as an evaluation and a critique. Your summary should indicate how the chapter fits into the argument of the book as a whole, and information from other chapters could be drawn upon in order to support your analysis. You need not consult additional sources beyond the book, but you are free to do so, if you wish.

In your introduction, grab your reader's interest, establish a context, and present your thesis. The body of the essay should include both summary and analysis, and well-chosen quotes will add considerably to its success. But don't use a quote when a simple paraphrase would do, such as in the case of presenting facts or data. Your conclusion should suggest an answer to the challenge — so what? One way to do this might be to suggest how your discussion of this particular chapter could lead towards a larger end — towards a defense or a critique of Diamond's entire line of argument.

Your guidance for technical and grammatical matters should be *The Everyday Writer,* which describes the format your essay should take and the way to document your sources according to MLA style in chapters 48-51. In appearance, your essay should resemble this handout. Your instructors will evaluate your essay according to the criteria described in "SPU University Scholars Program Criteria for Grades on Essays and Papers." Along with your paper, you will also submit a one-paragraph assessment of how your group functioned, including comments on each member of the group.

Notice that this kind of paper does not ask you to talk about your experience of reading the book (i.e., "At first I was really confused, but now I understand that Diamond's claim about the zebra makes a lot of sense"). Rather, you are to make a claim and prove it (i.e., "Diamond's argument that the zebra [. . .] is convincing, despite [. . .]"). In a formal academic paper, there are no rules against using personal pronouns, but some writers tend to include phrases such as "I think" that could easily be eliminated. Use personal references only if they help you to advance your case.

While this assignment still needs refinement, notice the way it includes clear deliverables that will be assessed, with both individual and group responsibility. It also includes lots of explicit instructions, examples, and modeling. Students find this to be a challenging assignment, but they have produced some remarkably creative and effective presentations, and four years later many of them still talk about this assignment and continue to wrestle with Diamond's ideas. The evidence of the papers and subsequent tests establishes that this activity produces in most students a firm grasp of Diamond's claims and some serious thought about the implications of those claims.

Lecturing and Learning

For many years, the primary method of instruction in American higher education has been the lecture. I will be the first to admit that I enjoy a well-constructed, clearly delivered, intellectually stimulating lecture. I also enjoy writing lectures — little mini-seminar papers in which I get to demonstrate the breadth of my knowledge, flourish verbal curlicues, and create memorable examples. Lectures also allow me to "cover" a lot of ground in an all-too-brief class period. And I'm a ham at heart: I enjoy "performing" in front of a class. Nonetheless, over my years of teaching, I have become increasingly convinced that lecturing is like salt — a little goes a long way. There are those few born lecturers — I'm sure you could name one or two — who can keep any size group on the edge of their seats, engaged and actively learning class after class, day after day. But be honest: Are you such a dynamic performer?

In Ken Bain's study titled *What the Best College Teachers Do*, his team "found no great teachers who relied solely on lectures . . . but we did find people whose lectures helped students learn deeply and extensively because they raised questions and won students' attention to those issues."[16] As Bain notes, lecturing can be an effective tool for learning, but it is only the rare instructor who has the dynamic personality and the communication skills to succeed in long periods of lecturing. But every teacher will do some lecturing and consequently needs to think carefully about *why* to lecture and *how* to lecture. Bain cautions that a lecture should not be used to present "an encyclopedic coverage of some subject, or as a way to impress students with how much the teacher knows."[17] In one of the most extensively researched studies of lecturing, Donald A. Bligh found that "the lecture is as effective as other methods for transmitting information," but is

16. Ken Bain, *What the Best College Teachers Do* (Cambridge: Harvard University Press, 2004), p. 107.

17. Bain, *What the Best College Teachers Do*, p. 107.

not as effective as other methods for teaching values, inspiring interest, or teaching skills.[18] A lecture can accomplish three things: (1) the presentation of information, (2) the clarification of ideas, and (3) inspiration for learning. But even the presentation of information needs to be considered carefully. Too often we rely on lectures to provide "first exposure" to basic information that would be more efficiently delivered outside the classroom — in a reading assignment, podcast, or PowerPoint slide show. What you can say in fifty minutes, students can read in fifteen.[19] If presentation of information is the primary activity in your classroom, why should students bother to attend an expensive, private, bricks-and-mortar institution, when they could read or watch an online lecture from the University of Phoenix?

There are a couple of instances, though, in which the lecture is an appropriate option for information presentation. Information that is not available in print (or on the Web) because the sources are out of date or the material is too advanced for students can be effectively delivered in a lecture, which may eventually evolve into a course packet or even a textbook. A lecture can also provide a useful summary or synthesis of information from a number of sources. Rather than having your students read five different texts about methodological naturalism, for example, you can bring five different perspectives on the topic together for them, identifying each theory's strengths, weaknesses, similarities, and differences.

Lectures work better if they are crafted in such a way as to build on or clarify ideas or information first encountered in another fashion, such as in a reading assignment or a lab activity. If students think that your lectures are merely a repetition of the material in the textbook, they will either (a) stop attending class, or (b) not do the reading. This is tricky because, as we have seen, repetition of information is essential for deep learning. Well-meaning instructors may lecture to provide such repetition, but any lecture that treats material covered in a text must go beyond merely repeating that information. Professors need both to insure that students do the reading before class (by means of easy-to-grade quizzes, written responses, etc.) and to construct lectures in such a way as to engage students with the material in a new way.

The third and potentially most powerful use of the lecture is to provide the students with a model (in the person of the lecturer) of intellec-

---

18. Donald A. Bligh, *What's the Use of Lectures?* (San Francisco: Jossey-Bass, 2000), p. 3.
19. Bain, *What the Best College Teachers Do*, p. 108.

tual curiosity, a passion for learning, devotion to a subject, ideal, or belief, and strategies of approaching problems and issues.[20] If you are bored by your own lecture, it doesn't stand a chance with students. If you are going to do much extended lecturing, you need to develop a charismatic, vibrant, droll (or witty) teaching persona that charms students into learning and retains their attention — whether that is because you are an enthusiastic but absent-minded professor, a dapper and elegant wordsmith, a quiet but dramatic poet, or a loud and wacky performer with garish ties. There isn't simply one model of a good lecturer; a lecturer needs a public persona that is compatible with her or his more private personality. As you present and work with information, you should be igniting your students' curiosity and helping them think.

A number of basic communication strategies will enhance lecturing. First and foremost, *Never read a lecture.* Nothing is more dull. Always speak extemporaneously from notes or an outline. Every lecture should include something that you are genuinely excited about, for that enthusiasm will manifest itself in some way, often unconsciously. Keep your students' attention by using eye contact, visual cues, and verbal tactics. I've found it a humbling experience to have an observer track the eye contact that I make during a class period. I, like most teachers unless they consciously work at it, tend to teach from one side of the room over the other. My lecture notes now remind me to look to the left at certain key points. Don't just stand at the podium or sit at the front of the room; walk around from one side to another; occasionally go down an aisle and talk from the back of the room. Moving objects, including talking heads, keep attention better than immobile ones. That's also why it's better to include visual examples whenever possible — short film clips, slides, photographs, drawings on the whiteboard, books or other tactile objects that you pass around. One Victorian literature professor brings whalebone corsets, Earl Grey tea, and lavender to class to help her students understand the physical world of Jane Austen.[21] PowerPoint slides should always include pictures or diagrams — not just text — and animated slides are better than static ones. Remember how brains learn best.

Effective verbal tactics include pausing and repeating when new

20. Bligh argues, "The inspirational role of lectures is grossly overstated" (*What's the Use of Lectures?*, p. 15).

21. See Amy Leal, "Dressing Literary History," http://chronicle.com/weekly/v53/i48/48b00501.htm.

words, names, or concepts are introduced, as well as writing the term on the board or overhead. This signals students that they should pay special attention. First-year and second-year students often need help in learning how to sort out key points and concepts from the flood of words, elaborations, explanations, examples, jokes, comments, and so forth surrounding these ideas. Bligh notes that pausing for a moment of silence to allow students to think is an important strategy to prevent interference, one of the chief causes of forgetting in lectures: "Silences provide time for consolidation and thought. Their timing requires the skill of an actor."[22] Always highlight the key points of the lecture at the beginning and return to them in a summary at the end. This may seem mind-numbingly repetitive to you, but it's necessary for students. A good way to test whether you have clearly delivered the information is to do a "one-minute paper" at the end of the class, which involves having the students answer two questions: "What was the most important idea in the lecture today?" and "What questions do you still have about this topic?"[23] It takes very little time to quickly skim these responses, and if you learn that your explanation of globalization theory completely confused two-thirds of the class, you can begin the next period by saying, "Your responses indicate that you're having some problems understanding globalization, so let's start by reviewing that concept." This strategy tells students that you listen to them, are concerned that they understand, and are willing to help them grasp the material. In addition, the one-minute paper is an easy way to take attendance, or give everyone a check mark for participation.

In the lecture's content, make a deliberate attempt to connect the material with student interests. As Bain says, "Start with the students rather than the discipline."[24] Give examples that relate to their lives. If you are presenting Aristotle's theories of friendship, for example, use examples of friendships from popular television shows or movies. If you are sorting out trans fats from other fats, list how much of each kind of fat is in the campus dining-hall pizza. Search for the hole in the students' mental pegboard to which to attach information. Another strategy is to begin the lecture with some kind of personal rhetorical question: How would you feel if your mother married your uncle immediately after your father mysteri-

22. Bligh, *What's the Use of Lectures?*, p. 32.

23. The one-minute paper was developed by Thomas A. Angelo and K. Patricia Cross, *Classroom Assessment Techniques: A Handbook for College Teachers,* 2d ed. (San Francisco: Jossey-Bass, 1993).

24. Bain, *What the Best College Teachers Do*, p. 110.

ously died? Tracing the history of an idea or the development of competing theories can be verbally sketched as a suspenseful drama: who will discover DNA first? Who has the best theory concerning urban poverty: Oscar Lewis or Janice Perlman? Peter Filene suggests asking a question that stirs up curiosity and then providing an answer with a vignette.[25]

Think of your lectures as a way of teaching students how to listen, learn, and think, rather than simply as an information dump. As a much-repeated quotation commonly attributed to Yeats says, "Education is not filling a bucket, but lighting a fire." If you provide lecture outlines in a handout, overhead, or PowerPoint slide, furnish only a skeleton, so that students must be actively engaged in taking notes. Stop occasionally and ask the class questions. "What was the most important point covered so far?" "Can anyone provide another example of unconscious stereotyping that they've noticed on campus?" "Who can explain the difference between metonymy and metaphor?" Ask students to put down their pens or close their computers for a moment and think about an issue. By posing rhetorical questions, asking students to repeat an idea that you've just presented, or requesting additional examples, you move the students into active learning.

While you are talking, stay alert to your students' responses. Do they look blank, intrigued, or puzzled? Are the boys in the baseball caps at the back of the room slumping down in their seats? Is there a group of three young women huddling over a computer screen and pointing? (I once observed a class in which a group of students spent most of their time shoe-shopping on the Internet.) Does the class laugh at your jokes? Does it feel like everyone is staring at you with a glazed expression? Or are they looking out of the window? How many people are yawning?

The most crucial aspect of lecturing is the Ten-Minute Rule: an audience's attention steadily increases from the beginning of a lecture until about ten minutes into the lecture, at which point it begins to go down. That's just the way the physical brain functions. After about fifteen minutes of straight lecturing, you've lost most of your audience, except for the handful who know how to process the material actively on their own. An effective classroom lecturer will never present nonstop content for fifty or ninety minutes. At the very least, he or she will provide a mental respite by telling a joke or a story, furnishing a visual or a tactile example, or pausing to take student questions. But there are a variety of ways in which extended lec-

25. Peter Filene, *The Joy of Teaching: A Practical Guide for New College Instructors* (Chapel Hill: University of North Carolina Press, 2005), p. 49.

tures can be effectively delivered as a sequence of mini-lectures interspersed with short, active-learning exercises. I never speak for more than fifteen minutes at a stretch in any class, because I don't think that I have a strong enough presentational persona or joke-telling ability (I tend to forget punch lines) to provide the necessary mental breaks. Besides, my primary goal is to have my students thinking, not just listening. I tend to break up my lectures a lot more frequently than every fifteen minutes, but that's the longest time I'd advise anyone to go without some kind of change of pace.

The simplest way to alter the pace is to pose a question. The more concrete the question, the better. "What do you think of this theory?" will produce responses only in a senior-level course. But unless you deliberately call on individuals — "Miss Jones, could you describe Ohm's Law for us?" — this strategy may engage only a small handful of the class, the eager beavers whose hands shoot up in the air at any opportune moment. Research on college class participation has shown that in classes of fewer than forty students, four to five students do about 75 percent of the talking, while in larger classes, participation levels drop even further.[26] And frequently, the talkers are male. To combat this problem, I've grown comfortable with making cold calls, but I explain to my students at the beginning of each term that I will do this and why. Extremely shy students have the option of talking with me and asking to be excused, but only a handful over the years have done so.

The pause, or short break, is another simple but effective way to break up a lecture. During the pause, students can fill gaps in their notes, compare notes with a partner, stretch and touch their toes, or do a quick writing exercise, perhaps listing pros and cons, or taking a certain stance.[27] Take five minutes for students to write a response, another five minutes to have several students read their responses, and then go on to the next lecture segment — unless a passionate discussion breaks out. "Think, pair, share" is an active learning strategy first proposed by Frank Lyman that has become widely adopted.[28] Stop your lecture to propose a challenging or

26. Susan Ledlow, "Using Think-Pair-Share in the College Classroom," http://clte.asu
.edu/active/usingtps.pdf.

27. Bligh notes that even a break as short as twenty-five seconds prompts attention levels to come back up and results in better learning performances. He concludes, "There is a strong case for short breaks and changes in teaching method in each period of teaching" (*What's the Use of Lectures?*, p. 52).

28. Frank T. Lyman, "The Responsive Classroom Discussion: The Inclusion of All Students," in *Mainstreaming Digest*, ed. A. S. Anderson (College Park: University of Maryland Press, 1981), pp. 109-13.

open-ended question, and give the class at least one minute of silence to think. This allows students to begin to formulate their answers by retrieving information from their long-term memory, re-examining a text, or looking over the notes they have just taken. Then have students form pairs, share their responses, and discuss their ideas for a few minutes. When you re-convene the class, you can ask for volunteer comments, or take a "vote" on a controversial issue; alternatively, you can omit the class discussion and ask each student to submit a brief written response. Because students have had a chance to think on their own and compare responses with someone else, they are much less reluctant to discuss their ideas with the class as a whole and more comfortable stating their opinions in writing. Robert Leamnson recommends interrupting the lecture for a five-minute study/performance period. Student groups of two or three review their lecture notes and then a one- or two-question quiz sheet prepared in advance is administered. The correct answers are then reviewed, which both initiates discussion and provides immediate feedback: "Knowing as soon as possible whether they are correct or not in their thinking is reinforcing if they are correct, or it will quickly dislodge wrong ideas if they are not."[29]

Every college professor relies to some degree or another on lecturing. But the evidence strongly suggests that none of us should exclusively employ the lecture if we wish to inspire our students to become active and engaged learners and that we should purposefully break up periods of lecturing with other activities.

Knowing and Loving: Facilitating Learning through Rapport

As we have discussed, to be an effective teacher, you must know and love not only your discipline but also your students. If you are able to think of each one as a miracle of creation, uniquely gifted with strengths, talents, and abilities, and to treat each student with respect and affection, you will help everyone learn. Believing that students are able to learn — even if they achieve different levels of mastery and have varying strengths — is a fundamental requirement for an effective teacher. Recognizing each one as being created in the image of God, even if you have to search for it, is an

---

29. Robert Leamnson, *Thinking about Teaching and Learning: Developing Habits of Learning with First-Year College and University Students* (Sterling, Va.: Stylus, 1999), pp. 68-69.

important pedagogical spiritual discipline. Praying for your students daily, especially the ones that are struggling, emotionally and/or academically, or those whom you personally dislike (there's always a few), helps immensely. And yet no experience of the new professor is as demoralizing as dealing with rowdy, disrespectful, unruly students. Nothing takes as much emotional energy or leads to such vocational doubt.

As the "Seven Best Practices of Effective Teachers" indicate, rapport is a crucial aspect of teaching and learning. Robert Boice, whose research on new faculty we have consulted before, has made an extensive study of the nature, frequency, and effectiveness of what he calls "Classroom Incivilities" (CIs) — actions that forestall or disrupt rapport. Boice concludes that the level of CIs is one of the first and most telling signs of success or failure in teaching, as measured in both learning outcomes and course evaluations, not to mention the personal impact of CIs on the novice professor; as Boice observes, "Initial classroom experiences too often make or break us as teachers."[30] Over several years of study, Boice found that "CI was more common than uncommon in the classes of all novice teachers I observed; it occurred disruptively and dishearteningly in over two-thirds of the courses of novices I tracked."[31] It also occurred more often in large-enrollment classes. With the influx of Millennial students into higher education, disruptive classroom behavior appears to have increased even more since Boice's 1990 studies,[32] at the same time that many pundits are lamenting the lack of common courtesy in general social exchanges. While such disruptive behavior might be less common at a mission-driven institution, it is overly idealistic to think that it will never occur. Despite opting and paying to attend a mission-driven institution, some students will be uncivil, and despite accepting a teaching position at a mission-driven institution, some faculty will also be uncivil in the classroom. For both students and faculty alike contribute to rapport-destroying classroom incivilities.

Through interviews and observations, Boice concluded that the following rank-ordered CIs were most commonly disruptive:

1. Teachers alienating students with negative comments and nonverbal messages

---

30. Robert Boice, *Advice for New Faculty Members: Nihil Nimus* (Boston: Allyn & Bacon, 2000), p. 81.

31. Boice, *Advice for New Faculty Members*, p. 97.

32. See the special issue of *New Directions for Teaching and Learning: Addressing Faculty and Student Classroom Improprieties* 99 (2004).

2. Teachers distancing themselves from students with fast-paced, non-involving lectures
3. Students talking so loudly that teachers and other students could not be heard
4. Students disrupting class by arriving late or leaving early
5. Students making sarcastic remarks and gestures
6. Teachers surprising students with tests or grades
7. A "classroom terrorist" making unpredictable, emotional, or intimidating comments[33]

Boice also discovered that such negative behavior patterns typically begin during the first few days of class. "The key initiator of classroom incivility," he claims, is the way that a teacher treats his or her students in the first few days of class. If instructors use "conspicuously positive motivators and strong immediacies" at the outset, lower levels of classroom incivilities of the type numbered 3, 4, 5, and 7 occurred.[34] If the instructor is initially cold and distant, students start acting up, and, left unchecked, this behavior will probably lead to a series of escalating incidents. Hence, the first few days of class are crucial. It is imperative that you work hard at creating a safe, hospitable learning environment during the first week of class, for once students suspect that you don't like them, or discover that you have a tendency to lecture at them for thirty or forty minutes at a time, or start browsing the Web or discussing last night's game in class, a terrible pattern is established that is difficult to break.

Novice teachers sometimes engage in brusque behavior because they are nervous and insecure. Boice found that when new teachers were attempting to be professional, business-like, or formal, or spent a good deal of time trying to establish their authority, students often (falsely) interpreted this behavior as impersonal, unfriendly, disdainful, or condescending. Yet instructors fresh out of graduate school or only a few years older than most of their students may feel as if they need to establish their credentials in order to win the respect of the class. The question of authority is often especially difficult for female faculty and faculty of color. Some students may respond to the authority invested in such faculty by means of their position with skepticism and resistance, perceiving identical behav-

---

33. Boice, *Advice for New Faculty Members*, pp. 86-87.
34. Boice, "Classroom Incivilities," *Research in Higher Education* 37, no. 4 (1996): 453; and Boice, *Advice for New Faculty Members*, p. 89.

ior in a differing light. While a white male teacher's persistent questioning may be seen as intellectually challenging, an African-American teacher's similar actions may be seen as hostile and argumentative.[35] On the one hand, you should never apologize or tell your students that you're feeling insecure about teaching. On the other hand, you shouldn't charge in on the first day of class and declare, "I have a Ph.D. from Harvard and my dissertation won a national award, so you need to listen to me." You want to convey both that you are pro-student and that you are in charge.

How to accomplish this? On the first day of class, give your students a sense of who you are as a person — your life story, values, enthusiasms, and dreams. Telling your students a little about yourself — including your undergraduate and graduate experience, why teaching and your topic excite you, your hopes for this class, your foundational beliefs, and even your own faith journey — will mitigate distance and facilitate trust. Especially if the nature of your course will challenge students' simplistic thinking and too-easy faith, it's important that they understand from the beginning that you are challenging them from a foundation of personal commitment. This is a crucial strategy for helping them move to critical commitment. You also should convey accurately the level and difficulty of the course, but in such a way that you don't come across as trying to scare students. Be demanding (high academic expectations are one of the Seven Best Practices), but supportive: "I know this is a difficult assignment, but I can help you work through it." I know of one professor who regularly told all the first-year students in his 1000-level course that it was highly unlikely that any of them were capable of doing the kind of work he expected. If that truly was the case, he should have re-classified the course or re-adjusted his expectations, instead of exercising a scare tactic that created an atmosphere of intimidation rather than of learning. As Bligh comments, "Fear . . . is not normally conducive to high student motivation."[36]

Boice places a high value on what he calls "immediacies," finding that when he coached new faculty on simple communication skills, they were better able to ward off classroom incivilities. Smiling, maintaining an open posture, leaning toward students when they are talking, and establishing eye contact are simple ways to create connections, yet it often took novice faculty weeks of deliberate work before they mastered such

35. Mia Alexander-Snow, "Dynamics of Gender, Ethnicity, and Race in Understanding Classroom Incivility," *New Directions in Teaching and Learning* 99 (2004): 21.
36. Bligh, *What's the Use of Lectures?*, p. 63.

skills.[37] Having someone observe your classroom can help you identify your own Achilles' heel in communication, and you can then write instructions into your lecture notes to be on guard against such unconscious behaviors.

The single most important act to develop rapport is learning your students' names. Students at private, teaching-intensive institutions expect this kind of personal recognition. Some instructors have an index card for every student that contains his or her name, photo (taken off the Web, or taken with a digital camera the first day of class), and some brief information. I use a seating chart, telling students that where they sit on the second day will become their assigned seat. That day I pass around a diagram of the classroom on which they sign on the appropriate spot (with the name they prefer I use), and I then keep this chart in front of me during class. When someone raises his or her hand, I can glance down and quickly locate the correct name. When students are working in small groups or doing some writing during the first two weeks, I purposefully concentrate on reviewing and learning the names of each row.

Probably the second most effective strategy to create rapport is to require all students to have a ten-minute visit with you in your office or campus coffee shop during the first two weeks of the course. Once a student has met and chatted with you personally, he or she is much more likely to drop in during office hours or when he or she needs help. Your office décor and the pictures displayed on your desk help your students realize that you are a person, while two people sitting in chairs talking with each other creates a personal rather than an adversarial dynamic. Obviously a required office visit is difficult to do with a class of a hundred students, but it may be worth the time investment for classes of twenty-five to forty students, especially if they are first-year students. I often will require an early visit at which I will return the first draft of a paper; by conveying some of my advice orally, I also save time in writing comments.

In addition to introducing yourself to the class, handling communication immediacies, learning students' names, and requiring a personal conference, there are two other strategies to keep student incivility out of your classroom: clearly conveying your expectations for student conduct, and taking action immediately if a rude incident does occur. While many of us may be surprised that students don't understand such basic rules as the importance of coming to class on time, not speaking when others are

37. Boice, *Advice for New Faculty Members*, p. 95.

speaking, reading other material or consulting an iPhone during class, I have found that many students are genuinely surprised when I rebuke them for such activities. Furthermore, different faculty may have different views on what makes up inappropriate behavior; I allow students to bring coffee and a sandwich to class, but some of my colleagues forbid food and drink. By clearly spelling out our behavioral expectations, we are further educating students about issues related to business etiquette and the effects of differing contexts. Some faculty have the students contribute to writing the classroom code of conduct, while others create their own and distribute it on the first day of class.[38] It's especially important to include clear descriptions of expectations and penalties regarding such things as tardiness, absences, late papers, early exams, illnesses, and so forth. I always include all of this kind of information in the official course syllabus. (See the Appendix for a sample syllabus template.)

When a student does act out in the classroom, you need to take immediate action. Subtle misbehavior, such as eye-rolling or online shoe-shopping, can be addressed in an individual conference after class, but any blatant incivility witnessed by the rest of the class needs to be addressed publicly. If a student makes a racist or sexist remark, you need to intervene immediately, explaining why such a comment is not appropriate. If a student rudely interrupts other students, or if a group is loudly whispering in the back row during a class discussion or lecture, you need to call them on it. I'm always on the lookout for an eager beaver or a classroom terrorist, and I will ask them to make an appointment with me, at which I will talk about their behavior and why it interferes with the rest of the class's ability to learn. Boice explains that exemplary teachers are able to turn the occasional moderate incident into a teaching opportunity. Faced with uncivil interruptions, such teachers kept their cool: "Expert teachers usually reacted respectfully, by listening carefully, as though the interruption had been offered up as a well-intentioned comment."[39] One of my colleagues, when rudely challenged by a student concerning a political point, responded, "Well, there's certainly another side to this issue. Would you like to prepare a rebuttal and present it in class next week? Why don't you come by my office so we can discuss it?" Would that I could be so quick and so forbearing!

38. A sample contract on classroom behavior can be found in Alan E. Bayer, "Promulgating Statements of Student Rights and Responsibilities," *New Directions for Teaching and Learning* 99 (2004): 84-85.

By designing and planning a course with clearly defined goals and activities for active student learning, carefully selecting your pedagogical bricks, and striving to foster rapport and respect in your classes, you have the ability to become an effective teacher — one who inspires and advances learning among a wide variety of students.

CHAPTER 5

The Faithful Professor:
Multiple Paradigms for Faith and Learning

The most distinctive aspect of the mission-driven college or university is the fact that Christian faith is a crucial part of its educational enterprise. Regardless of an institution's theological, liturgical, or historical tradition, its faculty will take seriously college students' hunger for meaning and believe that education includes addressing spiritual, philosophical, moral, and ethical issues. At the same time, however, professors at mission-driven institutions should be wary of proselytizing, indoctrinating, or encouraging simplistic judgments. Education involves seeking truth as well as conveying truth, humility as well as knowledge, criticisms as well as commitments. The search for truth lies at the heart of any educational enterprise, but the mission-driven institution maintains a holistic view of truth and persons that encompasses the truths of the heart and the soul as well as the mind.

In the days of the medieval university, Renaissance humanism, and the American Christian cultural synthesis, there was little controversy about the relationship of faith and learning, for they were assumed to be one and the same. But with the advent of the modern world, objective and subjective realms, faith and learning, the sacred and the secular were divorced and assumed different roles, responsibilities, and locations. In graduate school or the professional world, one pursued secular truth as revealed by observation, experimentation, and theorizing; in the private or religious world, one embraced a faith tradition that provided personal meaning and emotional solace. But the two didn't have much to do with each other.

In the 1950s, with the postwar expansion of American higher education, Christian scholars began thinking more seriously about the relationship of faith and learning, and a large body of literature ensued. In this same period, theologian H. Richard Niebuhr developed an influential typology of the relationship of Christian belief and the secular world in *Christ and Culture* (1951). Niebuhr does not claim that his five types are inclusive or mutually exclusive, but suggests that they represent a range of approaches to the relationship of Christ and culture. The full truth will emerge, Niebuhr contended, only in the providential historical interaction of all five.[1] Niebuhr's theologically informed types may inform the many subsequent models developed to talk about faith and learning. This chapter will identify the major voices and common language of this conversation. Naturally, I have my own preferences for how to talk about the complex ecology of faith and learning, which I will explain, and it is conceivable that your own institution, because of its history, theological affiliation, or educational philosophy, may prefer one approach over another. You should carefully explore your institution's stance toward faith and learning during your rookie years, for graduate study may have provided little training in thinking about the bigger picture or drawing connections among types of knowledge. Part of the task of a new professor at a mission-driven institution is to reflect on such issues, exploring both context and self, to discern the most authentic way in which to practice faith and learning. In the larger picture of mission-driven higher education, I think that multiple paradigms for relating faith and learning can be a strength, producing complementary practices that work within the academic Christian community to form a whole, with each approach adjusting and fine-tuning other approaches.

Institutions, persons, theologies, specific occasions of teaching, concrete practices of scholarship, audience — all impact the dance of faith and learning. Key factors include the discipline in which we work (art differs from biology) as well as our disciplinary specialty (the history of the discipline, the philosophy of the discipline, the discovery of new knowledge, the application of current knowledge, creation, interpretation, and so on). In teaching, types of courses and kinds of students will enter into the way we bring faith and learning together, just as in our scholarship, the audience and context will have an effect. Finally, theological commitments, faith traditions, and cultural backgrounds will also enter into the mix. Like Niebuhr's types, the models that this chapter discusses are not always mutually exclusive, although some approaches rule out other ones. Some models may simply be two different theoretical ways of describing the

---

1. H. Richard Niebuhr, *Christ and Culture* (New York: Harper, 1951), pp. 231-33.

same concrete activity. Models, by their very nature, tackle topics by employing metaphors, which may not always fit together tidily. Still, models are one of the best ways to illuminate some of the most common ways of thinking about faith and learning today.

Faith and Learning: Beginning Anew

One result of the Enlightenment was to divide faith and learning into distinctive areas or parts of life. Accepting this dichotomy, some conservative or fundamentalist traditions view modern learning with such a high degree of suspicion that their adherents contend that most, if not all, of the mainstream academic enterprise needs to be jettisoned in favor of a "Christian" approach based primarily upon the truths of the Bible. Ronald R. Nelson calls this school of thought *reconstructionism,* because it attempts "a radical reconstruction of the disciplines on . . . biblical foundations. The categories and epistemological presuppositions for any and all academic disciplines are to be found, they say, in the concrete revelations of the Old and New Testament."[2] Teachers and scholars need to become familiar with and employ biblical concepts and specific texts because the Scriptures are viewed as a major source of information about all academic areas. It is alleged that secular academic approaches are based on inadequate foundational beliefs and thus are epistemologically suspect and lead to faulty knowledge; therefore, standard academic practices must be jettisoned for new "Christian" disciplines based on scriptural truth. In Niebuhr's typology, this position is called "Christ against Culture."

In the first half of the twentieth century, many conservative Christian institutions of higher learning were birthed with the midwife of reconstructionism. Convinced that the learning found in the modern academy was irredeemably flawed, reconstructionist institutions promised to begin anew on biblical foundations. While such schools continued to emerge in the second half of the twentieth century, such as Jerry Falwell's Liberty University (founded in 1971), the reconstructionist approach today is more often found articulated in disciplinary terms as an alternative theory. Consider the practice of a "Christian psychology" that relies pri-

---

2. Ronald R. Nelson, "Faith-Discipline Integration: Compatibilist, Reconstructionalist, and Transformationalist Strategies," in *The Reality of Christian Learning,* ed. Harold Heie and David L. Wolfe (St. Paul, Minn.: Christian University Press, 1987), p. 325.

marily on a biblical model of personhood to employ as a guide in counseling, or Christian sociologists who identify the ideal structure of marriage and family from the teachings of Scripture. Jay Adams, for example, assumes that people's problems stem not from mental illness but from sin and advocates a biblical approach to counseling in stark opposition to secular methods. He clearly states that his approach is "not based upon scientific findings. My method is presuppositional."[3] Scientific findings should be accepted only when they illustrate and clarify biblical teaching. A few years ago, "scientific creationism" claimed status as a reconstructed science, while current debates consider whether the theory of intelligent design is a reconstructed science or a philosophical perspective, with differing definitions of science at the heart of the matter. In a reconstructionist approach, Christian learning is distinct from secular learning and unique in its practices. Maintaining the separate nature of two kinds of learning, those who would begin anew locate themselves solely in Jerusalem rather than Athens, using only the most minimal of information, processes, and procedures from the secular realm.

Faith and Learning: Separate but Equally Important

A second response also accepts modernism's dichotomy but places a high value on both spheres. Working with this assumption, one option for an educational institution that values both faith and learning is to use trained specialists in each area to carry out its mission. The faculty's responsibilities are primarily in the learning realm, focusing on objectively imparting cognitive knowledge and professional skills. Student development experts and/or campus ministry staff are responsible for fostering students' emotional and spiritual growth. In participating in extracurricular activities with students, faculty might contribute to such character-building elements of student development, but that is not their primary responsibility. Douglas Sloan calls this the *two-realms approach* and argues that educational institutions employing such a structure inevitably will move away, albeit gradually, from a concern with faith.[4] Others hold that this approach

3. Jay E. Adams, *Competent to Counsel: Introduction to Nouthetic Counseling* (Grand Rapids: Zondervan, 1970), p. xxi.

4. Douglas Sloan, *Faith and Knowledge: Mainline Protestantism and American Higher Education* (Louisville: Westminster John Knox Press, 1994), p. 6.

can be "a reasonable and sustainable way of maintaining an institution's religious identity."[5]

In an institution that uses the two-realms approach, issues of faith may be addressed in campus chapel programs, residence-hall Bible studies, or other kinds of religious centers, as a supplement to the learning that takes place in the classroom. The curriculum may even require students to take one or more specific courses in religion, the Scriptures, or theology. Faculty are expected to be supportive of these endeavors and may contribute to them by speaking in chapel, leading small groups, or working with students on service projects, but their primary task is to teach "in a kinder and gentler way," providing a "caring environment" for their students.[6] The content covered in most academic courses and the presentation of that material will not be affected by faith. For an example of the two-realms approach, consider Dr. P., a committed Christian who is active in her local church. She cares deeply for her students and treats them with respect. Dr. P. teaches her undergraduate psychology courses with a concern for facilitating student learning, employing a variety of active learning strategies, and she advises the student Psychology Club. In this capacity, she joins students in volunteer work at a local hospital and in fund-raising to support African psychologists working with traumatized refugees. She seldom mentions faith or religion in her introductory psychology course or her social psychology course, but she doesn't make disparaging remarks about faith, either.

Another approach to faith and learning that is theoretically similar although practically different has been called the *complementary* or *value-added* approach. Like the two-realms approach, it assumes that questions of objective learning are distinct from questions of subjective faith, but it differs in expecting faculty to address the more subjective issues stemming from faith and character in the classroom. Professors are responsible for imparting knowledge to and developing skills in their students, but they also are responsible for raising and addressing questions of ethics and values. Michael Hamilton and James Mathisen explain: "This view is neutral toward the prevailing intellectual culture. It assumes that secular knowledge and sacred knowledge do not conflict because they occupy different spheres. The

5. Larry Lyon and Michael Beaty, "Integration, Secularization, and the Two-Spheres View at Religious Colleges: Comparing Baylor University with the University of Notre Dame and Georgetown College," *Christian Scholars Review* 29 (1999): 75.

6. Lyon and Beaty, "Integration, Secularization, and the Two-Spheres View at Religious Colleges," p. 76.

two kinds of knowledge do not change each other in fundamental ways, but they can enrich each other."[7] Thomas Aquinas, the first great advocate of this view, held that natural law, perceivable by human reason, establishes the structures of the state and promotes the cardinal virtues (Prudence, Temperance, Justice, and Fortitude), which are completed for the Christian with the theological virtues of Faith, Hope, and Love, bestowed only through divine grace. Faith leads people to salvation, while learning promotes humanity's temporal well-being. Luther's "two-kingdom" theology is another tradition that has inspired a value-added approach: the Christian lives simultaneously in both the kingdom of nature and the kingdom of grace, both of which are under the rule of God. The paradoxical affirmation of both kingdoms, sacred and secular, may result in tensions, juxtapositions, and dialogue, but it provides a way for Christians to affirm both faith and learning. Niebuhr characterized these two kinds of approaches as "Christ above Culture" and "Christ in Paradox with Culture."

One contemporary scholar who practices a value-added approach is David G. Myers, who, in addition to writing several standard psychology textbooks, has co-written *Psychology through the Eyes of Faith* with Malcolm Jeeves. Myers and Jeeves distinguish between religious and psychological accounts of human nature, viewing them as different but harmonizing levels of explanation: "Psychological science offers a limited but useful perspective on human nature that complements the perspective of faith."[8] Avoiding the reductionism that sometimes arises with commitment to a discipline, they caution, "The methods of psychology are appropriate, and appropriate only, for their own purposes."[9] But psychology, just like biology or sociology, can support and enrich religious ideas and practices. Much of Myers's own work has been devoted to discovering correlations between what psychological research demonstrates and what Christians believe, as well as considering the ways in which psychological findings can be applied to issues of Christian life and community.

The value-added approach consigns questions of meaning and morality to religious ways of knowing that are distinct from academic disciplines

---

7. Michael S. Hamilton and James A. Mathisen, "Faith and Learning at Wheaton College," in *Models for Christian Higher Education: Strategies for Success in the Twenty-First Century*, ed. Richard T. Hughes and William B. Adrian (Grand Rapids: Wm. B. Eerdmans, 1997), p. 270.

8. David G. Myers and Malcolm A. Jeeves, *Psychology through the Eyes of Faith*, 2d ed. (San Francisco: Harper, 2003), p. 17.

9. Myers and Jeeves, *Psychology through the Eyes of Faith*, p. 11.

but nonetheless insists that these are significant issues to be addressed. In this approach, mathematical calculations in and of themselves are seen as neutral tools, but such calculations may be employed for good or for ill, to encourage a way of life or a way of death. The pragmatic goals of higher education to train students for a profession, such as medicine, teaching, business, or law, lend themselves to the value-added approach. Important questions include these: Why pursue this discipline or line of study? What results occur when a theory is put into practice? What kind of ethical guidance should be given to practitioners? Are professional guidelines sufficient for a Christian practitioner, or are there higher standards that should be applied?

Values can be "added" either as input or as output — prompting or informing initial learning as well as guiding a subsequent application. Values may motivate learning, scholarship, and vocation. For example, a concern to use one's education as a way of concretely loving one's neighbor inspires many Christians to enter service professions, such as counseling, social work, teaching, and medicine. One's ultimate commitments also may inform one's subspecialty; should a plastic surgeon specialize in the facial reconstruction of burn victims or in the latest Botox technology? Just as early American colleges were founded in order to teach the Greek, Latin, and rhetoric that every good minister was to employ, disciplinary learning today can be directed toward particular Christian applications in church or parish ministry, evangelism, or missionary work. One might study public relations and visual communication in order to use those skills to advance the cause of an organization like World Vision, the Mennonite Central Committee, or Catholic Relief Services; one might study anthropology and psychology to prepare for the mission field; or one might study business management in order to start a micro-lending program for AIDS orphans in Africa. By using learning overtly to fulfill the Great Commandment to love both God and neighbor, we bring faith and learning together in a complementary fashion.

Values are also at work in ethical conundrums of application and practice. Should sociologists assist fast-food chains in designing products that appeal to children or in developing effective strategies to encourage supersizing? Where should a health care provider draw the line between life and death? If a commanding officer orders that a prisoner undergo waterboarding, should the soldier follow orders? Professors may consciously raise ethical issues in any course, or curricula may include special courses which focus on business ethics, medical ethics, and environmental ethics.

Bernie Madoff, AIG, and the economic meltdown of 2008 are a few events that have prompted many to question how successful American higher education has been in ethical education, particularly in the realm of business. Perhaps some of the problem stems from institutions' wariness of pursuing moral formation and character development as part of their mission. Effective teaching for ethical living includes at least three elements: knowledge, commitment, and practice. Cognitive information, such as a professional disciplinary code of conduct or the details of legal compliance, is necessary but not sufficient to develop character. Analytical strategies for identifying, clarifying, and assessing the ethical issues that arise in a particular case also are necessary but not sufficient. We also must add the component of ethical commitment and practice, as the early American Puritan educators attempted to do with their concern for the role of the will. One's basic assumptions about human nature are key elements of this process. Are most people inherently morally good, with lack of knowledge operating as the primary cause of ethical slips, errors, or even downfalls? How does one teach someone to want to be good? Or, in Christian terms, how do we go about forming the conscience; how do we develop a moral imagination in our students?

There are many good guides to teaching ethics and moral development, so I will sum up only a few of the key components that should be considered. (See the sidebar following.) First, professors of any discipline at a mission-based institution need to develop a basic understanding of cognitive moral development as empirically identified in the work of psychologists such as Lawrence Kohlberg, Carol Gilligan, and James Fowler (all of which builds on William Perry's schemas of cognitive development). Second, teachers need to help students identify and recognize ethical problems and the ways that values enter into decision-making. This will entail teaching professional codes, presenting alternative moral rules, and helping students to identify and articulate their own personal convictions. In such "values clarification," students learn how to examine their lives in such a way as to identify their true, or authentic, values. However, as Arthur Holmes notes, "The problem with the values clarification movement was that it seemed to limit itself to a process without content, growth without direction."[10] Values clarification at the mission-driven institution should include some sense of direction, based upon biblical principles,

---

10. Arthur F. Holmes, *Shaping Character: Moral Education in the Christian College* (Grand Rapids: Wm. B. Eerdmans, 1991), p. 18.

Teaching Ethics

1. Draw on an understanding of cognitive moral development and subsequently assign appropriate learning experiences.
2. Identify pertinent systems of norms — i.e., professional ethical codes, specific cultural teachings, Christian theology and traditions.
3. Help students articulate and clarify their own values.
4. Help students recognize ethical questions and dilemmas that may arise.
5. Give students practice in ethical reasoning and applications.
6. Provide models of ethical reasoning and application, including yourself as a role model.
7. Confront students with human voices and faces through experiences, narratives, or visual embodiments.

---

natural law, Christian traditions, or theologically informed norms. This does not mean that all Christians will agree on how to resolve a particular ethical case, but we can agree on a common direction of love for God and love for neighbor, for a shared arc of peace, justice, and flourishing, even though we may disagree on how to reach that goal.

When we understand the process of student moral development, help them sort through and identify issues, and deliberately highlight the direction in which we are going, we must then provide practice in thinking through dilemmas before students encounter such issues in the working world and their personal lives. Such practice applications can be done through case studies, essays, and discussions, all of which provide valuable pedagogical strategies for ethical education. An accounting major might grapple with how she would deal with a case such as that posed in the Enron scandal; a pre-medical student might write a position paper on how he would anticipate treating an HIV-positive patient; English majors might debate whether the teaching of *The Adventures of Huckleberry Finn* is racist. Such exercises involving reasoning and argumentation teach, reinforce, and give practice in values identification, analysis, and decision-making.

But as many Christian educators have noted, forming students to live as thoughtful Christians goes beyond head knowledge to heart conviction; forming character involves inspiration as well as information. Role models, both professors and peers, play a crucial role.[11] Students need inspirational embodiments of ethical practitioners, respected people who grapple with hard questions and take thoughtful action. Professor P.'s volunteer work supporting the training of African psychologists is a significant implicit teaching device. One of the most difficult issues that mission-driven professors face in dealing with controversial moral or ethical issues in the classroom is whether or not to identify their own position on an issue under discussion, whether that be partial-birth abortion, gender discrimination in the workplace, or animal testing. I know many professors highly committed to developing students' moral character who never admit where they stand, alternatively arguing both or even multiple sides of a complicated case, with the goal of pushing students to exercise their own convictions rather than merely picking up and parroting "what the teacher wants." Yet such well-meaning reticence and aversion to proselytizing or preaching may also send a message that ethics ultimately are unfinalizable, relative, or not significant, that what one person decides is just as good as what another decides. Our students need to see us practicing critical commitment with both humility and conviction. Still, there are many different options of when to reveal one's position, and I seldom would do so at the outset of a course, an exercise, or a discussion. Whether it is as simple as committing to a particular interpretation of a story among multiple options or as complex as weighing both the positive and the negative moral implications of the development of a character or a plot, I try to model for my students that final step of taking a position, just as I show them the complex thought processes that should inform such position-taking. I may ask the students to voice and support their own claim in the form of a paper or presentation before I give my own. Or I may present my position and counter it with a critic who argues strongly in the other direction. And, of course, I never penalize a student for a well-supported and cogently argued ethical, moral, or interpretive stance that is different from my own, hard as it is for them to believe this.

Besides witnessing ethical thinking, students also can develop character through the practice of service-learning, taking intellectual knowledge and putting it into practice and thereby personally encountering the ethical dilemmas that emerge in any real-world setting. Since the 1990s,

11. For a discussion of the significance of role modeling, see Steven Garber, *The Fabric of Our Faithfulness: Weaving Together Belief and Behavior*, exp. ed. (Downers Grove, Ill.: InterVarsity Press, 2007).

American higher education has experienced a surge of service-learning programs. The service-learning movement distinguishes itself from community service by its emphasis on learning: it is a form of experiential education, with debts to John Dewey, in which academic study and community service combine to produce student learning. Key elements in service-learning programs include exposure to knowledge and skills through readings, lectures, and discussions, followed by the application of that knowledge and practice of the skills in a real-life situation providing some kind of service. A reflection component, requiring students to analyze and judge their service experience as well as to discover new knowledge and skills that they may have gained through the experience, is also crucial. Service-learning appeared first in professional schools and programs, such as business, nursing, education, and social work, but has since spread across the curriculum and into general education programs.[12] While acknowledging service-learning's pragmatic value in forming transferrable skills for the work world, the pervasive philosophy and rhetoric of the movement emphasizes the "rejuvenation of participatory democracy." American individualism, it is argued, has led to alienation, corruption, and selfishness. Service-learning "may renew a commitment to the common good as well as to individual accomplishment," the strengthening of social capital, and the development of civic virtues.[13]

Mission-driven institutions provide a faith-based rationale and theological grounding for this dedication to service. It is no coincidence that Jesuit universities with long-standing commitments to social justice and Wesleyan colleges with traditions of social service were early leaders in the service-learning movement. Service-learning simultaneously relies on and stimulates ethical commitments (to the poor, to justice, to democracy). Students who vaguely desire "to help others" may find both their expectations and their motivations challenged through a service-learning experience, such as working in a soup kitchen in conjunction with analyzing the social and political causes of homelessness. Human responsibility for service can be theologically grounded in a belief in human beings' solidarity through creation in the image of God, or the mutual self-giving community embodied in the Trinity, or the Judeo-Christian responsibility to love

12. Barbara Jacoby et al., *Service-Learning in Higher Education: Concepts and Practices* (San Francisco: Jossey-Bass, 1996), pp. 5-22.

13. Jordy Rocheleau, "Theoretical Roots of Service-Learning: Progressive Education and the Development of Citizenship," in *Service-Learning: History, Theory, and Issues*, ed. Bruce W. Speck and Sherry L. Hoppe (Westport, Conn.: Praeger, 2004), pp. 13-14.

the neighbor, or the Jesus-vision of the Good Samaritan. Preliminary studies of the impact of service-learning on student attitudes and practices show increases in civic engagement outcomes, empathy, and commitment to social justice.[14] One intriguing two-year study at a Jesuit university reveals that while social and civic attitudes were not significantly affected by service-learning involvement, students with service-learning experiences engaged in more spiritual seeking, and their beliefs became more intrinsically religious.[15]

Beyond such powerful influences provided by models and practice lies the more subtle character formation that occurs through stories, metaphors, and images. Film, literature, visual art, and music provide significant ways to develop empathy and new ways of thinking ethically and need not be limited to literature or fine arts classes. Reading historical accounts, political analyses, sociological dissections, and compilations of facts and statistics are all important ways of learning about the African-American experience of slavery, but viscerally encountering the experience as rendered in *The Narrative of Frederick Douglass* or Toni Morrison's *Beloved* often stirs one's heart in a mysteriously effective way. In Seattle Pacific's required social-science core course titled "The West and the World," for example, students read Chinua Achebe's *Things Fall Apart*, watch the film *The Mission*, and study a history textbook as complementary ways to learn about the interactions of the West and the world. One effective way to shape embodied character, according to Nicholas Wolterstorff, is through the development of empathy: "The disposition to struggle against some injustice can often be cultivated by evoking in the person empathy for those suffering under the injustice. And in my experience, one of the most effective ways of doing this, in turn, is by presenting to the person the human faces and the human voices of suffering — 'the voices of the night.'"[16]

14. See A. W. Astin et al., *How Service-Learning Affects Students* (Los Angeles: University of California, Higher Education Research Institute, 2000); R. E. Wideman, "Empathy Development in Undergraduate Students through the Cross-cultural Learning Experience," *Dissertation Abstracts International, Section A: Humanities and Social Sciences* 66, no. 2-A (2005): 494; and A. R. Roschelle, J. Turpin, and R. Elias, "Who Learns from Service-Learning?" *American Behavioral Scientist* 43 (2000): 839-47.

15. Matthew Bernacki and Frank Bernt, "Service-Learning as a Transformative Experience: An Analysis of the Impact of Service-Learning on Student Attitudes and Behaviors after Two Years of College," in *From Passion to Objectivity: International and Cross-Disciplinary Perspectives on Service-Learning Research*, ed. Sherril B. Gelmon and Shelley H. Billig (Charlotte, N.C.: Information Age, 2007), pp. 126-27.

16. Nicholas Wolterstorff, *Educating for Shalom: Essays on Christian Higher Education*,

Those human faces and voices can be encountered in service-learning, internships, field experiences, and works of literature, art, and other media — all of which provide creative ways to add value to learning through multiple ways of learning.

The Integration of Faith and Learning

By far the most prevalent way of talking about faith and learning in the past few decades has been with the language of *integration*. Especially at evangelical institutions, but increasingly at other kinds of mission-driven colleges, the integration of faith and learning has become an educational mantra. One of the biggest difficulties in talking about integration is the fact that it is such a protean term. For some, *any* kind of talk about faith and learning is termed integration, including the different kinds of value-added approaches discussed above. For others, integration designates a *specific* kind of connection between faith and learning. The confusion with the term is evident when one set of authors describes integration as primarily a Reformed concept; a former Wheaton College president claims it for a wide swath of theological traditions; a Reformed college president argues *against* using the term; and a relatively young conservative Catholic institution speaks of "the integration of the truths of the faith with the social, cultural, economic, and political developments in society."[17] The integration approach emerged in mid-century as a response to modernism's separation of facts and values, science and faith, the secular and the sacred. The word *integration* implies two distinct entities that need to be brought together. From a historical point of view, *re-integration* might be a better term, but the simpler language has prevailed.

Christian educators' original discussions of integration mirrored a widespread concern in American higher education. With the advent of the modern university, some educators became troubled by the fragmentation of meaning and the loss of unity that was a result of academic specializa-

---

ed. Clarence W. Joldersma and Gloria Goris Stronks (Grand Rapids: Wm. B. Eerdmans, 2004), p. 151.

17. Douglas Jacobsen and Rhonda Hustedt Jacobsen, *Scholarship and Christian Faith: Enlarging the Conversation* (Oxford: Oxford University Press, 2004), pp. 15-31; Duane Litfin, *Conceiving the Christian College* (Grand Rapids: Wm. B. Eerdmans, 2004), pp. 127-48; Carl E. Zylstra, "Faith-Based Learning: The Conjunction in Christian Scholarship," *Pro Rege* 26 (1997): pp. 1-5; http://www.avemaria.edu/aboutus/.

tion and the growing prestige of science. One response was to establish a common curriculum that featured courses in Western civilization or the "great books" as a way to discuss values, ultimate meaning, human nature, and transcendence.[18] Other educators, of the progressive school, proposed a cross-disciplinary curriculum based on student experience to provide unity. In 1937, L. Thomas Hopkins from Columbia University argued that deliberate connections needed to be drawn among the disciplines and noted, "In an age which is characterized primarily by fractionalism, by fragmented and segmented experience, it is natural that thoughtful persons should reach out for concepts of unity. Hence the popularity of the word *integration* in our time."[19] As the search for a holistic "integrated" approach to education continued, Christian educators began speaking about the integration of faith and learning. Ken Badley has traced the origin of Christian uses of the phrase to Frank E. Gaebelein, the headmaster of a Christian preparatory school in New York.[20] In *The Pattern of God's Truth: The Integration of Faith and Learning* (1954), Gaebelein states that a common educational problem is "How to achieve . . . unity? How to put together the diverse fragments that make up the raw material of education?"[21] The answer for Christian educators, Gaebelein claims, lies in the fact that all truth is God's truth. At "the heart of integration" is the "living union" of all disciplinary truth "with the eternal and infinite pattern of God's truth."[22] Gaebelein understood integration as a recognition and practice of the unity of all truths as grounded in ultimate Truth.

One of the most influential discussions of the integration of faith and learning appears in *The Idea of a Christian College* by Wheaton College professor Arthur Holmes, first published in 1975 and issued in a revised edition in 1987. Distinguishing *integration* from *indoctrination*, Holmes defines *integration* as being concerned with "the positive contributions of human learning to an understanding of the faith and to the development of a Christian worldview, and with the positive contribution of the Chris-

---

18. Jon H. Roberts and James Turner, *The Sacred and the Secular University* (Princeton, N.J.: Princeton University Press, 2000), pp. 108-22.

19. L. Thomas Hopkins, *Integration: Its Meaning and Application* (New York: D. Appleton-Century, 1937), p. 21.

20. Ken Badley, "The Faith/Learning Integration Movement in Christian Higher Education: Slogan or Substance?" *Journal of Research on Christian Education* 3, no. 1 (1994): 16.

21. Frank E. Gaebelein, *The Pattern of God's Truth: The Integration of Faith and Learning* (Oxford: Oxford University Press, 1954; rpt., Chicago: Moody Press, 1968), p. 10.

22. Gaebelein, *The Pattern of God's Truth*, p. 9.

tian faith to all the arts and sciences."[23] Like Gaebelein, Holmes argues that integration is not solely an intellectual activity, for it involves "the integration of faith into every dimension of a person's life and character."[24] He then identifies four approaches to the integration of faith and learning: (1) the attitudinal approach, (2) the ethical approach, (3) the foundational approach, and (4) the worldview approach.

In the first approach, one's personal motivation, attitude, and integrity while learning or performing an academic task originate in and are informed by one's Christian commitment. Holmes comments, "Especially in performance areas and in the disciplined development of skills . . . the attitude of the teacher or student is the initial and perhaps most salient point of contact with the Christian faith."[25] A pianist might engage in long hours of disciplined practice to honor his God-given talents and to celebrate God's gift of music and harmony, even though his performance of Beethoven's *Moonlight Sonata* sounds no different from that of any other gifted musician. A biologist might repeatedly perform painstakingly detailed laboratory procedures with patience and diligence, only to report the failure of a hypothesis, again motivated by an attitude of curiosity, obedience, and honesty. The Christian virtues of humility, faith, self-denial, and charity, as Mark Schwehn discusses, are vital to the academic vocation, and while the intellectual tradition of the academic disciplines may replicate or demand such virtues, it cannot generate them.[26]

The ethical approach to integration acknowledges that a positivist distinction of facts and values is specious, for "questions of justice and mercy haunt us continually, calling for active integration of factual understanding with moral values rooted in the Christian faith."[27] The very language we use to describe controversial issues is value-laden: pro-choice versus pro-life, the War Between the States versus the American Civil War. What counts as evidence is driven by values as well. Rather than the complementary approach — marshalling the facts and then moving to moral judgments — "The ethical approach to integration . . . must explore the intrinsic relationship between the facts and the values of justice and love, a

---

23. Arthur F. Holmes, *The Idea of a Christian College*, rev. ed. (Grand Rapids: Wm. B. Eerdmans, 1987), p. 46.

24. Holmes, *The Idea of a Christian College*, pp. 46-47.

25. Holmes, *The Idea of a Christian College*, p. 47.

26. Mark R. Schwehn, *Exiles from Eden: Religion and the Academic Vocation in America* (New York: Oxford University Press, 1992), pp. 44-65.

27. Holmes, *The Idea of a Christian College*, p. 50.

relationship that goes beyond the question of consequences."[28] Our deepest beliefs inform the questions we ask, the evidence that we count, and the answers we eventually reach. The previous discussion of educating for ethical proficiency and character explores some concrete ways to practice ethical integration. If we consider ethical questions regarding the application of knowledge (such as nuclear power, in vitro fertilization, or chemically caused depression) as essential and not easily divisible components of a discipline (as opposed to distinct, added-on issues of value), Holmes's ethical integration would be an apt description. But in actual classroom practice, as opposed to the teacher's mental model, the distinction between value-added ethics and integrated ethics might not be as readily apparent.

As a philosopher, Holmes spends the most time on his third type: the foundational approach. Here the scholar engages in interdisciplinary analysis drawing on history, philosophy, and theology to identify the foundational principles or governing assumptions of a discipline in order to compare them with the foundational assumptions of Christian faith. In the natural sciences, for example, empirical and mathematical methods assume the uniformity of nature and the validity of logic, two principles with which most Christians concur, on the basis that God created a world of natural law and rational order. Yet when scientists assume and argue that the natural world is the only thing that exists, the person of faith will disagree. The distinction between methodological naturalism and philosophical naturalism often becomes blurred in thinking and theorizing, and foundational integration asks us to interrogate our discipline and its practices in these philosophical terms. What effect will foundational Christian beliefs such as the creation of humanity in the image of God, the duty to practice self-giving love for one's neighbor, and the responsibility to work for peace and justice have on our understanding of the fundamental principles and practices of our disciplines?

Finally, Holmes states that "the most embracing contact between Christianity and human learning is the all-encompassing world and life view."[29] He contrasts this holistic understanding with the "intellectual polytheism" endorsed by the fragmented modern university, which excels in explaining and defining particulars but is unable to relate these particulars to each other in a coherent vision for life. A worldview, Holmes says, "is holistic or integrational. It sees things not just as parts but also as a

---

28. Holmes, *The Idea of a Christian College*, p. 51.
29. Holmes, *The Idea of a Christian College*, p. 57.

whole. It is a systematic understanding and appraisal of life, and none of the academic disciplines is exempted from contact with it."[30] Worldviews, he continues, are also exploratory rather than finalized, pluralistic rather than simplistic, and confessional rather than deducible.[31] Referring back to Holmes's initial definition of integration, we see that learning contributes to a Christian worldview even as that worldview will affect the way one learns. We will return to this dialogical aspect of worldview.

Holmes's initial nuanced and multifaceted discussion of integration became, in the hands of many subsequent writers, teachers, and publications, concentrated on the cognitive foundational approach. By the 1980s, talk of the integration of faith and learning had become pervasive in Christian higher education. In his seminal "Faith-Learning Integration: An Overview," William Hasker emphasizes that integration is a scholarly project involving cognition and intellect, not attitudes and values, as important as those might be: integration is "a scholarly project whose goal is to ascertain and to develop integral relationships which exist between the Christian faith and human knowledge, particularly as expressed in the various academic disciplines."[32] Playing on the association of *integral* with *integration*, Hasker suggests that such relationships are inherent and only need to be discovered and elaborated. Similarly, Harold Heie encourages students and faculty to develop *integrative questions*, those that can be addressed effectively only by drawing on the resources of both faith and discipline.[33] Issues of ethical applications clearly are integrative questions, and data-driven studies of the medical effectiveness of prayer, a spiritually sympathetic biography of Jonathan Edwards, and the theological significance of harmony and counterpoint are a few examples of integrative questions that have been addressed by Christian scholars.

Objections to Integration

The integration of faith and learning has encountered a number of problems over the course of its evolution into a definitional muddiness. First,

30. Holmes, *The Idea of a Christian College*, p. 58.
31. Holmes, *The Idea of a Christian College*, pp. 58-60.
32. William Hasker, "Faith-Learning Integration: An Overview," *Christian Scholars Review* 21 (1992): 234.
33. Harold Heie, *Learning to Listen, Ready to Talk: A Pilgrimage Toward Peacemaking* (New York: iUniverse, 2007), p. 170.

integration is conceptually and linguistically embedded in Enlightenment dualism; it begins by accepting the premise of the separate realms of faith and learning and then explores ways of bringing them back together. Value-added integrationists accept modernism's assumption that faith is informed essentially by the heart, while learning is informed essentially by the head. Sacred and secular thus enrich or complete each other. The cognitive integration of Hasker goes against the tendency of modernism to view faith as emotional, located in the heart rather than the head. But it does so by resorting purely to the head, insisting that education is only a cognitive activity. Postmodernism has revealed the inadequacies and inaccuracies of such dualism by deconstructing a simplistic differentiation of objectivity and subjectivity. What about the heart's pull to the discipline? What about the faith that is encouraged by the mind? What about the values implicit in the discipline? What about the ways that learning has affected the development of faith? By accepting dualism, the integration model often denotes overlap rather than the original unity to which the theory aspired. As Perry Glanzer comments, "Integration language . . . gives the impression that synthesizing is the primary task."[34]

The association of the term *integration* with the social and political turmoil of American race relations of the 1960s (its originating era) further accentuates the concept of two distinct entities that need to be brought together. Both the modernist context and the sociopolitical connotations of the word work against this model. Furthermore, the emphasis on foundational integration (at the cost of the attitudinal, ethical, and worldview approaches) that developed has prompted some scholars to call for "more" than the integration of faith and learning, which, they allege, unreasonably requires all Christian academics to become theologians and philosophers.[35] The integration of faith and learning may be a useful approach when one is studying the philosophy of science, but how applicable is it to a basic course in organic chemistry? Another criticism is that the integration approach is unnecessarily critical of the academic disciplines and modern learning, always seeking to critique or transform the discipline

34. Perry L. Glanzer, "Why We Should Discard 'the Integration of Faith and Learning': Rearticulating the Mission of the Christian Scholar," *Journal of Education and Christian Belief* 12, no. 1 (2008): 44.

35. Jacobsen and Jacobsen, *Scholarship and Christian Faith*, p. 24. Catholic traditions that speak of the integration of faith and learning (more often called "reason") typically require courses in philosophy and theology of all their students, and rely heavily on the work of philosophers and theologians in their teaching.

from a Christian perspective. To the extent that such a reformational approach is used, integration resembles Niebuhr's "Christ the Transformer of Culture."

Worldviews, Faith, and Learning

Advocates of the worldview approach disapprove of integration's acceptance of the dichotomy of facts and values, claiming that this results in a false dualism. Instead of beginning with such a division, the initial premise of worldview thinkers is that everyone has a worldview, a fundamental perspective that affects all of life, including learning. While many (although not all) forms of integration emphasize the overlap or union of two distinct spheres, the worldview approach assumes the existence of an all-encompassing Truth into which all other spheres, perspectives, practices, and truths fall. In emphasizing the unity of all truth in God's Truth, the worldview approach resembles the concern in American higher education for unity and transcendence found in early versions of integration. Yet, as with the theory of integration, educational scholars, philosophers, and theologians do not agree on what it means to think about faith and learning in terms of worldview. During recent decades, two different ways of thinking about worldviews have emerged: the *foundational* and the *narrative.*

Those who consider worldviews as foundational are concerned with the cognitive, intellectual, propositional nature of one's perspective on life. This stress is, in fact, a key element of the original term *Weltanschauung* (worldview) as articulated by the Enlightenment philosopher Immanuel Kant, who argued that every human being exercises reason — free from restrictions from religion or tradition — to construct a worldview.[36] Reason or rationality is central in this understanding. A Christian worldview locates human reasoning within the bounds of faith to articulate "a theistic system exhibiting the rational coherence of the biblical revelation."[37] For many evangelicals, worldview "is often used . . . as a synonym for theology, and that theology is still understood in the Protestant scholastic sense of a

---

36. A history of the concept of worldview is found in David K. Naugle, *Worldview: The History of a Concept* (Grand Rapids: Wm. B. Eerdmans, 2002).

37. Carl F. H. Henry, "Fortunes of the Christian World View," *Trinity Journal* n.s., 19 (1998): 163.

series of dogmatic propositions coherently organized and rooted in a divinely inspired, infallible and inerrant Scripture."[38] Although Catholic scholars do not as commonly use the language of worldview,[39] those working in the tradition of Thomas Aquinas similarly identify, explore, and apply philosophical and theological foundational principles to other disciplines.

The Christian worldview is thus associated with a set of propositions — perhaps as articulated in one of the historical creeds, catechisms, or other writings of the church — that can be diagrammed in comparison with other religions and/or philosophies.[40] For example, comparatively speaking, a Christian worldview defines the nature of reality as including both a transcendent realm (including God, the human soul, angels, and possibly other spirits) and a natural world; the naturalist worldview defines reality as consisting only of the material world; and a Zen Buddhist worldview defines ultimate reality as the Void, a nothingness that cannot be named or grasped, is neither physical nor transcendent. Like foundational integration, the foundational worldview approach to faith and learning consists of identifying the major premises of Christian belief as taught in Scripture and the orthodox tradition and then exploring how these principles should guide our thinking about all other matters, including learning and the academic disciplines.[41] Christian education is thus concerned with proclaiming and assisting students to grow in an intellectually grounded embrace of the Christian worldview. It involves catechesis, an explication of and instruction in the truths of the faith, as well as an application of those truths to disciplinary matters, whether social, political, artistic, or technological.

In its best forms, foundational worldview education identifies the ways in which all human beings operate with a set of often-unquestioned and unrecognized philosophical premises; it demonstrates the way that every position, even secular objectivism, relies on certain assumptions. A foundational worldview education establishes a rationally coherent system

38. Brian J. Walsh, "Worldviews, Modernity, and the Task of Christian College Education," *Faculty Dialogue* 18 (1992): 15.

39. Naugle explores the ways in which Roman Catholicism and Eastern Orthodoxy have employed worldview thinking. See *Worldview*, pp. 33-54.

40. See James W. Sire, *The University Next Door: A Basic Worldview Catalog*, 3rd ed. (Downers Grove, Ill.: InterVarsity Press, 1997).

41. *Shaping a Christian Worldview: The Foundations of Christian Higher Education*, ed. David S. Dockery and Gregory Alan Thornbury (Nashville: Broadman & Holman, 2002).

of Christian belief and pushes students to be philosophically attuned and grounded, to do important conceptual work in philosophy and apologetics that is a staple of a well-rounded liberal arts education. In its more limited forms, foundational worldview education provides answers but does not leave room for questions; it assumes that there is one easily identifiable and uniformly agreed-upon Christian worldview. It also may succumb to a triumphalism arising from dualism, drawing clear lines between a "Christian" worldview and other worldviews with the assumption that the Christian worldview as we articulate it is always more faithful to Truth in a "clash of worldviews."[42] As its governing metaphor suggests, the foundational worldview approach is a bottom-up approach, building on the "foundations" of Christian truth to construct the edifice of learning.

The *narrative approach* defines worldview not in propositional but in narrative terms. Rather than philosophical categories, it emerges from the basic dramatic plot of Scripture: creation, fall, redemption. It pays more attention to the contextual, communal, and historical aspects of one's perspectives. This approach has been most thoroughly explored by Brian Walsh and Richard Middleton in a number of places, and my account draws upon their work, with some greater elaboration of points related to narratology.[43] Worldview understood as narrative has seven characteristics:

1. It is a basic and inherent human attribute, found across all cultures regardless of whether the worldview has been consciously identified or transformed into the more technical sciences of philosophy or theology.
2. A worldview is religious, based upon a commitment to belief, not on subjective feelings, subjective opinions, or objective facts.
3. A worldview is social and communal, held by a group of people with traditions, practices, and cultures that embody and affirm this view of life.
4. The primary plot of worldview concerns human identity. Aristotle's

---

42. Charles Colson, Foreword, *Shaping a Christian Worldview*, p. xi.

43. Walsh, "Worldviews, Modernity, and the Task of Christian College Education"; Brian J. Walsh and J. Richard Middleton, *The Transforming Vision: Shaping a Christian World View* (Downers Grove, Ill.: InterVarsity Press, 1984); J. Richard Middleton and Brian J. Walsh, *Truth Is Stranger than It Used to Be: Biblical Faith in a Postmodern Age* (Downers Grove, Ill.: InterVarsity Press, 1995). See also Michael W. Goheen and Craig G. Bartholomew, *Living at the Crossroads: An Introduction to Christian Worldview* (Grand Rapids: Baker, 2008).

classic definition of narrative is that it is a presentation of a unified sequence of events. Unity and time are both key elements. A good plot has an identifiable beginning, middle, and end that cohere. Poor plots are episodic and random, without a clear direction or unifying principle. For example, picaresque narratives provide a series of chance events without clear unity beyond a central character who undergoes a variety of experiences — perhaps an appropriate metaphor for much education today. Genre fiction, on the other hand, is plot-heavy — sometimes following a prescribed plot so rigidly as to be trite or boringly predictable. A rigid foundational approach to faith and learning can become similarly generic. Unity, in plot, stems from direction, not only combination. One of the most articulate explanations of how narrative unity and time generate human meaning is that of Charles Taylor: "In order to make minimal sense of our lives, in order to have an identity, we need an orientation to the good, which means some sense of qualitative discrimination, or the incomparably higher [God]. . . . This sense of the good has to be woven into my understanding of my life as an unfolding story. . . . This is to state another basic condition of making sense of ourselves, that we grasp our lives in a *narrative*. . . . Our lives exist [in a] space of questions, which only a coherent narrative can answer. In order to have a sense of who we are, we have to have a notion of how we have become, and of where we are going."[44] A worldview plot treats who we are, where we are, what has gone wrong (what causes pain and suffering), and how things can be made better.[45]

5. As a narrative, a worldview may have logical inconsistencies, apparent paradoxes, and deep mysteries; stories don't always make logical or rational sense, even while they nonetheless convey truth.

6. A worldview is prone to the heresy of paraphrase, which lacks the full complexity, emotional resonance, and lived truth of a rich narrative.

44. Charles Taylor, *Sources of the Self: The Making of the Modern Identity* (Cambridge: Cambridge University Press, 1989), p. 47.

45. Middleton and Walsh were the first to articulate these four worldview components, although they used the singular pronoun, "I" (*The Transforming Vision*, p. 35). N. T. Wright suggests using a plural "we" to highlight the communal nature of worldviews, and he also adds a fifth component — "What time is it?" — to indicate that the Christian narrative is an ongoing story occurring in time in which we find our own role. See N. T. Wright, *Jesus and the Victory of God*, Christian Origins and the Question of God, vol. 2 (Minneapolis: Fortress Press, 1996), p. 443.

Although paraphrases are useful to a certain extent for purposes of discussion, they necessarily limit the full feeling, truth, and power of narrative.

7. A worldview is not static but rather is dynamically dialogical — both shaped by life experiences, traditions, and historical processes as well as shaping our life experience, choices, actions, and practices. The kind of family, neighborhood, or church in which one grows up has a tremendous impact on one's worldview, but opting to embrace a particular worldview also prompts someone to make certain choices about the way that he or she lives. If a worldview is frozen or stagnates, trouble will result, because the world is constantly changing, since God created us as historical, time-immersed beings.

The communal and dialogical aspects of worldview are extremely important for Christian educators, for they explain a great deal about what happens in college. Our students arrive with a worldview that has been formed by their families, churches, societies, and cultures, a worldview that often has not been challenged or tested by new information, different kinds of people, or unfamiliar experiences. This worldview may be radically inconsistent, formed by both a youth pastor and Facebook, family values and consumer culture, theism and paganism. While our worldview affects how we live, life experiences also affect our worldview. With the advent of new experiences and knowledge, creative tensions may emerge as inconsistencies are revealed, assumptions are challenged, and cognitive and emotional processing grows. Walsh suggests that such tensions often result in a worldview crisis, resolved by a revision in the worldview story, a conversion from one worldview to a completely different worldview, or an entrenchment that rejects or denies the new information or experience.[46] Common triggers of such worldview crises are going to college, with the accompanying new intellectual and social encounters; traveling or living in a foreign or unfamiliar culture; experiencing a major illness or loss of a family member or friend; going to graduate school; and so on. The question of the extent to which reason, physical discovery, personal experience, and other components of academic learning should impact one's worldview and affect one's faith is one of the most controversial elements of a Christian education. As we have seen, reconstructionists, complemen-

---

46. Walsh, "Worldviews, Modernity, and the Task of Christian College Education," pp. 23-25.

tarians, and foundationalists — both of the integration and worldview variety — provide different answers to this question. A narrative understanding of worldview provides more opportunity for intellectual and spiritual changes, for better or for worse; consequently, some may fear that it may lead to a loss of faith or Christian commitment, a rejection of the idea of the truth of the gospel or the authority of the tradition.

Teaching from a narrative worldview perspective can inspire a number of different practices. As in a foundational worldview approach, teachers will help students to understand what a narrative worldview is and to be able to identify and compare worldviews while studying subjects such as anthropology, history, and literature. For example, I ask students to identify the worldview of the Igbo people as depicted in Achebe's *Things Fall Apart* and then to explore the ways in which this communal understanding both resembles and differs from a contemporary American worldview, particularly in this society's ideas about what is wrong in the world and how it can be made right. Then we examine how a Christian worldview might learn from and critique both perspectives. Worldview analysis can also elucidate competing theories of economic behavior, sociological phenomena, or interpretive practices. While the strict logic of philosophical analysis has educational usefulness, establishing simple categories of "Christian" versus "Muslim" versus "Existentialism," for example, is not very useful in helping us move from disciplinary insights to growth in our conception of God, shalom, and life. Discussions of narrative worldview are better equipped to bring the positive contributions of human learning to the development of a Christian worldview.

A narrative worldview is vastly different from a foundational worldview, yet the differences between the two are not often recognized in mission-driven institutions or the literature on Christian higher education. The dominant mode of thinking has been that of foundationalism, either that of integration or worldview, which involves philosophical categorization and analysis. This has immense educational usefulness and value, but it is only one way to relate faith and learning. As may be evident, I am a strong advocate for the narrative worldview approach. Yet the narrative worldview model also has difficulties. Narrative worldviews are sometimes described in terms of an umbrella or all-encompassing arc, under which all other truths fall, or from which point all genuine truth is perceived. The visual imagery of world*view* emphasizes the importance of perspective, of an angle of vision. But this metaphor has two significant limits: it prematurely solidifies the worldview, ruling out its dialogical development, and it limits our grasp of the physical, embodied aspect of narrative understanding. Human beings live, practice, and enact their stories as well as examine, identify, and retell those stories. To that end, I'd like to propose a new model for Christian education: faithful learning within God's story.

The Faithful Professor: Living and Telling the Story

Given the fact that so many different factors, including pedagogical objectives, scholarly tasks, disciplinary practices, and theological commitments, enter into the relationship of faith and learning, I don't believe there is one "right way" to talk or think about this association. Relating faith and learning will look different in different instances or cases. Ultimately, at a mission-driven institution, I believe that the goal should be to practice *faithful learning* in all of our roles: teaching, scholarship, creative production, and community service. Faithful learning, as I will describe it, incorporates both head and heart, intellect and piety, the fault lines that characterize modernity. In our postmodern age, it may be advantageous to move beyond the approach of integration and foundational worldviews to a different model, for the objective/subjective dichotomy is no longer the standard fare of all the academic disciplines, despite its continuing dominance in parts of the sciences. The narrative worldview approach is more attuned to these changes, but has been repeatedly colonized by foundational approaches, and I have little hope that either *integration* or *worldview* are recoverable terms, despite the strengths and possibilities of each. Faithful learning attempts to draw on those strengths and possibilities even as it moves beyond them.

The language of *faithfulness* is not new; in recent years several Christian educators from a variety of traditions have employed this language.[47] But we also find Nicholas Wolterstorff, perhaps the leading thinker in Reformed educational philosophy, shift during the course of his career away from *integration* and *worldview* language to the language of *faithfulness*, a move that can be clearly traced in *Educating for Shalom: Essays on Chris-*

---

47. See, for example, *Faithful Learning and the Christian Scholarly Vocation*, ed. Douglas V. Henry and Bob R. Agee (Grand Rapids: Wm. B. Eerdmans, 2003); and *Didache: Faithful Teaching*, an online journal sponsored by the Nazarene Theological Seminar (http://didache.nts.edu/). I'm indebted to Randy Maddox, now William Kellon Quick Professor of Theology and Methodist Studies at Duke Divinity School, for introducing me to this phrase during presentations at the SPU New Faculty Seminar.

tian Higher Education, a collection of Wolterstorff's speeches and essays over a thirty-year period. As early as 1987, Wolterstorff was arguing that "the aim of Christian learning is *not to* be different or distinctive but to be *faithful,*" and subsequent essays also turn to the language of faithfulness.[48] Similarly, a collection of essays from professors who served as "The Calvin Worldview Lecturer" between 1998 and 2006 is entitled *Faithful Imagination in the Academy,* and attempts "a move away from triumphalism and toward dialogue with the academic mainstream."[49] After the clarion call of *The Outrageous Idea of Christian Scholarship,* George Marsden has subsequently written of the terminological problem of "Christian scholarship," which invokes imperialism, the religious right, or witnessing, concluding, "The more helpful general term is 'faith-informed' scholarship."[50]

Faithful learning, as I will define it, begins with an ecological assumption of a relational whole consisting of a transcendent Triune God, created human beings, and a created and evolving natural, social, and cultural world. Because of this complex ecology, the process of learning includes both head and heart, intellect and piety, thought and practice. Referring to the historical Scholastic/Pietistic division in one of his haunting hymns, Charles Wesley asks the Holy Spirit to bring together both sides: "United the pair so long disjoined,/Knowledge and vital piety; Learning and holiness combined,/And truth and love, let all men see."[51] Neither learning nor piety is sufficient, his brother John Wesley explains: "We know indeed that wrong opinions in religion naturally lead to wrong tempers, or wrong practices; and that consequently it is our bounded duty to pray that we might have a right judgment in all things. But still a man may judge as accurately as the devil, and yet be as wicked as he."[52] In the history of American Christian higher education, however, we find repeated instances of either piety being emphasized at the cost of knowledge, or knowledge being

48. Wolterstorff, *Educating for Shalom,* p. 106.

49. Janel M. Curry and Ronald A. Wells, Introduction, *Faithful Imagination in the Academy: Explorations in Religious Belief and Scholarship* (Lanham, Md.: Lexington, 2008), p. 3.

50. George M. Marsden, "Beyond Progressive Scientific Humanism," in *The Future of Religious Colleges,* ed. Paul J. Dovre (Grand Rapids: Wm. B. Eerdmans, 2002), p. 44.

51. Charles Wesley, quoted in Paul Wesley Chilcote, *Recapturing the Wesleys' Vision* (Downers Grove, Ill.: InterVarsity Press, 2004), p. 69.

52. John Wesley, "On the Wedding Garment," Sermon 127, in *John Wesley's Sermons: An Anthology,* ed. Albert C. Outler and Richard P. Heitzenrater (Nashville: Abingdon Press, 1991), p. 563.

emphasized at the cost of piety. It is easy to err on one side or the other, to privilege head or heart, to insist that only the cognitive represents Christian (academic) learning versus Christian (personal) formation; or to slap a devotional moment on a class opening or tag a Christian moral to the end of an interpretation. Both head and heart, however, are integral aspects of education, as learning theory demonstrates: passion increases cognition, personal connection facilitates retention, repetition and practice embody wisdom, and application improves analytical abilities. Faithful learning is a comprehensive act in which all aspects of the learner — intellect, spirituality, imagination, emotion, memory, practice, and sociability — are involved.

Faithful learning relies on the testimony of the physical world and the embodied nature of humans. It employs "perspectival realism": "Realism advances the claim that there is a definite 'something' that lies outside our own perception. Perspectival, on the other hand, turns our attention to our own particularities and roles played by our biases, traditions, genders, and the like."[53] Faithful learning is postmodern to the extent that it acknowledges the significant role of perspectives, of the "privileged cognitive access" that stems from our narrative identity and embodied creatureliness.[54] Yet in its deliberate embrace of the truth of the Christian story, its affirmation of a meta-narrative, God's story, faithful learning is markedly different from much postmodern thought. Faithful learning is modern in that it acknowledges the value of reason as a gift from God and the reality of the physical world, even as it points to the limits of reason and the material.

Consequently, faithful learning is not an eternal, universal concept but rather is a historical phenomenon: changing, developing, and unfolding in time. Faithful learning in the twenty-first century looks different from the faithful learning of the sixteenth century. Wolterstorff elaborates: "Christians who wish to be faithful in their scholarship — faithful to their Lord, faithful to their fellow believers, faithful to their fellow human beings, faithful to the earth — never have any other choice than to engage in learning in the particular form in which they find it in their particular time and place. Always trying to alter it, but still always engaging it."[55] The truths and practices of the academic disciplines and current scholarly con-

---

53. Susan M. Felch, "Words and Things: The Hope of Perspectival Realism," in *Faithful Imagination in the Academy*, p. 25.

54. Wolterstorff, *Educating for Shalom*, p. 237.

55. Wolterstorff, *Educating for Shalom*, p. 172.

versations call us to engagement and dialogue. As we learn, discover, and create knowledge, data, art, theories, and interpretations, faithful learners will sometimes say yes and sometimes say no. Unlike monologue, dialogue goes both ways and allows for the possibility of changing one's mind. Once again, Wolterstorff describes this process succinctly:

> On the interactional model . . . Christian faith and the theoretical disciplines are such that we must expect conflict — that is, disequilibrium — to emerge repeatedly. . . . We who are committed to engaging in learning in fidelity to our Lord must acknowledge that sometimes the revision required to bring our faith and our learning into satisfactory equilibrium should go in one direction, and sometimes, in the other direction. Sometimes the best recourse is to revise something in our complex of Christian belief, other times, to revise something in what learning offers us.[56]

Starting from our own position, we listen to others and are willing to practice self-critique and correction, requesting and relying on the Holy Spirit's guidance.

One of the more remarkable and often overlooked elements of faithful learning is that it is not necessarily distinctive learning. There are various theological explanations for this, ranging from Catholic sacramentalism to Calvinist common grace to Lutheran two-kingdoms, but all stem from the beginning of the story: God's good and blessed creation. To those who are searching for a distinctive Christian mathematics or literary theory or psychology, Wolterstorff responds, "The aim of the Christian learning is *not to be different or distinctive* but to be *faithful*. Let the differences fall out as they may. . . . Fidelity in the field of scholarship will yield plenty of difference. But difference is not the goal; indeed, Christian scholars should be delighted when others accept their view."[57] Sometimes Christian and non-Christian scholars will be in agreement; other times they will not. Sometimes Christian teachers will facilitate learning in exactly the same way as non-Christian teachers; other times they will not. External signs, overt practices, and specific code words are not always necessary in faithful learning, although they may appear at appropriate moments. Faithful learning, in both teaching and scholarship, might be either implicit or ex-

---

56. Wolterstorff, *Educating for Shalom*, p. 197.
57. Wolterstorff, *Educating for Shalom*, p. 106.

plicit. Faithful learning thus weaves together the strengths of different Christian traditions: the Catholic embrace of reason, the Calvinist focus on perspective, the Wesleyan concern with spiritual formation, and the Anabaptist emphasis on radical action.

Practicing Faithful Learning

Depending on the context — the discipline, the learning occasion, the topic, the audience — faithful learning (and thus teaching) may involve many of the different practices of relating faith and learning that this chapter discusses: consideration and examination of motivation; identification, analysis, and comparison of foundational assumptions or propositional worldviews; concerns with ethical and moral decision-making; conscious analysis of narrative worldview; and deliberate formational practices to remember and embody the Christian story. Faithful professors will overtly name these acts both for themselves and for their students.

In their first years of teaching, all professors at a mission-driven institution should perform the hard intellectual work of identifying the metaphysical, epistemological, and ethical assumptions of their discipline or subdiscipline for themselves, no matter how applied their teaching and scholarship may be in practice. And then they must help students to think about and work through some of these issues. While such foundational issues may easily arise in a history-of-the-discipline course, a course in ethics, or a senior capstone, even a nuts-and-bolts course such as Basic English Grammar or College Mathematics should be situated or contextualized for the students in terms of the ways in which the particular story told by the discipline or topic of study fits into the Christian story. The Dutch thinker Abraham Kuyper famously claimed that every square inch of creation belongs to God, which means that every mathematical formula, grammatical oddity, and biochemical reaction is part of a larger story, which Christians understand as God's story. One goal in teaching can be to help students learn how to situate the minute elements as well as the grand theories or practices of a discipline within a coherent whole. We can probe issues such as "Why should a Christian study X?" and "How does X fit into the larger picture of God's good creation?" If all of life is connected by and through God, we should not be surprised to find that every action has a ripple effect, touching other people, nonhuman beings, and the natural world. This divine ecology means that ethical and moral decisions and consequences are unavoidably connected, much as we would prefer to separate "neutral" knowledge from the ethical use of such knowledge. Such meta-narrative contextualizing can be done in the syllabus, at both the opening and the conclusion of a semester, and in small comments and reminders throughout the term. The design of majors, minors, and the general education curriculum should be constructed to provide students with experience in thinking in both foundational and big-story terms. Faithful learning will thus embrace both curricular unity and ethical sensitivity.

Faithful professors will help their students learn to recognize, develop, and affirm a Christian worldview, both foundational and narrative, but they will also acknowledge that the Christian story can be told with slightly different emphases and interpretations. Christians often hold opposing positions. Consider the differences, for example, between the Mennonite pacifist position and the traditional Catholic just-war position. Even the basic narrative of creation-fall-redemption is told with different emphases in different traditions: for example, faithful Christians will differ in their view of the extent to which creation remains "good," the degree to which human beings maintain free will, and the temporal scope of sanctification. Our goal should be to assist students in developing a Christian worldview — in both foundational and narrative terms — that comports with their personal experiences and participates in a Christian tradition and community. We should help them reach a more conscious apprehension of previously unconsciously held perspectives and encourage them to make deliberate choices and commitments for their own beliefs and practices.

Recognition of the dynamic, dialogical process of worldview development will encourage humility, dialogue, and discipline. In retrospect, we recognize the limits that historical or cultural blinders have imposed in the past, deforming understandings of the Christian worldview, as in the Inquisition, the Crusades, and the Christian endorsement of slavery. Narrative worldview analysis can examine ways in which the Christian church has been called to be more faithful to God's Word and Truth by revising its worldview in the light of truths uncovered by reason, experience, or new perspectives. Galileo's radical re-visioning of "Where are we?" or Frederick Douglass's reprimand to slave-owning Christians concerning "Who are we?" are two such examples. With such errors in our past, we must deliberately seek out opposing voices and different perspectives for conversation and dialogue. In the process, we may find confirmation, affirmation, rebuke, revelation, and even correction. Sociologists talk about the concept of triangulation, moving in on a concept from three different points of view in order to reach a more complete understanding. I like to ask students to examine a phenomenon or a theory by identifying two different Christian perspectives and one non-Christian perspective and then comparing, contrasting, and choosing one perspective or a new combination of views.

Faithful learning acknowledges that the educational process is not hermetically sealed in the classroom, laboratory, and library. Service-learning, travel abroad, civic engagement, residential life, student leadership positions — all contribute to one's unfolding understanding of God's story. The spiritual discipline of personal and communal practices such as Scripture reading, meditation, prayer, worship, participation in the sacraments, and acts of service help train our minds, bodies, and souls to perceive God and God's kingdom in all that we do.[58] When Christian students from sheltered backgrounds express fear that they might lose their faith if they go to graduate school and encounter dangerous ideas and competing worldviews, I encourage them not to neglect spiritual workouts, which will reinforce and inform their growing Christian worldview. Just as physical exercise releases chemicals in the brain that encourage neuron connections (i.e., learning), so spiritual exercise creates the habit of seeing and worshiping God in all of our life. We need to remember and to live our story, not merely be able to see it or to diagram it. John Wesley held that for most believers, theological convictions take the form of an implicit worldview framing the practice of their lives rather than a fully developed philosophical system. Such a theology or worldview did not automatically appear at the time of conversion but needed development, and Wesley had a deep concern to form a Christian worldview in believers. To this end, he not only developed a rigorous lay education program with an extensive course of reading provided in his fifty-volume *Christian Library* but also held that the spiritual disciplines were necessary for nurturing and shaping the worldview that frames the temperament and practice of believers' lives in the world. Real theological activity for Wesley was not systematic theologies or apologetics; instead, it took place in carefully crafted liturgies, hymns, sermons, prayer books, spiritual biographies, autobiographies, devotional practices, and spiritual

---

58. For an intriguing approach to the relationship of worship and worldview, see James K. A. Smith, *Desiring the Kingdom: Worship, Worldview, and Cultural Formation* (Grand Rapids: Baker, 2009).

exercises and disciplines. Head and heart, knowledge and piety were both crucial aspects of growing as a Christian.

Although it includes careful analysis, cautious judgments, and articulations of Christian perspectives, faithful learning ultimately returns to issues of motivation and attitude. It grounds all learning, teaching, and scholarship in/as a fearless exploration of God's cosmos — anthropological, biological, chemical, economic, educational, geographical, geological, literary, mathematical, musical, physical, political, psychological, sociological, theological, technological, visual — as a means of praising God and worshiping God forever. We must encourage our students to practice learning to the glory of God and the love of the neighbor. Richard Mouw says, "We can get beyond merely embracing the tensions between piety and learning by fostering a piety *for* learning, by becoming the kind of people who see deeply into the reality of things and who love that reality — for the Savior who shed his blood for us also descended into the deep places of the creation so that he might fill all things. Jesus not only rules over every square inch of the creation, he also *loves* those square inches."[59] As a faithful professor, I try to model for my students that rigor of thought and depth of love.

59. Richard J. Mouw, "The Maturity Mandate: A Sermon," in *Keeping Faith*, ed. Ronald A. Wells (Grand Rapids: Wm. B. Eerdmans, 1996), p. 5.

CHAPTER 6

How Outrageous Is Faithful Scholarship?

George Marsden's landmark *The Outrageous Idea of Christian Scholarship* (1997) takes its provocative adjective from responses that characterized Marsden's case for Christian scholarship as "loony" or "like proposing something from a Martian point of view."[1] However, there are other ways in which the practice of scholarship, much less Christian or faithful scholarship, at a mission-driven institution might be considered outrageous. With a few exceptions, such as Notre Dame and Baylor, few mission-driven institutions are research universities with extensive scholarly expectations or commensurate institutional support. In the face of a 3/3 or even a 4/4 teaching load, the prospects of maintaining a research agenda are daunting. What does faithful scholarship look like or mean at a teaching-intensive, mission-driven institution?

Fresh from the intensive focus on scholarship in graduate training, most newly minted faculty begin their careers with strong commitments to research and writing. They are eager to turn their dissertation into a book, to unpack further the data they collected in graduate work, or to set up their own lab and research program, even while wondering how to combine teaching and scholarship successfully. Few graduate mentors will have provided a model for this kind of professional life. More uncertainty may arise from questions about how scholarship is viewed in one's new context. What are the expectations for tenure and promotion? How is scholarship defined? Does one have to produce "Christian" scholarship,

1. George M. Marsden, *The Outrageous Idea of Christian Scholarship* (New York: Oxford University Press, 1997), pp. 5, 7.

whatever that might be? During their first years at an institution, young professors may struggle to identify the right kind of scholarship to practice in their new context. And new faculty joining an educational mission after a professional career may find it even more difficult to adjust to scholarly expectations, practices, and production after a time away from academic culture. Underlying these pragmatic questions, new faculty may also feel a nagging tooth of self-doubt. Am I truly a scholar? How strong are my academic abilities? Was my successful graduate work a fluke? Old hands refer to such self-questioning as "the imposter syndrome," and many faculty experience this kind of fear during their pre-tenure years.

This chapter will consider the outrageous idea of producing faithful scholarship at a teaching-centered, mission-driven institution, although its advice should also prove helpful for those joining mission-driven institutions with strong research agendas. First I will consider the variety of ways in which the academy defines scholarship, with some reflection on the idea of Christian or faithful scholarship. Then I will examine some common objections to scholarship found in teaching institutions, argue that scholarship in one form or another is a crucial part of any professor's academic vocation, and offer some practical advice on how to succeed as a scholar as a new faculty member at a mission-driven institution.

Defining Scholarship

In graduate school, particularly in a Ph.D. program, scholarship is typically defined as contributing new data, theories, or interpretations to a field of study through a process of experimentation, discovery, and publication. Graduate programs seldom worry about formal definitions of scholarship, assuming that their apprentices will absorb the concept as they read published scholarship, assist in labs, take graduate seminars, write papers, and learn the practices of the discipline. In order to earn a Ph.D., candidates in most disciplines are expected to make a new contribution to a field, not merely to sum up or repeat previous work. American higher education inherited this definition of scholarship from the German research university at the end of the nineteenth century and has pragmatically operated with such a definition, albeit uncomfortably at times, ever since.

Responding to this discomfort and recognizing that American higher education includes many different kinds of institutions with diverse missions, the Carnegie Foundation for the Advancement of Teaching, under the leadership of Ernest L. Boyer, conducted an intensive study of the role of the American college professor resulting in *Scholarship Rediscovered: Priorities of the Professoriate* (1990). This brief volume, often referred to as "the Boyer report," examines the range of activities that make up the work of the professoriate and calls for multiple models of scholarship. The standard definition of scholarship, the report posits, does not accurately describe academic work in disciplines outside the traditional arts and sciences, nor is it pertinent to institutions that prioritize teaching over research. Boyer states,

> We believe the time has come to move beyond the tired old "teaching versus research" debate and give the familiar and honorable term "scholarship" a broader, more capacious meaning, one that brings legitimacy to the full scope of academic work. Specifically, we conclude that the work of the professoriate might be thought of as having four separate, yet overlapping, functions. These are: the scholarship of *discovery;* the scholarship of *integration;* the scholarship of *application;* and the scholarship of *teaching.*[2]

Boyer's four-part definition has had a huge impact on higher education and subsequent discussions of faculty responsibilities, with numerous institutions using his categories to re-conceptualize faculty roles and even to rewrite promotion and tenure guidelines. Many mission-driven institutions specify that scholarship in any of these categories is equally respected and similarly rewarded. Other institutions have opted to prioritize one or two of the categories. Some mission-driven institutions place a particular emphasis on the scholarship of integration, understood in a context-specific way as referring to overtly Christian scholarship.

In Boyer's model, *the scholarship of discovery* refers to the traditional search for knowledge that characterizes graduate research. The scholarship of discovery is investigative, involving the uncovering of new information, facts, data, matter, theories, or interpretations. One may discover a planet, a cure for cancer, an unknown historical text, or a new philosophical argument. In the creative arts, sometimes overlooked in more traditional definitions, the scholarship of discovery refers to the creation of a new work of art: composing an opera, writing a novel, painting a canvas, constructing a

---

2. Ernest L. Boyer, *Scholarship Reconsidered: Priorities of the Professoriate* (New York: Wiley, 1990), pp. 15-16.

sculpture, taking a photograph, or recording a song. Boyer's second category, *the scholarship of integration,* entails synthesis rather than investigation; it refers to "scholars who give meaning to isolated facts, putting them in perspective. By integration, we mean making connections across the disciplines, placing the specialties in larger context, illuminating data in a revealing way."[3] In the secular academy, the scholarship of integration typically refers to cross-disciplinary or interdisciplinary work, but at many Christian institutions it includes being able to articulate the way in which one's scholarship and faith come together, are part of the same meta-narrative. Some colleges even require an "integration essay" of publishable quality and length as a precondition for tenure, no matter what the discipline of the faculty member.

In *the scholarship of application,* the scholar asks, "How can knowledge be responsibly applied to consequential problems?" and "Can social problems *themselves* define an agenda for scholarly investigation?"[4] This model of scholarship reflects the mission of the nineteenth-century land-grant institutions and is also pertinent for the professional disciplines. It is an apt approach for American scholars who recognize a democratic responsibility to serve the larger community, to bridge the gap between town and gown by dedicating intellectual resources to tackle social and economic problems. For scholars at mission-driven institutions, it reminds us of the possibility of directly serving the church through scholarship. Finally, and perhaps most influentially, Boyer endorsed *the scholarship of teaching.* Boyer's discussion of this point is brief and vague, mentioning the teacher's need to know the discipline, reach students, and learn from the act of teaching. Boyer tends to emphasize the knowledge that can be acquired through teaching, but subsequent developments of the concept of scholarship of teaching in various programs, grants, and publications sponsored by the Carnegie Foundation define it as reflecting on, studying, and even experimenting with the most effective ways to teach a particular discipline or topic. Some institutions accept an extensively researched teaching portfolio as evidence of such scholarship; others may require a peer-reviewed publication or presentation of such work in order for it to "count" as scholarship in the promotion and tenure process. Of Boyer's four categories, the scholarship of teaching has had the most impact on large sectors of higher education.

Most of us recognize scholarship when we see it, or at least we do

3. Boyer, *Scholarship Reconsidered,* p. 18.
4. Boyer, *Scholarship Reconsidered,* p. 21.

within our own discipline, but a common faculty role at a mission-driven institution includes assessing the scholarship of those outside of your field. University-wide faculty promotion committees often must make such judgments, even when the input of an outside expert in the discipline or subdiscipline is considered. Consequently, it is beneficial both for institutions and for individuals to articulate a general definition of scholarship that works across the disciplines, from Art to Zoology. One such succinct definition is found in *Scholarship and Christian Faith: Enlarging the Conversation:* "Scholarship is disciplined and creative reflection on the natural and humanly constructed world disseminated for the benefit of others and judged by appropriate standards of excellence."[5] It may be useful to consider whether this definition applies to your own discipline, field, and work as a means of testing its effectiveness. Although its parameters may not extend far enough (How about the reflection on God that takes place in some forms of theology and philosophy?), this definition includes four crucial components: discipline, creativity, dissemination, and peer review. The Jacobsens explain the importance of the first two components:

> Human beings may be curious and creative by nature, but scholarship involves the honing of those natural skills into disciplined excellence. Scholarship involves effort: thought, practice, creative energy, the risk of failure, and the joy of success. Some of this effort is in a sense preparatory, focusing on the development of necessary skills and the acquisition of necessary knowledge for our chosen fields of interest. But on top of that, scholarship requires the hard work of researching one's projects, carefully developing one's own perspective, and then sharing those new, intelligently crafted insights with others. . . . All of this takes time, and it also requires creativity. Sheer work alone does not make one a scholar; scholarship necessarily mixes sustained effort with creative insight. Take away the hard work and all we have is effluent self-expression; take away the creativity and all that is left is the cataloging or repetition of what others already know.[6]

Despite the stereotype of the isolated academic, scholarship entails community. Pure creativity, without attention to what others have known or

---

5. Douglas Jacobsen and Rhonda Hustedt Jacobsen, *Scholarship and Christian Faith: Enlarging the Conversation* (Oxford: Oxford University Press, 2004), p. 123.
6. Jacobsen and Jacobsen, *Scholarship and Christian Faith*, p. 123.

done, lacks discipline, while the production of knowledge or ideas without submission to the scrutiny of others also does not constitute scholarship. I tell my students that writing a poem in your journal is a creative act but is not a scholarly act until someone reads and critiques that poem. Constructing an interpretation of a short story without paying any attention to the ideas and opinions of other scholarly readers similarly fails to be scholarship, although it may represent good undergraduate work. Relying on these four criteria also means that the general task of keeping up with one's discipline by reading academic journals or attending conferences is not scholarship, for dissemination and peer review are not involved.

Scholarship, as I am defining it in agreement with the Boyer report, can occur across a full spectrum of fields as one engages in the particular practices of discovery, creativity, and methodology appropriate to the search for truth in one's discipline. The most valued form of dissemination may vary with the discipline — from a book to an academic journal, from a refereed conference presentation to a juried art exhibit, from an article in *The Wall Street Journal* to an essay in *The Christian Century*. For most humanities scholars, the publication of a book by a university press represents the highest scholarly achievement, but for social and natural scientists, numerous peer-reviewed articles, preferably with a listing as a first author, is the academic Golden Fleece. For those in computer science and engineering, in contrast, peer-reviewed Web-based publications or conference proceedings are valued more highly because of the timeliness with which such information can be disseminated in a rapidly changing field. It is important that such disciplinary differences be understood and that educational institutions clearly identify the forms of dissemination that are prized and rewarded. Does a book published by William B. Eerdmans count toward tenure and promotion in the same way as a book published by the University of Michigan Press? Or would it be viewed more (or less) favorably in your context? You will need to educate yourself about your institution's precise definitions and scholarly expectations. To what extent has your new academic home embraced the Boyer report? Does it define scholarship traditionally or more broadly? And how does it comparatively value Boyer's four models? Consult your faculty handbook, discuss these issues with your mentor or department chair, and pay attention to the kinds of scholarly work done by your new colleagues, especially those receiving tenure during your first few years at the institution.

The variety of ways to practice faithful learning that were discussed in Chapter 5 are as applicable to scholarship as to teaching. One key difference, however, arises with the question of audience and context. While teaching at a mission-based institution involves tact and discernment, overt affirmations and explorations of one's faith commitments are always appropriate and may even be expected. The same cannot be said for scholarly dissemination. Good writing or speaking is always context-specific, and just as an article written for one journal might need to be adjusted in terms of organization or vocabulary for another, so the degree to which one is explicit about the ways in which faith has inspired, affected, or provided resources for one's scholarship may differ. Faithful scholarship need not always be overtly labeled or identified as Christian scholarship in order to be faithful. An essay written for *Christianity and Literature* or *Christian Scholars Review* may take a very different rhetorical stance than one intended for *PMLA* or the *Journal of Social Psychology,* even as the basic discovery, claim, or interpretation proposed might remain the same. Some mission-driven institutions may prefer or even require that their faculty engage in overtly Christian scholarship, and there are many peer-reviewed scholarly journals across the academic disciplines that welcome such work. Other scholars may work in disciplinary areas or publish in venues in which their Christian faithfulness need not be overtly proclaimed and may, in fact, be detrimental. Some may desire to do good disciplinary work and gain scholarly recognition first before "outing" themselves as Christians or explicitly discussing the ways in which Christian foundational principles or a Christian meta-narrative enter into and form their work. Others may be called to bring the wisdom and discoveries of their discipline to the Christian community, serving as translators and educators by publishing in venues such as Baylor University Press, Baker Publishing, or University of Notre Dame Press. And a few may move back and forth between two audiences — writing one essay or book for a secular academic audience, followed by another for an explicitly Christian audience. Shaping one's scholarly trajectory in such terms of audience and levels of explicitness should be a matter of individual discernment of calling, gifts, and opportunities.

Scholarship: Cons and Pros

After the heady air of graduate school, new faculty may be surprised to encounter resistance to scholarship arising from some in their new world, including parents and trustees, college advancement officers and admissions personnel, student life and academic administrators, and — perhaps most unexpectedly — senior faculty. This opposition will typically appear as unarticulated assumptions or beliefs rather than overt arguments. The primary reason most mission-driven colleges downplay or even neglect scholarship is the fact that their identity is first and foremost that of a teaching institution. We position ourselves in the market premised on this identity, and our college Web sites, viewbooks, and advertising stress our commitment to teaching. This identity as a teaching institution is one that we are proud of, and rightly so, particularly when the research institution is regularly lambasted for its irresponsible use of research funds, neglect of student needs, and elitist attitudes. Horror stories abound — first-year classes of 700 to 800 students crammed into a cavernous lecture hall, peering at the indistinguishable figure of the professor lecturing below; full professors who haven't taught an undergraduate class in ten years; researchers who spend two hours a week in the classroom but thirty hours a week in the lab. During the past two decades, numerous reports, beginning with the Boyer report, not to mention pronouncements by various Secretaries of Education and other political figures, have issued strong calls for reform in our institutions of higher learning with respect to the role of teaching.

But let's be realistic. Few mission-driven institutions are in danger of succumbing to these problems. Rather, in a kind of reverse elitism, they sometimes suspect those who conduct research and publish extensively as perhaps not being the best teachers. Formal reward structures may reflect this bias; how many institutions that honor a "Teacher of the Year" also honor a "Scholar of the Year"? While the research institution tends to overemphasize research at the cost of their teaching mission, mission-driven institutions can overemphasize teaching and service at the cost of their responsibility to conduct scholarship. It is not unusual at such institutions to overload faculty in terms of teaching assignments, summer-school duties, advising responsibilities, and committee service, all at the cost of the life of the mind.

This leads to the second argument against expecting scholarship that I have heard — usually from faculty themselves: "The time and resources that support scholarly work are not available at our institutions." We face different expectations than faculty at research institutions. Our responsibilities are unique because we are committed to helping our students learn in the context of their faith how to lead more thoughtful and effective Christian lives. Consequently, we have heavier teaching loads, and we are expected to participate in the college community in more extensive ways

— attending chapel, counseling students, serving as academic advisors, speaking in dorms, having students over to our homes. We don't have the necessary laboratories, start-up funds, libraries, travel funds, academic grants — and, above all, time — to be scholars.

Besides — and here's a third common argument against scholarship — what good do research and writing do? The pressure to publish or perish has resulted in a huge outpouring of seldom-cited, mediocre, unread essays and books aimed at an increasingly smaller readership of narrow specialists. There is a great deal of frivolous and unimportant scholarship produced today, especially in the humanities and social sciences. Academic publication often appears to be nothing more than an elaborate game that rarefied scholars play for the sake of promotion and prestige — not because it is meaningful or makes a difference. Within Christian circles, as Michael Hamilton points out, many believe that "most specialized scholarship has no practical impact on [the] Church or on society," a view that reflects a broader secular prejudice against research scholarship. Americans tend to be skeptical of what occurs in what they derisively term "the ivory tower." For example, Hamilton notes that scholarly research was one of the favorite targets of Senator William Proxmire's Golden Fleece Awards in the seventies and eighties, awarded for "the most outrageous examples of federal waste," such as the four hundred thousand dollars Ohio State spent to invent a six-legged robot, or the millions of dollars devoted to finding out if drunk fish are more aggressive than sober fish.[7] Academic scholarship often appears to be nothing more than some elaborate game that highbrow scholars play for the sake of promotion and prestige — not because it is meaningful or makes a difference.

Now obviously this is not the kind of scholarship for which I want to make a case. However, with the able assistance of the media, this is what enters many people's minds when scholarship is mentioned. Nonetheless, legitimate questions about the value of scholarship can and should be asked, and combined with an admirable commitment to teaching and deplorable resources to support scholarship, such questions at times result in a prejudice against research and scholarly work. Historically, many mission-driven institutions have not had a strong tradition and culture of scholarship, so you may not find a robust system of expectations and support at your school. Your senior faculty may have few scholarly irons in the

7. Michael S. Hamilton, "The Elusive Idea of Christian Scholarship," *Christian Scholars Review* 31 (2001): 14-15.

fire and be faintly discouraging about any desire on your part to write a book, apply for an NSF, or publish in one of the top journals in your field.

The tide is changing, however; ever since Mark Noll took the evangelical community to task in *The Scandal of the Evangelical Mind,* a concerted effort has been made to encourage and support more scholarship by Christians. Both the Lilly Fellows Network and the Council for Christian Colleges and Universities have sponsored programs encouraging their member institutions to promote, support, and value scholarship. In the 1990s, the Pew Charitable Trust provided generous support for Christian scholars on the model of the National Endowment for the Humanities, and numerous centers supporting scholarly work have been established since that time, including the Calvin Center for Christian Scholarship, the Baylor Institute for Faith and Learning, and the Pepperdine Center for Faith and Learning. More and more mission-driven institutions are instituting or increasing scholarly expectations for promotion and tenure. Such changes reflect a growing recognition that scholarship can play a vital role in the mission of an institution, but such change also can be awkward as senior faculty find themselves in the position of evaluating junior faculty on the basis of different criteria than they themselves met, fully cognizant that if they were to go up for tenure or promotion to full professor at the present time, they would not be qualified. Senior faculty who have not been active scholarly may feel either threatened by newer faculty with scholarly ambitions or envious of more recent institutional support for research.

Learning about your institution's history in this respect may provide glimpses of potential hidden land mines. I strongly believe that an institution should never significantly increase expectations for scholarly achievements without also providing additional support for such work, but I also am convinced that research and scholarship, as broadly defined by Boyer, should be an essential part of every faculty member's job description. Following Marsden and Noll, many writers have advocated for increased production of Christian scholarship, including C. Stephen Evans, Joel Carpenter, and Richard Hughes.[8] Like them, I believe that the production of

---

8. Mark A. Noll, *The Scandal of the Evangelical Mind* (Grand Rapids: Wm. B. Eerdmans, 1994); Richard T. Hughes, *How Christian Faith Can Sustain the Life of the Mind* (Grand Rapids: Wm. B. Eerdmans, 2001); C. Stephen Evans, "The Calling of the Christian Scholar-Teacher," in *Faithful Learning and the Christian Scholarly Vocation,* ed. Douglas V. Henry and Bob R. Agee (Grand Rapids: Wm. B. Eerdmans, 2003), pp. 26-49; Joel Carpenter, "The Mission of Christian Scholarship in the New Millennium," in *Faithful Learning and the Christian Scholarly Vocation,* pp. 62-74.

faithful scholarship is an important Christian calling that can be carried out in a variety of ways, including work at secular institutions or research-intensive universities. In what follows, I will make the case for the crucial role of scholarship at the teaching-sensitive, mission-driven institution in both theological and practical terms.

Scholarship as Tending the Garden

The astonishing opening act of the biblical drama, creation, establishes one reason to pursue scholarship, especially the scholarship of discovery. After fashioning the Garden of Eden, God gave humanity the responsibility to tend that garden. Although under the influence of Platonic idealism, the church too often envisions the Edenic paradise as immutable and changeless, the original creation was not frozen perfection. Herbs and trees turned to seed, birds and fish reproduced, human beings were "to be fruitful and multiply and fill the earth," as well as "to till" the new creation (Gen. 1:11-12, 22, 28; 2:15).[9] All Christians have a responsibility to work as co-creators with God to develop the abundant potentials of creation: the immense variety of the natural world, the multitudinous possibilities of social structures and relationships, and the limitless prospects of the aesthetic imagination. Discovering mammoth stars or miniscule insects, creating compelling stories or astonishing paintings, positing new theories or explanations are all ways that we bring "to fruition the possibilities of development implicit in the work of God's hands," thus engaging "in the ongoing creational work of God."[10] But competent cultivation, as any gardener knows, goes beyond merely adding more shrubbery. One must encourage and govern growth by tilling: removing unruly growth, pinching wild shoots, deadheading petunias, and pruning the box shrubs. In *Paradise Lost*, Milton visualizes prelapsarian gardening in this way: Eve props up heavy rosebushes with myrtle bands, while Adam dexterously trains the climbing ivy in this most British Eden. In discovering more about the creation and conceiving new ways to organize, explain, and employ that creation, we act in the image of the Triune God, reflecting "the mind of the maker."[11] William A. Barry, S.J., writes, "God wants a world in which we work in harmony with God's inten-

9. All biblical references are to the New Revised Standard Version.
10. Al Wolters, *Creation Regained: Biblical Basics for a Reformational Worldview,* 2d ed. (Grand Rapids: Wm. B. Eerdmans, 2004), pp. 43-44.
11. Dorothy L. Sayers, *The Mind of the Maker* (New York: Harcourt Brace, 1941).

tion in creation; a world in which God is active and we are active; a world in which, indeed, we cooperate with God in developing the planet."[12]

In the act of creation, God also expressed delight, as is indicated in the sevenfold chorus of "it was good." The goodness of creation was both practical and aesthetic: Eden's numerous trees were not only "good for food" but also "pleasant to the sight" (Gen. 2:9). God's creation provides not only sustenance but also delight, as the psalmist celebrates:

> You cause the grass to grow for the cattle,
>   and plants for people to use,
> to bring forth food from the earth,
>   and wine to gladden the human heart,
> oil to make the face shine,
>   and bread to strengthen the human heart. (Ps. 104:14-15)

Research, scholarship, and creativity make possible a fuller savoring of the extravagant beauty and complexity of God's creation. Every piece of information about God's creation, no matter how trivial — down to the number of hairs on our head — is valuable in God's sight.

With the infamous second act of the biblical drama, sin entered the world, encumbering the development of the garden, distorting the true beauty of Milton's rosebushes and ivy. While we are to continue to develop and delight in God's good gifts, sin presents the scholar with a new task: adding our efforts to God's redemptive activity, working to bring about the kingdom of God. The biblical idea of shalom — a right relationship between ourselves and God, others, and the natural world — indicates that it is not only our souls that need redemption but also the material, social, and cultural world. In the scholarship of application and teaching in particular, the scholar advances God's kingdom by working for shalom, striving to love the neighbor by meeting needs, ameliorating suffering, healing disease, working for peace and justice, striving to live in harmony with the natural world by treating it with love and respect, practicing earth-keeping and ecological awareness.

People with intellectual gifts and academic resources thus are called to practice scholarship as a way of glorifying God and advancing God's kingdom. As Perry Glanzer states, "The Christian academic vocation primarily

---

12. William A. Barry, S.J., *Here's My Heart, Here's My Hand: Living Fully in Friendship with God* (Chicago: Loyola Press, 2009), p. 4.

involves the *creation and redemption of scholarship.*"[13] In developing and redeeming God's good gifts through our intellectual work, we act as good stewards. The parable of the talents suggests that when God gives us a resource, we should work to increase that resource, not just hide it away. We are all called "to be faithful over a few things," as Matthew describes the two obedient servants (chapter 25). This story also proposes that different servants receive different gifts, just as the body of the church that Paul describes in First Corinthians has many different parts. Some work for God's kingdom and glorify him forever by growing flowers, others by being full-time parents; some are politicians; others are plumbers. And then there are those of us who have been designated the professorial part of the body; we have been given the gift of an ability to think critically and creatively, to analyze, synthesize, and deduce; to make connections and uncover insights. We have been called to produce science and sociology, math and music, psychology and philosophy. God gave us these intellectual abilities and then gave us the opportunity to develop them by providing — often through providential means — a graduate education. That education, as we have discussed, has many problems, but the one thing that it does well is to prepare us to be scholars, which is, ironically, the one thing that new faculty at Christian colleges may discover has little usefulness or status in their positions. Far too often their intellectual talent is then either hidden away in the earth or carried back to the secular institution; this happens when some of our most promising junior faculty members, frustrated by their inability to continue their research and writing, leave positions at mission-driven schools. Both individuals and institutions, then, have a responsibility to promote and produce scholarship.

Even though your work may be difficult to explain to your parents, your scholarship is capable of contributing to shalom. Every piece of good scholarship, no matter how minor, provides a small contribution to the larger progress of learning, even if that contribution occurs at the bottom of the academic food chain. George Slanger, a professor of English, describes this well:

> At the top of a mountain sit brooding Douglas Bush and Northrop Frye and Jacques Derrida and other luminaries, those who have shaped our

13. Perry L. Glanzer, "Why We Should Discard 'the Integration of Faith and Learning': Rearticulating the Mission of the Christian Scholar," *Journal of Education and Christian Belief* 12, no. 1 (2008): 43.

thinking, our reading, our lives, and our teaching. But in my vision, they sit so high because many scholars with lesser abilities and greater distractions have built the mountain spoonful by spoonful. Great scholarly minds spring forth not, like Athena, from the skull of Zeus but from scholarly enterprises of which we are all a part.[14]

In contributing our grain, or spoonful, or even shovel of sand to the scholarly enterprise, we have the opportunity to testify to the world about the length, height, breadth, and depth of God's wisdom. Our initial impressions about the frivolous nature of research can be misleading. As Hamilton points out with reference to some of Proxmire's awards, "research on the six-legged robot led to a better prosthetic knee" that has helped thousands of people to walk without pain, and studies of drunken fish may help us better understand human aggression and alcoholism. When scholars "[toil] in the trenches of their disciplines, wrestling over long periods of time with arcane theoretical and technical questions," they seldom know when their work will bear pragmatic fruit. Hamilton explains, "The scientific reason why we cannot know beforehand which scholarship will be practical is that there are too many variables that lie outside anybody's control. The theological reason is that God controls the outcomes of human endeavor, and he often has big surprises up his sleeve."[15] The Christian scholar's call is to be faithful, even in small things and even when outcomes are uncertain. Just because some scholarship today is silly or produced for selfish purposes doesn't mean that all scholarship is. The scholarly choices that we make are important. Faithful scholarship should not be "research that has been ground out in long, soul-deadening nights of fear and loathing," as Slanger poetically phrases it.[16] Faithful scholarship should not be produced for the purpose of personal prestige, career fame, or even tenure. Faithful scholarship should emerge from the depths of our true selves out of a desire to glorify God and a willingness to utilize our strongest gifts.

If Christianity does provide a true view of the world, despite the sinful blurriness raised by historical, cultural, and personal limits, faithful scholarship has the potential to make discoveries that are unavailable to other

14. George Slanger, "A Chair's Notes toward a Definition of Scholarship in the Small State University," *ADE Bulletin* 118 (1987): 29.

15. Hamilton, "The Elusive Idea of Christian Scholarship," p. 20.

16. Slanger, "A Chair's Notes toward a Definition of Scholarship in the Small State University," p. 28.

approaches, to provide answers that have been overlooked, to offer solid grounds on which issues of justice can be pursued. A commitment to the Christian gospel, the historical resources of the church and its confessions, and the application of a Christian worldview may provide some access to truths that other perspectives may miss.[17] The faith-informed ways in which we answer the basic worldview questions — Who are we? Where are we? What's wrong? How can wrong be made right? — may creatively and positively influence our research into breast cancer, broken families, depression, multiculturalism, the Internet, globalization, performance art, or nationalism. Asking even slightly different questions with the goal of glorifying God and loving our neighbors may produce new insights, interpretations, and recommendations.

Beyond fulfilling the theological mandate to practice scholarship, faithful scholarship at a mission-driven institution also provides significant pragmatic benefits for the institution, the faculty, and the students. Producing peer-reviewed research and creative work will improve our reputation and institutional rankings, much as most academics profess to dislike such measures. Similarly, especially if an institution offers graduate programs, producing scholarship may be a crucial part of receiving and maintaining secondary accreditations. Conducting research and producing scholarship also promote personal and professional renewal. All faculty — new and seasoned alike — will benefit from some kind of scholarly activity to help them stay intellectually alive, to allow them to escape the cranky-old-professor-with-yellowing-notecards syndrome. This is more than simply a matter of keeping up to date in a field, staying on top of the latest developments in string theory, cultural studies, or state requirements for teacher preparation. Slanger argues that well-done scholarship makes professors "more wakeful." He writes,

> When we have an ongoing project, we are put on alert. Things jump out of the newspaper or out of passing conversations because they challenge or confirm the point we are groping toward from week to week. Even our hasty perusal of professional journals becomes more palatable and more productive because we read them with a mind primed to receive

17. Of course, other perspectives will also contain access to truth, including truths that Christian perspectives may overlook. By claiming that faithful Christian scholarship has the possibility to achieve unique insights, I do not intend to take the triumphalist stance that only Christian scholarship can achieve truth.

information about a research project. Something that would otherwise go unnoticed will stick because we think, "I can use that."[18]

Scholarship also benefits our students. If we remain active scholars, our courses and curriculum will reflect the latest information and theories and remain on the cutting edge of the discipline. We will provide role models of passionate lifelong learners with intellectual curiosity and solid discipline. If we engage in research projects to which our students can contribute, they will learn much by that participation. And our scholarly activities provide an important way for us to maintain contact with the larger academic world, which can be advantageous in helping our students gain admission to graduate school, apply for scholarships and fellowships, and discern their own future callings.

The Teacher-Scholar

Academics often are highly conflicted about the relationship between teaching and scholarship. Philosophically and intellectually, we say one thing; pragmatically and emotionally, we feel another. Common wisdom holds that scholarship enhances teaching, that the two are two halves of the same coin. That is why a research-based Ph.D. is a typical prerequisite for faculty employment. Research repeatedly demonstrates that most professors believe that teaching and research are positively related. For example, one British survey found that 90 percent of academics claimed that in order to be a good university teacher, one must also be active in research.[19] The two activities are seen as mutually supportive because of the belief that research is necessary if we are to keep on top of new developments in our fields and so be effective and up-to-date teachers, as I have argued above. In general, academics believe that research enhances teaching more than teaching enhances research, and that the link between the two activities is stronger at graduate than at undergraduate levels.[20]

18. Slanger, "A Chair's Notes toward a Definition of Scholarship in the Small State University," p. 30.

19. A. H. Halsey, *Decline of Donnish Dominion: The British Academic Profession in the Twentieth Century* (Oxford: Clarendon Press, 1992).

20. Mohammad Qamar uz Zaman, "Review of the Academic Evidence on the Relationship between Teaching and Research in Higher Education" (United Kingdom Department

On the other hand, when we begin to cultivate our own scholarly crop, we may come to view teaching and scholarship as competing or even contradictory roles. Have you ever heard yourself or a colleague say, "I'm so busy grading papers that I don't have time to do my own work"? The uneasy relationship between teaching and scholarship is reflected in titles of essays about teaching and scholarship. A cursory literature review shows repeated instances of words such as "balancing act," "dilemma," "tension," and "conflict." So although we think that research and scholarship enhance our teaching, we also think that the time we spend teaching prevents us from engaging in scholarship.

Some of these contradictions are outlined in a 1996 essay in the *Review of Educational Research* that conducts a meta-analysis of over fifty studies of the relationship between research and teaching. The authors, John Hattie and H. W. Marsh, identify a number of models of the possible connections between teaching and scholarship and the predicted relationship between the two — negative, positive, or zero. In what they call the "conventional" model, the assumption is that "research performance is a prior condition for good teaching," so the two activities will have a positive relationship. The assumption of the "scarcity" model is that given the scarcity of time and energy, commitment to one role inhibits the development of excellence in the other role. The two activities will have a negative relationship.[21]

Those of us who struggle to allocate the proper amount of time to both teaching and scholarship tend to believe quite strongly in the scarcity model, but Hattie and Marsh found little evidence that time spent on teaching and time spent on research are negatively correlated. Time spent on research is positively correlated with productivity — that is, the more time you spend on scholarship, the more likely you are to have something published. But there is little evidence that the amount of time spent on teaching is related to the success of your teaching. In fact, as we discussed previously, most faculty members, especially new faculty members, spend too much time preparing to teach; they over-prepare. But the correlation between teaching and research is zero, not negative. In addition, when time devoted to research increased, teaching time seldom decreased on a

---

for Education and Skills, Research Report RR506, 2004), p. 5. The Web access is http://www.dcsf.gov.uk/research/data/uploadfiles/RR506.pdf.

21. John Hattie and H. W. Marsh, "The Relationship between Research and Teaching: A Meta-Analysis," *Review of Educational Research* 66 (1996): 507-42. Similar findings are reported in Zaman, "Review of the Academic Evidence on the Relationship between Teaching and Research in Higher Education."

one-to-one basis. More time spent on scholarship is more likely to come from leisure or family time.[22] One caveat here: talking about "time spent on teaching" is confusing because this can be measured as the amount of time spent per hour of class (preparing, grading, responding, etc.) or in terms of teaching load or contact hours. Obviously, teaching twenty credit hours a week versus ten credit hours a week will make a big difference in the amount of time available for scholarship. The study refers to what happens when a teacher spends ten hours a week outside of class for every contact hour versus three hours a week for every contact hour. Mohammad Qamar uz Zaman suggests, "It is possible that initially the roles of research and teaching may enhance each other until a threshold level is reached where increasing effort spent on one operates to reduce the quality of the other due mainly to the limitation of time. A single study examining this proposition using U.S. faculty data finds that up to 8 hours per week of teaching are indeed facilitative of research."[23] Hattie and Marsh conclude, "The common belief that research and teaching are inextricably entwined is an enduring myth. At best, research and teaching are very loosely coupled."[24]

Being a productive scholar doesn't necessarily detract from being an effective teacher, but neither does it necessarily enhance one's teaching, as the common wisdom model holds. One response to this data might be to cut the umbilical cord between research and teaching, either by seeing them as two unrelated responsibilities or by designating some faculty as teachers and others as researchers, but this is not Hattie and Marsh's recommendation. Instead, they write, "It should cease to be surprising that the relationship between teaching and research is zero, and it would be more useful to investigate ways to increase the relationship. . . . The strongest policy claim that derives from this meta-analysis is that universities need to set as a mission goal the improvement of the nexus between research and teaching."[25]

One of the advantages of a meta-analysis is that it provides some useful information that allows us to weigh the many variables involved. After all, there are various ways to measure "good" teaching and "good" scholarship, and thus to measure the relationship between the two. Hattie and

22. Hattie and Marsh, "The Relationship between Research and Teaching," p. 509.
23. Zaman, "Review of the Academic Evidence on the Relationship between Teaching and Research in Higher Education," p. 5.
24. Hattie and Marsh, "The Relationship between Research and Teaching," p. 529.
25. Hattie and Marsh, "The Relationship between Research and Teaching," p. 533.

Marsh found that the scenarios in which the correlation between teaching and research is greater than zero are (1) in the social sciences (as opposed to the natural sciences), (2) when peer ratings of teaching are used (as opposed to self-rating), (3) when indicators of the quality of publications (as opposed to sheer quantity) are used, and (4) in colleges or liberal arts institutions (as opposed to the research university). Here are a few of their additional findings: "Good researchers are a little more likely to be better prepared as teachers. . . . Good researchers and good teachers are more enthusiastic, have greater breadth of coverage, are more committed to teaching, and appear more knowledgeable." The critical mediator appears to be that researchers have better organizational skills and use their time more carefully. Students find that faculty who are active in research are slightly more available, give more feedback, and are quicker to return student work. Active researchers are also seen as more demanding, with higher standards, lower grades, and more required work. Students don't work any harder for them or think that they are more interesting or enthusiastic. They do find them to have clearer presentations, be better prepared, and have more explicit expectations. Yet, ironically, students saw most active researchers as less knowledgeable, perhaps because their knowledge was more specialized or narrow than general.[26] Zaman's meta-analysis found two British and one Australian study with strong, positive student perceptions of faculty research. Undergraduate courses in which research is integrated are seen as "current and intellectually exciting," although some course content was seen as being skewed toward faculty research.[27]

What these sometimes conflicting and tentative findings suggest is that we should think more carefully about the relationship between teaching and scholarship. There is much that we can do, both individually and institutionally, to improve this relationship. As an administrator charged with the responsibility of encouraging faculty to excel as teacher-scholars, I wrestled with the challenge. One of my responsibilities as director of the SPU Center for Scholarship and Faculty Development was "to promote a campus climate in which research, writing, creating, teaching, and learning are understood and valued as Christian vocations." SPU's Center is unusual in that its mission encompasses both scholarship and teaching. It's more typical to have distinct centers for teaching and distinct centers for

26. Hattie and Marsh, "The Relationship between Research and Teaching," p. 529.
27. Zaman, "Review of the Academic Evidence on the Relationship between Teaching and Research in Higher Education," p. 4.

scholarship. But the mission of the SPU Center for Scholarship and Faculty Development is to support "the teacher-scholar." At most mission-driven institutions, I would argue, the professorial role should be that of the hyphenated "teacher-scholar"; the professor's primary task is to help students learn, but he or she facilitates that learning through scholarly work. We are not scholars at research institutions, and the kind of scholarship that we do should always inform and improve our teaching. Being a good teacher-scholar involves a hyphen, not a slash. Our teaching and our scholarship will both flourish if we consciously develop a symbiotic relationship between the two rather than an oppositional one.

Grafting Teaching and Scholarship Together

Most faculty need training in how to be a teacher-scholar; few of their graduate-school mentors will have taught them this difficult art. One way of conceiving of this hybrid role is to argue that the pure act of doing research and writing enhances teaching by means of modeling. Teacher-scholars show their students what a scholar does, even if the topic they are working on has no relationship to their curriculum. For example, I might bring into a class an essay on which I am working — primarily to show my students all the crossed-out sections, arrows, and pasted-together fragments. Writing is a process, I say, a long and arduous process, and I certainly don't sit down at my computer and just churn out publishable prose. But another way to combine teaching and scholarship is to conduct research and pursue writing projects that are inherently related to and enhance one's teaching. There are several concrete ways to graft together teaching and scholarship to produce more fruits of learning. Grafting is a horticultural process in which a cutting, called the *scion*, is inserted into a root-and-stem base called the *stock;* some varieties of flora can reproduce only in this fashion. Growing up on my family's azalea farm, I learned how to graft at an early age: slicing the top off the stock, making a vertical slit in the remaining stem, honing the end of the scion into a wedge, inserting it into the stock's incision, and winding a string to bind the two together temporarily. The grafts were then kept warm and humid until the two parts had grown together, producing a new plant. In grafting together teaching and research, we need to think about the different kinds of relationships that can be fruitfully cultivated.

In terms of teaching and scholarship, which is the stock and which is the

148

scion? Too often, professors adapt their curriculum to fit their research, but students, especially first- and second-year students, tend to perceive such highly specialized studies as irrelevant. There's no question that up-to-date research should affect curriculum, but we seldom find professors adapting their research agendas to better fit what they are teaching. One study of select liberal-arts colleges found that 58 percent of academics indicated that changes in their scholarly agenda determined or importantly influenced the shape of their teaching. Only 6 percent claimed that their teaching program set their scholarly agenda.[28] But what if professors intentionally chose research projects that were inherently related to the subject matter that they taught? Initially this might be difficult for those who have recently come from working on a dissertation that might be highly specialized and esoteric. One's graduate trajectory almost invariably directs one to a narrow plot in the garden of learning, and that trajectory may need to develop a new direction once one's teaching career begins. For example, I wrote my dissertation on the early novels of Herman Melville, and while I have regularly taught *Moby-Dick* and some of Melville's short stories, I haven't read or discussed *Typee, Oomo, Redburn,* or the rest of the early works in many years. New faculty may be wise to shift or redirect their research track, the niche in the discipline in which they will engage, in response to their teaching. Let me illustrate with a personal example.

For the past twenty-five years, because of a teaching assignment I was given early in my career, I've been researching and writing in the field of African literature, a field that barely even existed during my graduate school days. For many years, one of my most successful courses was in African literature. I don't think this is coincidental. Background reading that I did for the course helped in my writing; I had my students write essays on authors on whom I was working so that we could discuss ideas together. Their ideas often stimulated my own. If I were assigned to teach a general education course with no specific syllabus, I chose to teach an African novel on which I was writing. But this system worked both ways: I also chose what African novel to write on based upon whether it would teach well or fit into the syllabus of a specific class. In this way, my teaching assignments provided the stock for my scholarly scions. As I moved into the field of faculty development, my research and publication areas shifted again, as the work I did designing faculty workshops and seminars led to and prompted my writing projects.

28. Hattie and Marsh, "The Relationship between Research and Teaching," p. 512.

For those in the sciences and social sciences, developing ways to encourage and utilize undergraduate research is a way to simultaneously teach and conduct scholarship. Again, the choice of a research agenda is important: Faculty need to consider what they and their students can accomplish with the given resources at their institutions. Obviously you can't use a nuclear accelerator, but what could you do and what could undergraduates assist with? One social-psychologist that I knew conducted research into what causes people to support mass-transit projects. When Seattle voters had a huge mass-transit initiative on the ballot, he had three different classes distributing surveys and collecting data. He brought a draft of his subsequent analysis to class and had students read and comment on it before he submitted it for publication. And many of my colleagues in the hard sciences regularly involve students in their research projects; because one biology professor at SPU specializes in pond snails, many senior honors projects on *Lymnaea Stagnalis* have been produced over the years. Recent research into teaching science has highlighted the superiority of a "discovery" or "problem-based" model for learning, which means that developing and assigning portions of our own research projects to students can be an effective instructional strategy.

Increasing resources are now available for designing, developing, and supporting undergraduate research. The national leader in this area is the Council on Undergraduate Research (CUR), whose mission "is to support and promote high-quality undergraduate student-faculty collaborative research and scholarship."[29] CUR's focus is to provide research opportunities for faculty and students at predominantly undergraduate institutions. It "believes that faculty members enhance their teaching and contribution to society by remaining active in research and by involving undergraduates in research." It offers faculty development programs and assists administrators in improving and assessing the research environment at their institutions. It also advocates for undergraduate research to state legislatures, private foundations, government agencies, and the U.S. Congress. CUR's Web site has a wealth of resources, including information on the annual conference, publications such as *Broadening Participation in Undergraduate Research: Fostering Excellence and Enhancing the Impact,* a Web Guide to Research for Undergraduates (WEBGuru), and a list of journals publishing undergraduate research. CUR's focus, however, has been on the sci-

---

29. Council on Undergraduate Research, http://www.cur.org/.

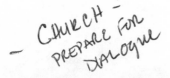

ences, and more work needs to be done to encourage and support undergraduate research in the humanities.

A third strategy for grafting teaching and scholarship together involves changing direction in order to work in the scholarship of teaching, a relatively new and growing field, but one seldom promoted in graduate school. The scholarship of teaching does not entail a chemist or a political scientist becoming a professor of education; rather, it involves exploring the specific ways in which chemistry or political science are best organized, taught, and mastered. It requires that the scholar be knowledgeable about the disciplinary field as well as investigate learning theories and pedagogical techniques that are especially appropriate for the discipline, topic, or skill. Again, I know an engineering professor who began her career at a state university where there were many resources available for conducting the scholarship of discovery, but who, upon taking a position at a teaching institution, has redirected her research into questions of how engineering can be most successfully learned on the undergraduate level and how to involve more women and minorities in the field. A plethora of journals are now devoted to the scholarship of teaching and learning both in general and in disciplinary areas.[30]

Cultivating Yourself as a Teacher-Scholar

In addition to redirecting or adjusting your scholarly trajectory in response to your current context, grafting your curriculum and your scholarship together in new ways, you can personally promote your growth as a teacher-scholar in several ways. Even if your position entails a heavy teaching load, you can maintain an active scholarly life by promoting a personal climate for research. The following guidelines can help.

1. *Have realistic expectations.* If you do not have a position at an R1 institution, do not expect that you will be as productive a scholar as those who do. Younger faculty at mission-driven institutions may feel discouraged about their inability to write a book or conduct a major project during their first years of teaching. The expectations instilled in graduate school are not being met; professional reality is not cohering with professional socialization. After a few years, it is easy to become disillusioned, to let scholarship slide completely, since, after all, it isn't much appreciated in

30. For a bibliography of SOTL resources, see http://www.indiana.edu/~libsalc/SOTL/.

this context. Here's a reality check: A comprehensive study of hundreds of novice professors at a variety of institutions showed that during the first two years, over two-thirds of new faculty produce virtually nothing, despite having had highly ambitious plans earlier.[31] New faculty need to realize that they will have little time to spend on research, writing, or creating because they will be scrambling to put together syllabi, lab assignments, lectures, and discussion questions.

I know how you feel. In my first two years as a professor, I was responsible for teaching four courses a semester, and none of them were repeated until my third year on the job. New professors at mission-driven institutions also need time to think about their discipline in new ways, ways that have not been taught in graduate school. How does this material relate to or impact faith? What's the relationship between my Christian commitments and my discipline? How can I be a faithful professor? Given all the other adjustments you will be making, don't expect too much of yourself as a scholar during your first few years.

2. *Have an ongoing project.* Even in your first few years on the job, however, always have at least one project that you are working on, at least mentally. Remember George Slanger's description of how this makes one "more wakeful"? I like to think about the ongoing project as Perlite, a white siliceous rock that gardeners use in potting mixes to provide aeration and moisture retention. Both home gardeners and commercial growers have found that a little bit of Perlite facilitates superior plant growth. That project may be at the initial stage of brainstorming or at the finishing stage of tracking down the final references, but when someone asks what you are working on, you should always be able to name your current intellectual passion, your pressing question, your area of high awareness. Many new faculty will have left graduate school with untouched research data or early drafts that may provide this first project. For those in the humanities, revising a dissertation chapter or writing a book review for a professional journal are manageable small projects. For those in the sciences, working on a major grant proposal may be a good option.

3. *Work in brief, regular sessions during the academic year.* Some plants do best if they are allowed to dry out completely before they are watered; others do better with a small but consistent amount of watering each day. Scholarship is like the latter. Both new and experienced faculty should

---

31. Robert Boice, *Advice for New Faculty Members: Nihil Nimus* (Boston: Allyn & Bacon, 2000), p. 103.

conduct some scholarly work during the academic year. In order to accomplish this, you need to set aside a specific time for scholarship, even if it is no more than a couple of hours a week. Block that time off in your calendar, close your door, and don't answer your phone or read your e-mail during that time.

During my first few years of teaching, I set aside two hours each Thursday to research, write, or read; that's all the time I could find. I told my students and colleagues why I would be unavailable during those two hours, and they understood and respected my decision. Since then, I've learned more about what helps faculty succeed in scholarship through the research of Robert Boice. One of Boice's studies measured the writing habits and outputs of newly hired professors. One group were "binge-writers," cranking out their scholarship in huge chunks during weekends or vacations; the other group wrote in brief, daily sessions, day in and day out. The regular writers wrote more pages per week, submitted more manuscripts, and had many more manuscripts accepted for publication at the conclusion of the six-year study. Boice recommends that new professors begin with as little as ten to fifteen minutes of daily writing, reading, or thinking in order to develop the constant and moderate working habits that facilitate scholarship.[32] During the rookie years, the quantity of finished products is less important than developing a scholarly habit. Perhaps you might try to regularly read one or two of the most significant journals in your field as well as plugging away on a small part of your ongoing project — conducting the literature review, writing summaries, reading background material, and so on.

4. *Choose manageable targets.* After your first two years in a teaching-extensive position, deliberately move into more intensive scholarly work, but select modest scholarly projects. While scaling down your scholarly expectations, don't abandon them altogether. Always have a goal, but keep that goal manageable: short articles or essays, little segments of a research project, data collection from small samples, incremental progress on a book manuscript, or preliminary research on a grant proposal. Few faculty at mission-driven institutions need to write a book every two years in order to progress toward tenure; we have the luxury of taking our time, of enjoying our research and writing rather than just grinding it out. Although some among our professional subculture may view our situation with dismay, I would like to suggest to you that we are, in fact, singularly

32. Boice, *Advice for New Faculty Members,* pp. 137-56.

blessed. The lot of the faithful teacher-scholar is a happy one, to paraphrase Gilbert and Sullivan.

Because I've taught at mission-driven institutions throughout my career, I've never had to publish or perish, unlike my graduate-student friends who accepted jobs at state institutions or large research universities. One friend of mine spent the first years of his career at a state school in the South, where he taught five classes a semester and was expected to publish a book during his first four years of employment in order to stay on tenure track. Others found plusher jobs, at private liberal-arts institutions or at research universities, where they typically taught only three or even two classes a term, but were still expected to produce that book in short order. It took me eight years to write my first university-press book, and since then I have published five books, but each has been a labor of love, not a survival strategy. Each was written because I wanted to write it, because I was excited about the topic and the process and because my scholarly project has been one way for me to serve God.

5. *Use your summers wisely.* Most plants have particular times of year in which they set their buds or generate their energy for the coming year. Think of summer as that time. If you attempt to do too much during the academic year, you might become so burnt out that you need the entire summer to recover. Why not just admit that you won't be able to finish your current project this term, since you have two new courses and a demanding committee assignment? Put in your thirty minutes a day on the project to keep it moving forward, but then dedicate a month of your summer to that project. On the other hand, don't take the entire summer off and then complain that you don't have any time for scholarship.

One of the (few) luxuries of being a college professor is the greater flexibility one has in terms of how one spends one's summers. And some new faculty may opt to take the entire summer off, preferring to spend time with family and friends. (We'll talk more about these kinds of decisions in the next chapter.) But we also need to realize that our ability to "flex" will come at some cost, and at mission-driven institutions, that cost typically is the amount of time one has for research and scholarship. Professionals in other careers typically work eight to ten rigidly scheduled hours a day throughout June, July, and August. I'm delighted that I have the privilege to adjust my hours on campus in order to attend my son's soccer games; to take a couple of days off to help my parents during a health emergency; or to take a week off to go on a mission trip with my church. But I also know that if I choose to spend my entire summer traveling or gardening or remodeling or being with my son, I should not be frustrated that my scholarly project is not advancing.

6. *Apply for both internal and external support.* New professors should investigate both internal and external opportunities to apply for support. Many institutions have faculty research programs that assist in initially setting up a lab or getting a one-course teaching reduction to kick-start a research project. Small as these internal grants often are, begin applying for them as soon as possible. They are often competitive, and you may need to apply a few times before you receive one. Internal grants, though, provide significant leverage and support for external grant applications. An agency such as the National Endowment for the Humanities or the National Science Foundation will look more favorably on a project that has been tested or begun with support from your home institution. Thoroughly investigate the varieties of external opportunities that are available, including the big federal agencies, large private foundations and corporations, disciplinary associations, and local businesses and area foundations. Also be aware that many federal agencies sponsor specific programs targeted for teacher-scholars — those with primary responsibilities for undergraduate education and relatively large teaching loads.

Investigate whether your institution provides faculty with the services of a grant writer or a sponsored research office, and be sure to enroll for any grant-writing workshops that are offered. Two common mistakes faculty make in working with grant-writers or officers are either expecting them to write the entire grant or, alternatively, paying no attention to the advice and editing they provide. University grant-writers characteristically do not write a grant *for you;* after all, you have to generate the research question, design the research strategy, do the literature review, and demonstrate your knowledge of the field. But a university grant-writer will work *with you* to complete the grant-writing process as successfully as possible. First-time grant-writers may be surprised to discover that faculty grant-writing is not a Lone Ranger activity; chairs, deans, budget offices, advancement offices (which enter into the process when a grant-writer applies for foundation support), and other university bodies may need to be informed and/or approve of the grant application, and a grant-writer or a grants office can help you negotiate these institutional mazes. Grant officers can provide boilerplate language and institutional data; check the application against the original Call for Proposals; coordinate with the university finance office to shape a budget with accurate salaries, benefit calculations, student salaries, and percentage of overhead; and apprise you of required institutional approvals and signatures, not to mention proofreading the entire document when you reach the final stages; additionally, they will submit a federal grant through the byzantine online system of grants.gov. While you are indubitably the disciplinary expert, the grant-writer or grants office indubitably will be the grants expert, and you may be surprised to discover how much you can learn about the process. Such a complex activity involving many parties takes time, so it is crucial to begin the process as early as possible, allowing plenty of time for gathering the necessary information, approvals, and feedback. Dashing off a grant proposal in one or even two weeks and expecting institutional help is unreasonable, and will, more often than not, result in a poor proposal being submitted.

Grant-writing is time-consuming and discouraging, but if you don't apply for a grant, you will never get one. And if your application is rejected, apply again. The common wisdom in the grant world is that for every grant someone receives, he or she has applied unsuccessfully for three other grants. It took me four attempts to win an award from the National Endowment for the Humanities, even though I was applying to programs limited to non-R1 faculty. I've written three books made possible by support from outside agencies, but I've also applied for countless grants and fellowships that I have not received.

7. Design a long-term scholarly plan. Home gardeners plan ahead. How big will this tree get? When will the asparagus start producing? For scholarly trajectories, five-year plans are common, allowing you to design how to use your summers, sabbaticals, and grant opportunities. Planning and application for sabbaticals, fellowships (such as a Fulbright), and grants often needs to be done as much as two years in advance. For an inspiring but somewhat daunting description of five-year scholarly plans, consult *The Academic Self,* by Donald E. Hall, who teaches at Cal State, Northridge. Hall teaches a 4/4 course load, but he has managed to carve out time for scholarly research and writing, and his advice is concrete and specific.[33] Keep an idea book, but also select and order projects, estimating out how much time they will take. Break the projects into component parts and schedule your time accordingly. Hall advises that you figure out approximately how many days and hours you will need to complete a specific process, drawing on your knowledge of how you have worked in the past. Many academics are quite unrealistic about how much time they need to

---

33. Donald E. Hall, *The Academic Self: An Owner's Manual* (Columbus: Ohio State University Press, 2002), pp. 43-65.

complete a project, as many an academic journal editor can attest. Don't promise to write three articles over one summer, complete a book in a year while teaching fulltime, or write an NSF grant in a month. When drawing up your plan, account for the time that journals and publishers will take to have your manuscript read and evaluated, which can be anywhere from six weeks to two years. In their guidelines for submission, most publishers will list their typical turn-around time. But even when a manuscript is accepted, realize that additional steps of copy editing, proofreading, and possibly indexing will add additional months until the time of publication. So if you have three years to get a peer-reviewed article published in order to meet the requirements for tenure or promotion, you cannot wait until one year before the deadline to start.

8. *Try, try again.* In general, submit your work initially to your ideal journal or publisher — the top one in the field, the most respected, etcetera — as long as the work is suitable in topic, approach, and tone for that publication. But also construct a list of five to six additional potential publishing venues, including the name of the appropriate editor, and any stylistic, organizational, or informational changes you would need to make. If your first submission is rejected, send out the piece as soon as possible to the next publication on your list. If you've received some reader comments, consult them to see if they suggest any ways to strengthen the manuscript without making it a completely new work. But don't despairingly stuff the letter and the manuscript away in a file and let them sit there for the next six months. One of my early mentors told me to turn around and send the manuscript out to the next publication on my list the day after receiving a rejection, but I've found that I often have to make small tweaks to make something suitable for a different publication. I think it should go out again within a month, if at all possible.

As the years pass, it is possible to always have two or three pieces out under consideration. Meanwhile, you can be working on your current new project, occasionally pausing to deal with proofreading and source-checking for a project in the final stages of publication. Your scholarly production rate will by no means look like that of a university researcher, but there is no cause for shame in that at all.

A few years ago, one of my colleagues came into my office and slumped down on a chair. "I'm feeling really guilty," he confided. "I'm on sabbatical, but I just can't seem to get going."

"What's the problem?" I asked.

"I just can't decide which of four projects I should do," he said.

"They're all fascinating, and I've wanted to work on them all for years." My colleague had gone ten years without a sabbatical, as a consequence of being department chair and director of a major campus program, so he had put his scholarly interests on hold for quite a long time. Now he was experiencing a bad case of sabbatical block.

"What are the four projects?" I asked, and he excitedly talked about each at some length. He clearly had a passion for all four. "Which one of these projects would be the most useful for your teaching?" I then asked. He thought for a moment, and then named one. "Do that," I advised. "Projects always take longer than you think, so you need to be prepared to be finishing up this work while you're teaching. Which one would enhance your teaching and mesh best with it? That's how I'd decide."

I'm happy to say that my colleague followed this advice, wrote two scholarly articles that were both published based on his sabbatical work, and continues to lecture on this particular topic both in his own courses and in several other courses on campus. He figured out how to be a true teacher-scholar.

CHAPTER 7

Beyond Professing Alone:
Becoming an Academic Citizen

During the last two decades, higher education has developed a renewed interest in educating for civic engagement. Such a concern is perennial; it stretches as far back as Plato's Academy, a republican institution educating the future leaders of Athens, through John Dewey's promotion of democratic education as teaching for civic involvement, to the present day. Most recently, this ideal has been articulated in the face of a growing apprehension that individualism, one of America's distinctive strengths, ironically has also become one of its most dangerous weaknesses. From *Habits of the Heart: Individualism and Commitment in American Life* (1985) to *Bowling Alone: The Collapse and Revival of American Community* (2000), sociologists have traced Americans' increasing tendency to disengage from community. In *Bowling Alone*, Robert Putnam drew on twenty-five years of data to show that Americans at the turn of the twentieth century signed fewer petitions, belonged to fewer community organizations, attended church less often, participated in fewer volunteer activities, socialized less often with friends and neighbors, and even bowled alone rather than in leagues. The fear that dwindling social capital may weaken American democratic structures has resulted in numerous programs to increase the civic participation of students through volunteer work, service-learning, and other forms of community involvement. Faculty support of such programs has grown: in 2007-08, the majority of college faculty (55.5 percent) considered it "very important" or "essential" to "instill in students a commitment to community service," an increase of 19.1 percentage points since the previous survey in 2004-05.[1]

---

1. Robert N. Bellah et al., *Habits of the Heart: Individualism and Commitment in Ameri-*

However, even the best-designed and well-funded program to engage students in civic activities will not be effective if professors do not model what it means to be a part of a community. If Americans increasingly are bowling alone, American faculty members increasingly are professing alone. Although the role of the professor has traditionally been seen as threefold — teaching, research, and service — the third leg of the educational stool has become especially shaky. While requirements for community service commonly appear in faculty handbooks, faculty service and leadership are becoming endangered species. Clark Kerr, former chancellor of the University of California system and originator of the term *multiversity*, states that during the last half of the twentieth century, academic citizenship has become imperiled as the academy has moved from a traditional to a postmodern paradigm: "In the traditional paradigm most faculty members were part of a particular academic community as the center of their lives, and they took their on-campus citizenship responsibilities very seriously." Postmodern faculty have less commitment to their local academic community and are more interested in their own intellectual pursuits.[2] Eugene Rice declares, "Getting faculty to change the way they think about their work — moving from an individualistic approach ('my work') to a more collaborative approach ('our work') — is a critical transition that challenges deeply rooted professional assumptions."[3] Committee work and participation in faculty governance are often viewed as temporary irritations, hoops that must be jumped and that can be abandoned once tenure has been achieved.

Many aspects of the academic life encourage individualism over community. We college professors are an ornery lot. Many of us entered this profession because we liked the independence it offered, the freedom to do our own thing in the classroom, library, and lab. The dark impetus occasionally lurking behind the sacred cow of academic freedom is the attitude

---

can Life (Berkeley and Los Angeles: University of California Press, 1985); Robert D. Putnam, *Bowling Alone: The Collapse and Revival of American Community* (New York: Simon & Schuster, 2000); Thomas Erlich, *Civic Responsibility and Higher Education* (Westport, Conn.: American Council on Education/Oryx Press, 2000); and Linda DeAngelo et al., *The American College Teacher: National Norms for the 2007-2008 HERI Faculty Survey* (Los Angeles: Higher Education Research Institute of UCLA, 2009).

2. Clark Kerr, "Knowledge Ethics and the New Academic Culture," *Change*, January/February 1994, pp. 9-10.

3. Eugene Rice, "From Athens to Berlin to LA: Faculty Work and the New Academy," *Liberal Education* (Fall 2006): 12.

that "no one, least of all administrators, can tell me what to do." Just try to get a faculty to agree on general education revision, establishment of a core curriculum, time schedule changes, or transitioning from quarters to semesters, and you'll have plenty of evidence of our difficulty in participating in an academic community. How many of us know what goes on in other faculty members' classrooms? What books are our colleagues assigning, and what issues are they discussing? How many of us know what writing and research projects our colleagues are laboring over? How many of us turn to our colleagues for assistance when a student asks a difficult theological question or when an essay cries out for accurate grounding in a discipline other than our own? Being a university professor involves an extraordinary degree of autonomy, while paradoxically the operations of the academy are deeply rooted in community and collegiality.

The natural inclination for academics to be independent introverts makes sense, given the structures within which we are trained and work. Graduate training, David Damrosch notes, promotes isolation: "Students go from working in courses to working with a few professors for the doctoral orals, and then working alone in the library to complete a dissertation, often under the guidance of a single sponsor."[4] The broader loyalties that have been inculcated through our training, for the most part, are loyalties to the guild, to the profession, to our discipline. When we begin our professorial careers, we find ourselves with a degree of autonomy available in few other professions. John B. Bennett comments,

> Professors . . . have extraordinary control over what they actually do and how they do it. Selection of research areas, choice of methodology and approach, determination of pace and intensity — all are largely decided by the individual. Parallel freedoms exist with respect to teaching responsibilities — symbolized, reinforced, and extended by the separate classrooms into which colleagues or outsiders are rarely invited.[5]

A number of recent developments in higher education have also fed the decline in academic citizenship. The massive increase in part-time and

4. David Damrosch, *We Scholars: Changing the Culture of the University* (Chicago: University of Chicago Press, 1995), p. 10. Damrosch's observation is not as applicable to graduate work in the sciences, which often entails a higher degree of collaboration than work in the arts, humanities, and social sciences.

5. John B. Bennett, *Collegial Professionalism: The Academy, Individualism, and the Common Good* (Phoenix: Oryx Press, 1998), p. 19.

non-tenure-track appointments, which typically do not require committee work, curricular design, advising duties, and other institutional activities, have reduced the number of faculty available to assume service responsibilities. The difficulty in finding permanent academic positions and the rise of "freeway faculty" increases the difficulty of developing campus community. At the other extreme, we find the scholastic entrepreneur so neatly satirized by David Lodge in his classic academic novel, *Trading Places*. Although few academic superstars exist and even fewer are recognized by the American public in general, the celebrity mentality lingers. Writing in *The Chronicle of Higher Education*, an administrator who moved from a private research institution to a state university commented on the differences in the culture, noting that her former colleagues "were people on the make, plotting their next professional move — passing through from somewhere else and eager to take the next plane, train, or BMW out of town. When the semester ended, they rushed off to their 'places' in New York, New England, London, or Paris."[6] She was excited to join an institution with a commitment to the surrounding community.

Whether because of scarcity or stardom, postmodern academic life has become increasingly mobile: today's professors, like today's business-people or computer gurus, move from job to job, from institution to institution, from town to town, and from church to church. Very few will spend their entire career at one institution, as faculty in the past have done. (So far, I've taught at three different institutions over the course of my career.) At urban colleges and universities, financial pressures result in faculty living farther and farther from campus, making it more difficult for them to participate in campus life outside of teaching hours. The research institution's crucial role in socializing new faculty and in serving as a (questionable) model for the rest of higher education results in an emphasis on research and publication at the cost of service and leadership. Furthermore, in a time of increasing economic uncertainty and the rise of disciplinary specialization, fierce departmental allegiances develop rather than institutional loyalty, manifested in battles over curricular turf, budget allocations, and student credit hours. Rather than a community of those who seek to advance truth and learning through a variety of complementary practices and perspectives, American higher education too often is a battleground of contending power centers. Our personal temperament, professional so-

---

6. Natalie Henderson, "Trading $80 Wine for Cheap Cookies," *The Chronicle of Higher Education*, 3 August 2007, p. C4.

cialization, institutional structures, economic pressures, and contemporary rootlessness all work against collegiality and community. The real difficulties of a fluctuating job market, combined with the individualistic ethos of graduate school and the idealization of autonomy in both American and academic culture, reinforce academic individualism.

Instead of having an exclusive concern with the success and shape of a personal career, a professor joining a mission-driven institution should be willing to be rooted, connected, and committed to the success of the institution as a whole. Ideally, one should "join" the mission, not merely sign a contract. Many faculty today desire this kind of connectedness. In a national study on faculty work and rewards, the American Association for Higher Education found that at every type of institution, "faculty express a longing for an older and spiritually richer academic culture, one that placed greater value on the education of students and on the public responsibilities of scholars, one that nurtured community and collegiality instead of promoting competition for resources and prestige."[7] The mission-driven college or university may be capable of offering such a spiritually richer culture, for it typically identifies community as a core value and prizes team players rather than superstars, faculty who embrace the broader mission rather than their personal success. Theological rather than political commitments tend to underlie this embrace of community: God's Trinitarian nature, humanity's creation in the image of God, our human responsibility to love and serve others.

Yet even when a mission-inspired identity revolves around something other than the task of developing future citizens, liberally educated individuals, or a highly trained labor force, that ideal can easily be lost in day-to-day functioning. Also, a theological and rhetorical endorsement of community can be used to discourage dissent and shut down healthy discussion. As in the formation of any community, working together toward a common goal often exists in tension with disagreeing over how to reach that goal. Defining institutional identity around such issues as an allegiance to the transcendent and Triune God, a common sense of values and virtues, and the flourishing of learning through both teaching and scholarship is critical for creating a center for community, but disputes about the precise location of communal borders often work against vibrant community life. The great mystery of community consists in affirming a center

---

7. Clara Lovett, "Listening to the Academic Grapevine," *AAHE Bulletin*, November 1993, p. 3.

but being willing at times to adjust the borders. Both unity and diversity contribute to the strength of an institutional body.

Learning how to become a vital part of an academic community is thus a huge challenge for any new faculty member. Entering any new community is always fraught with uncertainties as one gradually becomes familiar with the community's central identity, the social practices sustaining it, its unspoken expectations and norms, its hidden landmines, and the contentions at its borderlands. For example, at Seattle Pacific there have been periodic discussions about the failure of some faculty to participate in certain events that other faculty believe are crucial to our community identity. Attendance at our annual faculty lecture has been poor; faculty senate meetings draw fewer and fewer participants; the lack of faculty attendance at chapel is constantly lamented by certain voices. During one of these discussions, newer faculty members noted that it was difficult to know, given the plethora of events on campus, what one should attend and what one could opt not to attend. Faculty could spend twenty hours a week participating in community events as varied as concerts, chapel, athletic games, public lectures, presidential forums, current event debates, and so on.

Clearly, colleges and universities need purposeful programs to initiate faculty into community as well as into teaching and scholarship. Wise mentors should advise newer faculty about the most significant traditions and events on a campus. And wise administrators should be constantly vigilant to avoid scheduling too many campus events of overriding importance. When "a major campus event in which the entire community should participate" takes place three times a week, no event will appear genuinely important. On the other hand, newer faculty sometimes fail to realize that becoming an active, contributing member of the local academic community is an essential part of their academic task. Mission-driven institutions need reminders, rituals, structures, and conversations whereby they articulate a common vision and facilitate commitments.

Becoming an esteemed and effective academic citizen will look different at different institutions, so once again, contextual reflection is essential. But all new faculty should devote energy and develop commitments to three basic areas of community life: committee work, curricular matters, and collegial relations.

The Abyss of Committee Work

On most college campuses, it's hard to find many enthusiasts for committee work, although there is always the odd one or two (who may go on to become administrators). Most professors will tell you that committee work is the bane of their existence. And yet a hallmark of American academic life as it has evolved from the British and Continental systems is the shared governance system, in which faculty, administrators, and trustees share responsibility for the operations of the college or university. The American Association of University Professors (AAUP) composed its first statement on the governance of higher education in 1920, "emphasizing the importance of faculty involvement in personnel decisions, selection of administrators, preparation of the budget, and determination of educational policies." Further refinements of the initial statement culminated in the AAUP's 1966 "Statement on Government of Colleges and Universities."[8]

If faculty want to continue a shared governance system, committee work is essential. Nothing irritates administrators more than faculty who loudly and publicly criticize an institutional policy but then refuse to work to reform or replace that policy. Faculty can be experts at diagnosing problems, but then be reluctant to contribute to an attempt to solve those problems, alleging that this is what the administrators are supposed to do. Donald Hall comments, "Too often we simply complain that 'someone' should do 'something' about a situation that we perceive, but we never seem to find the energy, the motivation, the collegial goodwill, or the hours in the day to do something about it ourselves."[9] Yet if administrators take matters into their own hands, issuing top-down policy changes in areas in which the faculty share governance, a howl of protest will resound across faculty discussion boards and around departmental coffeepots. For those new faculty members entering the academy from other areas of professional life — law, nursing, business, engineering — this phenomenon is often one of the most puzzling social practices to encounter and manage.

The degree to which your new institutional home shares governance among faculty, administrators, and trustees most likely will differ in some ways from the exact recommendations of the AAUP, and your faculty

---

8. See "American Association of University Professors," http://www.aaup.org/AAUP/issues/governance/.

9. Donald E. Hall, *The Academic Self: An Owner's Manual* (Columbus: Ohio State University Press, 2002), p. xx.

handbook is the best source to consult to gain clarity on these matters. While procedures for the selection of administrators and budgetary decisions are not always seen as areas of shared responsibility, most institutions affirm that personnel decisions regarding faculty hiring and determination of educational policies are key areas for faculty to play major — if not determining — roles in governance.

At one mission-driven institution, faculty had complained for years about the athletic scholarship award policy, arguing that given the mission of the institution, the size of the student body, and the funds available for financial aid, such scholarships should be severely reduced, if not abolished by a change in divisional status. When a new provost from outside the institution was appointed, she learned of these complaints and created a task force to study the issue and make recommendations. The athletic director, the alumni director, and one coach were appointed to the task force; then the provost, wanting to get faculty input on an issue that appeared to be important to them and judging that scholarship policy was an area in which faculty shared governance, attempted to find several faculty to serve on the task force, only to meet resistance. The responses she heard included these: "Why can't the administration take care of this? I just want to focus on my teaching and advising." "Why are faculty continually asked to do things outside their major responsibility of teaching and scholarship? I serve on far too many committees already." "I don't know anything about athletics and scholarships."

As in so many situations in our muddled lives, there was truth in many of these replies. Many faculty members had excellent reasons for turning down this provost's request, and I don't mean to imply that you should always accept an appointment to a task force or a committee. (In fact, we'll talk about the importance of saying no in Chapter 8.) I also have no doubt that some institutions and administrators ask far too much of their faculty in terms of this kind of service. But as faculty we can't have it both ways: if we want to improve our institution, be responsible academic citizens, exercise our privilege of shared governance, and contribute to the advancement of the mission, we will at times have to do toilsome but necessary committee grunt work.

A theoretical commitment to the importance of contributing to the common good of one's institution can only go so far, though, when one is faced with the mind-numbing reality of committee work. The truth of the matter is that professors are notoriously inefficient when it comes to committee work. Some academics' inclination to hear themselves talk poses as great a danger to effective committee operations as it does to facilitating student learning. While committee work unquestionably can sink one into an abyss, there are a few ways to remain in the sunlight. New faculty should commit to participating in committee work, but also exercise strategies to make committee service less boring, time-consuming, and unrewarding.

Attitude plays an important role. Committee work can be seen as a burden or an opportunity, as a waste of time or an investment in community, as a dull obligation or an intellectual challenge. Working on a campus-wide committee or task force provides rare opportunities to get to know colleagues from other departments and areas of the university. New friends can be made; conversations can move beyond the sometimes repetitive concerns of departments to broader philosophical and theological issues regarding institutional mission. Committee work can also provide the opportunity to make other aspects of our work easier: designing a new advising system with clearer expectations of what students will do before their advising appointments, some standard file-keeping procedures, and a process for an equitable distribution of advising load will eventually make your own advising work less demanding or confusing.

My first faculty committee assignment as a young professor was to the Faculty Social Activities Committee, which planned the annual faculty Christmas party, the spring picnic, and other social events. I strongly suspect that I was appointed to this committee because I was a woman (a rare phenomenon at this institution), but, frankly, planning social events has never been one of my strongest gifts. Yet I know other faculty members who take great delight in strategizing about ways to bring faculty and their families together in creative, community-building practices. If you have the ability to choose or give input into your committee assignments, always request to be placed in an area of interest, expertise, or passion. I'd hate serving on our Faculty Intercollegiate Activities Committee, but the Faculty Development Committee and the Undergraduate Curriculum Committee have provided me with wonderful opportunities to learn new things and generate good programs and policies. One school of thought holds that junior faculty should join committees that have the least amount of work, but I think it is more important to join a committee that does work in which you are interested, work that you find intellectually stimulating and communally valuable.

Lest I seem too idealistic, however, let me hasten to add that even with inspiring areas of concern and a positive attitude, committee work can be soul-numbing. In some cases this is because the work could be more efficiently done by administrators or staff, so faculty leaders should regularly monitor the assignments and activities of committees. There may be instances of committee structures that have outlived their usefulness or areas in which faculty deliberately agree to give up input and decision-making, turning some operations over to the administration. But there are also ways to help committees function more efficiently and effectively. Some are mundane but effective: scheduling all of the meetings for a term at the beginning of that term, using a written agenda to define a focus and stick to it, and keeping and distributing minutes as a record of what has been decided. (I once belonged to a faculty body whose leader was opposed on some unclear grounds to minute-keeping, preferring that we all just talk and gradually reach a decision. After about three years, I realized that we were having some of the same conversations and remaking decisions that we had already made a few years earlier. I requested that we start keeping minutes and volunteered to do so.) Sometimes it is efficient to use subcommittees to accomplish certain tasks, because it is easier to find meeting times for only two or three people and decisions can be reached more quickly. Faculty committees should also realize that they do not always represent a consensus opinion. Before bringing a major policy recommendation to your faculty senate, do some informal temperature-taking of faculty opinion or use a tool like Survey Monkey to test the waters. Although everyone on the committee may hate the latest classroom technology addition, a majority of the faculty may, in fact, appreciate it. The most important rule for efficient committee functioning is simple: respect each other's time. This means arriving on time, staying on task, and adjourning on time — none of which are professorial strengths.

In *Good Start: A Guidebook for New Faculty in Liberal Arts Colleges,* Gerald Gibson proposes several principles for new faculty engaged in committee work, including, "Do your homework. Don't be bashful. Help keep the train on the track." Gibson's advice about preparing for meetings is insightful:

> It is amazing what an edge one can have in a group enterprise simply by doing a little homework. You will discover early on that most committee members are faithful in attendance, but that they devote little or no time to issues on the agenda except during meeting times. There is a strong tendency to consider it to be the responsibility of the committee chair — but no one else — to think about things between meetings. It is far better to set aside maybe half an hour between times to review the

agenda, minutes of past meetings, and other relevant materials, and to make a few notes to take back to the next meeting.

Prominent among the notes should be your own ideas about possible solutions to problems before the committee, disposition of items on its agenda, and/or initiatives that it might profitably take. With this modest amount of preparation, you will find it much easier not only to participate, but to become a leader in committee work — and thus in setting directions. You will also contribute significantly to the efficiency with which the group operates.[10]

While you may feel that it is the chair's responsibility to keep the train on the track, any committee member, even a newbie, can assist in keeping committee discussion going in useful directions. Gibson notes, "Committee discussion is prone to meander rather than to move purposefully toward conclusion. In part this traces to the lack of homework done by most members between meetings, and thus to the use of scheduled committee time for 'thinking out loud,' an activity that seldom proceeds in a straight line and often takes the group off on tangents."[11] But having done your homework, you are in a good position to suggest specific proposals to provide a focus for discussion. It's more effective to present such ideas as thought experiments or rough ideas that need refining so that you don't come across as imperious or overbearing.

Besides providing concrete talking points, you can also subtly suggest ways to move your work along. Many institutions and committees prefer to operate on the basis of group consensus on some matters, but this form of decision-making can be extremely time-consuming. Gibson advises,

> One process that you might suggest the committee use to determine the degree of group accord — and to push the train back onto the track — is that of employing written opinions. When there has been a reasonable amount of discussion on some matter — say, whether a new course being proposed to the Curriculum Committee rates high, medium, or low in furthering the curriculum goals of the college — each committee member is asked to write down an individual opinion on a piece of paper and pass it to the chair. The chair then lists the results on the board for all to see; whether there is consensus becomes immediately clear.

10. Gerald W. Gibson, *Good Start: A Guidebook for New Faculty in Liberal Arts Colleges* (New York: Anker, 1992), p. 156.
11. Gibson, *Good Start*, p. 157.

Straw votes, ranking of priorities, and the use of subcommittees are other ways to keep a committee functioning efficiently. Gibson notes, "You may be surprised at how useful strategically timed proposals for processes of closure can be in moving the group along, reducing the effects of unhealthy dynamics (such as domineering personalities), and coming to sound conclusions. You may also be surprised at how welcome your ideas for keeping the train on track turn out to be."[12]

Irresponsible committee behavior bears an uncanny resemblance to irresponsible student behavior: attending erratically, arriving late or leaving early, failing to carry through on your assignments, issuing long-winded and self-indulgent proclamations. But it's amazing how easy it can be to be responsible, facilitate the group's work, and — consequently — help improve your institution.

Curriculum and Community

The high degree of autonomy that professors enjoy makes it tempting to think that what takes place in our classroom is entirely up to us, within the standards of the discipline in which we have been trained, of course. Parker Palmer points out that teachers are among the few public professionals who practice essentially in isolation from their peers: "Lawyers argue cases in front of other lawyers, where gaps in their skill and knowledge are clear for all to see. Surgeons operate under the gaze of specialists who notice if a hand trembles, making malpractice less likely. But teachers can lose sponges or amputate the wrong limb with no witnesses except the victims."[13] I've known those who take offense merely at being asked to turn in a copy of their syllabus to their chair or dean, alleging that this interferes with their academic freedom. Yet if we view the professor's central role as contributing to the mission of the institution, and that mission has student learning at its heart, academic citizenship includes a high degree of communication and cooperation with respect to curricular matters, both departmentally and across campus.

I'm not saying that all professors should follow a top-down mandated curriculum with uniform daily assignments and activities, which is some-

12. Gibson, *Good Start*, pp. 157-58.
13. Parker J. Palmer, *The Courage to Teach: Exploring the Inner Landscape of a Teacher's Life* (San Francisco: Jossey-Bass, 1998), p. 142.

times the practice in elementary and secondary education. Rather, academic citizenship entails that faculty talk with each other on a regular basis about what goes on in their classrooms; share their syllabi and assignments; jointly analyze the shape of the major, minor, or general education programs; and examine collectively the degree to which their students are learning and what they are learning. What happens in any individual course is only a small portion of a complex educational mosaic. Rather than contributing our course chip and then sitting back to let the students assemble the fragments as they may, we should help them create a coherent picture, one in which different chips work together to produce a work of art. Again, this is not mandating a rigid uniformity; the completed educational mosaic will look different for each student, depending on the courses, professors, and extra-curricular experiences that go into its composition. But — to continue to press this analogy — if all the mosaic chips are round, a square chip will provide problems; if all the chips are exactly the same shape and color, no picture will emerge. Instead, deliberately shaded variations and contrasts in color can work together beautifully.

Curriculum and Community: General Education

During your initial year at a new institution, you needn't set out to master the entire college curriculum, but you should begin to pay attention to these issues. The first important move is to learn where your courses fit into the overall curricular structure either of the department or of the school, and to inquire, if your chair has not informed you, about any community-established learning objectives or activities. If you will be teaching courses in the general education (GE) program of your institution, it is also crucial to learn your institution's philosophy of and method of categorizing general education courses. But even if your teaching assignments are limited primarily to departmental offerings or graduate courses, it's helpful to become familiar with the way that the undergraduate college curriculum is structured. At the very least, on the undergraduate level, you will be working with students who have taken or are taking the GE curriculum, and you can work purposefully to connect your course with some of their other learning. And if you are one of the few professors at mission-driven institutions who work solely with graduate students, it is nonetheless useful to have a basic grasp of the undergraduate curriculum so that you can contribute meaningfully to faculty discussions and evaluations.

As we saw in Chapter 2, the curricular structure of American higher education has undergone many changes over the past two hundred years, and it continues to evolve. The nineteenth century witnessed a move away from a classically based curriculum to the elective system, in which students took a specialization along with a number of electives. As major concentrations were developed, different versions of general education also grew. While a school's mission usually played a major role in the particular kind of GE it embraced, institutional history, financial resources, staffing, the ever-expanding knowledge base, social shifts, educational trends, and student expectations all contributed to its evolution. Given these numerous factors, we find a tremendous variety in GE programs, which can resemble loose, baggy monsters awkwardly stitched together both by happenstance and by philosophy. Almost nothing is as daunting to an academic community as GE revision, which often involves years of committee work, countless meetings, nasty turf battles, and a good deal of hurt feelings. General education programs tend to balloon over time, with additions of new courses and tinkering with old courses more common than a complete overhaul of the system, which may explain some oddities that you might find at your institution.

Up until this point, I have been loosely speaking of "general education" as that course of study required of all undergraduates in addition to the specific requirements for a major or a minor. General education can include specific courses that every undergraduate is required to take *(core courses)*, or a set of course categories from which students make selections of courses *(distribution requirements,* sometimes referred to as a "cafeteria" program). A true core course is taken by every single student; some institutions, for example, require Western Civilization or Introduction to Literature. More common are area distribution requirements, such as requiring one course in physical science selected from a menu of options. Many schools' GE programs involve some combination of core and distribution courses, and college catalogs and institutions often refer to a cafeteria system as their "core." To add to the complexity, different secondary accrediting standards (for business, education, engineering, health sciences, etc.) may necessitate different GE requirements. For example, a college might have a standard GE requirement of two years of a foreign language, but exempt students majoring in electrical engineering from this requirement because of the large amount of strictly sequenced courses needed for this major. Education students may be required to take Introduction to Psychology or Educational Psychology to fulfill their social-science GE distribution rather than having the same smorgasbord of choices as other students.

Institutions will use different terms for these curricular categories (and the term *core* is widely misused), so be sure to identify the exact vocabulary and structure of your institution's GE curriculum. Some other common terms include *competency, foundational,* and *exploratory* courses. Competency courses are basic skills courses such as college writing, mathematics or statistics, oral communication, and foreign languages. Recently, in one instance of the continuing expansion of knowledge, institutions have added competency requirements in areas such as computer literacy, Internet research and law, and intercultural or multicultural proficiency. Mission-driven institutions also often have a category of *foundational* courses, including courses in Bible, theology, spiritual formation, church history, worldview studies, or philosophy and critical thinking, which are viewed as the essential building blocks for college-level study.

After a period of decline in the mid-twentieth century, true core programs are becoming more popular, within both mission-driven and public institutions. Some selective institutions such as the University of Chicago and Columbia University are renowned for their long-standing interdisciplinary core programs, while St. John's College offers nothing but a "Great Books" core curriculum. A true core program can take one of two forms. The first resembles a taste of St. John's approach — a common sequence of interdisciplinary text-based courses in world classics and (possibly) other texts of major cultural significance. The Association for Core Texts and Courses, based at St. Mary's College of California, supports such text-based efforts to provide a liberal education.[14] A second kind of true core program features a sequence of interdisciplinary, often team-taught courses organized by broad themes, such as Appreciating Beauty, The Person in Society, Multicultural America, The West and the World, Faith and Science, and Living in the Physical World. This kind of core is promoted by the Association of American Colleges and Universities in *College Learning for the New Global Century* (2007) and the Liberal Education and America's Promise (LEAP) initiative.

There are two standard philosophies of general education that inspire perennial faculty debate: the *introductory model* and the *relevance model.* In the introductory model, courses provide an introduction to the discipline — basic concepts, ways of pursuing knowledge, vocabulary, skills,

14. See http://www.coretexts.org/.

and methods. Students who complete such a course are ready to move on to a more specialized course in the major. Within this model, students take a range of such courses, such as Introduction to Psychology, Introduction to Economics, and Introduction to Music, in order to gain a sense of the broader educational picture. While a few specific courses may be required (some mission-driven schools, for example, require Introduction to Philosophy or Introduction to Theology), most of the system involves distribution requirements for the arts and humanities, physical and biological sciences, and the social sciences. One student might take Introduction to Art History to fulfill an arts requirement, while another might take Introduction to Film. A first-year student might take General Biology I, a standard survey and laboratory course covering the scientific method, the chemistry of living organisms, the organization of cells, and the foundations of genetics and molecular biology. If she or he opts to become a biology major, General Biology II would follow, but the first course could also fulfill a GE science requirement, with no additional biology course work.

In the relevancy model, the goal of general education is not to provide a detailed introduction to a discipline's specialized vocabulary, processes, and theories, but rather to give students some ways of thinking about or employing the discipline in their ordinary lives — learning, for example, how issues in science might affect them personally, how to appreciate a variety of kinds of music as a non-musician, how families function because they themselves are and will be members of families, and how the American political system operates so that they can participate as informed citizens. Again, a cafeteria approach might be taken, with students given the option to choose general education courses within certain broad parameters to cover a range of approaches to knowledge. In this model, general education biology courses might include those focusing on human nutrition, marine biology, and environmental biology, but all three courses would cover the basic concepts of the chemistry of living things, their structure and function, and their interactions with the environment, and include applications to current issues and possible Christian responses and assessments. No attempt would be made to "cover" all the specialized material of General Biology I or to teach the use of CSE documentation (Council of Science Editors).

This brief survey of the imprecise vocabulary and competing philosophies of general education provides a framework in which to locate your own institution's practices and controversies. In your teaching, you will need to learn your institution's expectations for GE courses, whether a specific course serves two purposes (both GE and entry to major), and with what knowledge and experiences students will be arriving in your class. If students have all read *The Narrative of Frederick Douglass* in their freshman core course, you need to think about how that might affect your Introduction to American Literature course. If they have no common textual experiences, will they arrive with some understanding of the different ways in which disciplines raise questions, or define knowledge, or understand evidence? Having discussions with faculty across disciplines, participating in curriculum workshops, and even sitting in on core or GE courses are all good ways to become more curricularly assimilated.

Similar issues, of course, will arise in terms of courses within a major or a minor, although the content and approach will be more familiar and less difficult to grasp. But regular department meetings to discuss the shape, content, and activities of courses in the major can provide a more clearly structured and purposefully interrelated education for your students. You will need to learn if you are expected to teach your discipline's standard documentation system in an introductory course, or if you can expect that this information has been or will be conveyed to students in another course. Where within the major do students learn how to explicate a poem/conduct a case study/write a lab report? As a new faculty member, you are in a good position to request that your department have occasional curriculum-centered meetings to help you adjust, but such communal discussions will prove useful and interesting to all your colleagues. In fifteen minutes, an instructor could provide a brief introduction to a course, distribute the syllabus and assignment sheets, and talk about course goals and content. It's fascinating to hear what's going on in other classrooms, and such conversations can be fruitful for your own teaching.

Curriculum and Community: Assessment

Communal conversations about curriculum lead usefully to what has come to be branded as the academic scarlet letter: Assessment. For many professors, the requirement that faculty develop comprehensive educational assessment programs outweighs even committee work as the most dreaded aspect of their work. Faculty opposition to assessment may take the form of indifferent undermining, passionate resistance, or *pro forma* activities; in my experience, only a few professors enthusiastically embrace assessment as a way to improve student learning. Without denying that many so-called assessment activities are pure busywork or window-dressing, and while admitting that the prospect of a meeting devoted to assessment often causes me to develop narcolepsy, I would suggest that participating in level-headed outcomes assessment programs is an essential part of our professorial call. Faculty opposition to assessment appears elitist and illogical to the public, for most people are asked to demonstrate in some way or other that their work has positive outcomes. Assessment discussions again require us to move beyond thinking about "my course" and "my teaching" to the impact of an entire major, program, or educational experience.

Higher education's outcomes assessment movement is a direct result of public demands for greater relevance, accountability, and access to higher education. Following the No Child Left Behind Act of 2001, politicians began to consider how to improve college and university education, which was popularly perceived as being inefficient, expensive, and sometimes irrelevant. The contentious debate over congressional re-authorization of The Higher Education Act in 2008 included serious consideration of establishing a national accrediting body and a standardized national test for all college graduates, rather than continuing the existing system of regional self-governing accrediting bodies and self-defined institutional diversity. State-funded institutions faced greater scrutiny by legislatures and governors, with demands to demonstrate that their costly programs were successfully preparing students to enter the American workforce and public square. Accountability became the watchword, and some form of outcomes assessment is now conducted in every state,[15] with institutions scrambling to implement assessment programs in response to regional, professional, and disciplinary accrediting agencies. Expect to hear about assessment sooner rather than later in your new position.

The fact that the demand for accountability is coming from external constituencies, including the Congress, state legislatures, and media pundits, is at the heart of some of the faculty resistance. Some politically radical faculty view the assessment movement as driven solely by conservative politics; other faculty regard external demands for accountability as an infringement on their academic freedom. Mission-driven institutions, highly dependent on external constituencies for funding, may feel similar pressures; their administrators are more concerned with the views of par-

---

15. M. Nettles, J. Cole, and S. Sharp, "The Landscape: Tracking a Subtle Storm: Assessment Policies in Higher Education," *Change* 30 (1998): 47-51.

ents, alumni, and donors than those of the state legislature, but they also regularly face questions about the added value of an expensive, private, mission-based education. The most frequently voiced faculty objections to outcomes assessment, however, include genuine questions about the effectiveness and efficiency of strategies for assessing learning. We find a blend of such concerns in the following confession by Benjamin Baez, writing in *Academe,* the journal of the AAUP:

> I have accreditation fatigue. My university and the college of education in which I teach are preparing for reviews by the Southern Association of Colleges and Schools, the Florida Department of Education, and the National Council for Accreditation of Teacher Education.
>
> Accreditation processes, in the name of assessment and accountability, wind up reducing what is, in my opinion, inherently unmeasurable — teaching and learning — to things that can be put into a language of accounting, a language that lends itself to neat little matrices. This accounting then comes to represent what we do, who we are, and how we are to be judged.
>
> But what most fatigues me is not this reductionism, which I was prepared to deal with, thinking that perhaps by learning the language of accreditation I could more effectively argue for increasing the number of faculty in the college. What gives me fatigue is that I have come to learn that I am surrounded by faculty members who do not seem to understand core academic values such as academic freedom, professional autonomy, and shared governance.[16]

Since Baez is facing three accreditation reviews, his fatigue is understandable, and it points to one of the foremost difficulties of a non-centralized system. He then claims that teaching and learning are "inherently unmeasurable," or at least irreducible to the "language of accounting." There is an important difference between these two positions, which Baez skirts: perhaps teaching and learning are measurable in other ways than the language of accounting or in "neat little matrices." Yet Baez himself wants to employ this rhetoric in order to use the assessment process to make a case for hiring more faculty. Finally, he sees his colleagues' acquiescence to the process as a betrayal of essential academic values:

16. Benjamin Baez, "Faculty Forum: Accreditation Fatigue," *Academe,* http://www.aaup .org/AAUP/pubsres/academe/2009/MJ/col/facfor.htm.

When I complain at meetings, for example, that accreditation reviews seem to be dictating to me how I should teach my classes, assess my students, develop my syllabi, and so on, and that these decisions are essential to the academic profession, my colleagues see me as an unruly child. They consistently tell me that no one is forcing anyone to do anything and, more patronizingly, that I need to understand that "if we do not get accredited we are going to have to close our college."[17]

Baez does not seem to even consider the value of questioning whether students are learning or not, of examining in some way the effectiveness of his school's educational program. As Gerald Graff (president of the Modern Language Association in 2007) argued, "To see outcomes assessment as merely a conservative dodge designed to distract everyone from structural inequality ignores the ways our own pedagogical and curricular practices contribute to the achievement gap. . . . This view is remarkably complacent in its suggestion that nothing in our house needs to change."[18]

Clearly, how assessment is conducted is of monumental import — in terms of both the workload and the legitimacy of the measurement. But blanket opposition to the idea of assessment as constituting a threat to faculty is, I believe, counterproductive and self-serving. We should care about whether or not our students learn, and we should welcome ways to discern how to improve their learning. Furthermore, given the exorbitant tuition costs at most mission-driven institutions, we should be sensitive to issues of stewardship, of using those tuition dollars prudently. If we want reasonable ways to identify our successes, and if we are willing to acknowledge that some of our educational programs might be less than successful, we need to be willing to work on appropriate means of assessment. Joshua Smith, Bruce Szelest, and John Downey state, "Institutions that effectively utilize the mandates provided by accreditation and state governments and simultaneously encourage faculty and staff to embrace outcomes assessment are more likely to meet the needs and wishes of both constituencies. This form of collaboration is essential for outcomes assessment to be truly beneficial to those for whom it was intended, the students."[19]

University assessment programs usually examine student learning in

17. Baez, "Faculty Forum."

18. Gerald Graff, "Assessment Changes Everything," *MLA Newsletter*, Spring 2008, p. 4.

19. Joshua S. Smith, Bruce P. Szelest, and John P. Downey, "Implementing Outcomes Assessment in an Academic Affairs Support Unit," *Research in Higher Education* 45 (2004): 406.

the respective majors, general education programs, and individual courses. Three central principles of assessment are (1) using multiple measures of learning, rather than relying on one standardized test such as the GRE;[20] (2) employing narrative or qualitative measures as well as quantitative measures, particularly for more subjective learning objectives; and (3) "closing the loop" between assessment and improvement by using the information gathered through assessment to change in order to improve. Smith, Szelest, and Downey note that when institutions focus their energy solely "on testing and reporting rather than using testing and reporting as a means for feedback and improvement," assessment appears overwhelming.[21] But faculty enjoy talking about specific students, courses, and programs, and assessment programs involving such communal conversations are not onerous or irrelevant. For example, a department might hold a meeting at the conclusion of the academic year to discuss what its senior seminar papers reveal about the strengths and weaknesses of the program and what improvements this information suggests for the major, minor, or individual courses. This does not necessarily entail a whole-scale redesign of one's program; one or two changes might be implemented, and the next year's assessment include an analysis of what improvements, if any, are seen from the changes.

Assessment work is inherently communal, as Graff observes:

Once we start asking whether our students are learning what we want them to learn, we realize pretty quickly that making this happen is necessarily a team effort, requiring us to think about our teaching not in isolation but in relation to that of our colleagues. The problem is not that we don't value good teaching, as our critics still often charge, but that we often share our culture's romanticized picture of teaching as a virtuoso performance by soloists, as seen in films like *Dead Poets Society, Dangerous Minds,* and *Freedom Writers.* . . . For all its obvious value, ex-

---

20. Trudy W. Banta describes multiple modes of assessment, including the National Survey of Student Engagement; surveys of alumni and employer satisfaction; retention and graduation statistics; and measures of the proportion of students engaged in experience-based learning opportunities such as undergraduate research, study abroad, and service-learning. See "Can Assessment for Accountability Complement Assessment for Improvement?" *Peer Review* 9, no. 2 (2007), http://www.aacu.org/peerreview/pr-sp07/pr-sp07_analysis2.cfm.

21. Smith, Szelest, and Downey, "Implementing Outcomes Assessment in an Academic Affairs Support Unit," p. 406.

cellent teaching in itself doesn't guarantee good education. The courses taken in a semester . . . may all be wonderfully well taught by whatever criterion we want to use, but if the content of the courses is unrelated or contradictory, the educational effect can be incoherence and confusion. . . . Outcomes assessment [makes] us operate not as classroom divas and prima donnas but as team players who collaborate with our colleagues to produce a genuine program.[22]

Curriculum and Community: First-Year Seminars and Senior Capstone Courses

During the last few decades, two curricular developments have been embraced by many mission-driven institutions: first-year seminars and senior capstones. First-year or freshmen seminars began to multiply in the 1980s as part of the widespread calls for undergraduate education reform led by the Carnegie Foundation, among others. With research demonstrating that students' success and retention were significantly affected by their first-year experiences, many comprehensive campus initiatives were born that included orientation, advising, mentoring, residence-hall life, wellness, character formation, academic assistance, and first-year seminars. In 1986, the National Center for the Study of the Freshman Year Experience, under the leadership of John N. Gardner, was founded at the University of South Carolina, and it remains a leader in this field. In 1999, Gardner created the Policy Center on the First Year of College (later renamed The John N. Gardner Institute for Excellence in Undergraduate Education) with a mission to improve the first-year experience through enhanced student learning, success, and retention. The Gardner Institute administers a comprehensive, voluntary, self-study process known as Foundations of Excellence® in the First College Year and sponsors new publications about the first-year experience.[23]

On the academic side, the first-year seminar plays a crucial role in the liminal experience of commencing a college career, with first-year semi-

---

22. Graff, "Assessment Changes Everything," p. 3.

23. See http://www.jngi.org/. Recent publications include B. Barefoot et al., *Achieving and Sustaining Institutional Excellence for the First Year of College* (San Francisco: Jossey-Bass, 2005), and M. L. Upcraft, J. Gardner, and B. Barefoot, *Challenging and Supporting the First-Year Student: A Handbook for Improving the First Year of College* (San Francisco: Jossey-Bass, 2005).

nars "almost as commonplace on college and university campuses as freshman English."[24] Two types of courses exist: the orientation course and the freshman seminar. Orientation courses stress student development and teach particular academic skills and personal coping strategies, along with introducing students to various parts of an institution. They are sometimes taught by student-life staff. The first-year seminar, on the other hand, "is more concerned with the student's academic adjustment and development and is more intellectually based. It is often taught by the faculty, perhaps the student's academic adviser. The seminar content may be incorporated into an already existing course or may be initiated as an interdisciplinary offering."[25]

Since 1988, the National Survey on First-Year Seminars has gathered data on the content, administration, staffing, and assessment of first-year seminars. In 2006, the most common type of seminar at reporting institutions was the extended orientation seminar (57.9 percent), but, in an increasing trend, 53.8 percent of the respondents offered some type of academic seminar. About 28 percent of respondents offered academic seminars with uniform content; seminars with variable content were offered by 25.7 percent of the respondents. Courses ranged from one to three credits (with orientation courses more likely to be one credit and academic courses three credits), enrolled an average of sixteen-to-twenty students, and, for the most part, were assessed by letter grades. Private institutions tend to incorporate the first-year seminar into their general education programs, while public institutions more often count it toward elective credits. The key objectives of such courses were developing academic skills (64.2 percent) and orienting students to campus resources and services (52.9 percent). At 90 percent of the institutions, faculty teach the first-year seminar.[26] At mission-driven institutions, first-year seminars often include an introduction to the religious tradition and educational mission of the institution; because of the orientation component, most first-year faculty are not asked to teach in such programs until they themselves become

24. A. Jerome Jewler, "Elements of an Effective Seminar: The University 101 Program," in *The Freshman Year Experience: Helping Students Survive and Succeed in College* by M. Lee Upcraft, John N. Gardner, and Associates (San Francisco: Jossey-Bass, 1989), p. 198.

25. Virginia P. Gordon, "Origins and Purposes of the Freshman Seminar," in *The Freshman Year Experience*, p. 191.

26. Barbara F. Tobolowski and Associates, *2006 National Survey of First-Year Seminars: Continuing Innovations in the Collegiate Curriculum* (Columbia, S.C.: National Resource Center for the First-Year Experience and Students in Transition, 2008), pp. 97-98.

more accustomed to their new campus culture. Most institutions offer specific training for teaching first-year seminars, which you would be wise to take, if it is not mandatory.

Two examples of first-year seminars at mission-driven institutions demonstrate the variety of approaches. The first is an orientation course but is taught by faculty. Goshen College, a Mennonite institution in Indiana, requires all first-year students to enroll in a one-credit colloquium course involving a set of activities introducing students to academic life: "Colloquium students learn about the resources and values of Goshen College, process the changes that happen at college, and find encouragement to grow socially, spiritually, psychologically, and academically. The colloquium class introduces competency requirements in information literacy and begins to document students' academic learning."[27] Taught by a faculty member who also serves as the students' academic advisor for the first semester, each colloquium is attached to another one-to-four credit course, providing the students with a cohort experience. The second example is an academic seminar — with a disciplinary focus but with common learning objectives in writing. At the University of Notre Dame, first-year students take a University Seminar, a small, writing-intensive seminar taught by a faculty member. Each seminar fulfills one of six university disciplinary requirements: a class in philosophy, theology, history, the social sciences, literature and fine arts. The seminar introduces students to the paradigms, content, methodology, or problems of their discipline and to that discipline's conventions for academic writing, including a research paper.

The joys of teaching first-year seminars are many, and you should explore the possibility of adding such a course to your repertoire in the future. The small class size and special nature of such courses provide unique opportunities to get to know students personally and provide intellectual mentoring, which may be different from the mentoring they previously experienced from youth pastors or high school teachers. First-year students tend to be energetic, excited, motivated, and eager to learn. They are thrilled about entering this new academic world, even while they are often intimidated and unsure of themselves. Their bright shiny enthusiasm has not yet tarnished into cynicism and ennui. They are eager to please, attempt new things, and push themselves. First-year seminars also provide an effective way to recruit for your major by exposing students to new

27. See http://www.goshen.edu/catalog/033General-Education/.

ideas and areas of thought, getting them excited about pursuing questions in sociology or philosophy or history that they may not have even realized existed. Although the students seem to get younger every year, first-year seminars provide an unparalleled opportunity to engage students in the life of the mind and the mission of your institution.

A natural outgrowth of the first-year experience movement has been the renaissance of the senior capstone course, which provides a transition out of academic life into society. The growing popularity of such courses also is an attempt to address the problem of curricular fragmentation, and the rhetoric of the "Senior Year Experience Movement" emphasizes the coherence that the capstone brings to the curriculum and the creation of interdisciplinary connections.[28] The senior capstone revival thus is reminiscent of the senior moral philosophy course of nineteenth-century American collegiate education, which was designed to provide unity and coherence to the college curriculum, synthesizing four years of study in an attempt to help students draw connections among ideas, make ethical applications, and develop a comprehensive worldview. As disciplinary specialization, the elective system, and secularization transformed American higher education, the traditional senior capstone course fell away like an unnecessary appendage. New general education requirements in the arts and humanities replaced the old capstone course in providing connections, applications, and worldviews. Now the capstone has returned, but with some significant changes.

In 2000, Jean Henscheid conducted an analysis of senior seminars and capstone courses across American colleges and universities. Of the responding institutions, 549 institutions (77.6 percent) indicated that they offered a senior seminar or capstone. The majority of capstones were discipline- or department-based courses, intended to culminate learning within the major and to incorporate the student into a disciplinary community. Connections among courses in the major were explored, and transitions into the world of work or further study were facilitated. Such capstones may involve an internship or service-learning component, addressing the concern of senior college students for obtaining employment after earning their degrees. Engineers "try out" being an engineer by completing a senior project; education students do "practice" or student teaching; history majors write a major historical research paper. Henscheid observes, "The survey indicates that the

---

28. Jean M. Henscheid, *Professing the Disciplines: An Analysis of Senior Seminars and Capstone Courses* (Columbia, S.C.: University of South Carolina, National Resource Center for the First Year Experience and Students in Transition, 2000), p. 3.

culminating academic experience at America's colleges and universities most frequently caps not the whole of college, but a specialized piece of that experience."[29] The old capstone ideal of identifying and promoting unity in the college curriculum has been abandoned. In summary, "the evidence is weak that in senior seminars and capstone courses undergraduates are primarily engaged in reflection on learning in the general education curriculum or in learning that links general education to the major."[30] The reality of capstone courses with respect to providing unity and coherence is not living up to the rhetoric.

As might be expected, capstone courses are slightly more common at private institutions than public institutions, but schools with medium selectivity were far more likely to offer such courses than either those with high selectivity or those with low selectivity. Perhaps this reflects the fact that private, mission-driven institutions are more likely to include capstone courses in their curriculum. Nonetheless, the principal finding of the survey must still apply to the majority of faith-based institutions: senior seminars or capstones are designed primarily as a culmination of the major and a transition from the study of a discipline into the world of work or graduate studies. The rhetorical desire to provide unity and coherence is significant, but the "inward focus" of most current capstones reflects the continuing primacy of academic disciplines in the academy.[31] Mission-driven institutions may be uniquely situated to rethink the nature and practice of the senior capstone. If they are to do so, they must consciously develop and articulate the "uni" in the university, the central commitments and beliefs that hold together what Yeats called "the widening gyre." If capstones are to help students recognize the unity of the curriculum, the place of a major in the larger body of knowledge, and the importance of living out their faith in every area of life, these courses must be structured in ways that differ from the prevailing academic norm and overtly draw on the mission of the institution.

Collegiality and the College

Of all the requirements for successful job performance on the part of a professor, collegiality may be the most obscure. Many contested tenure

---

29. Henscheid, *Professing the Disciplines*, p. 4.
30. Henscheid, *Professing the Disciplines*, p. 139.
31. Henscheid, *Professing the Disciplines*, pp. 139-40.

and promotion cases revolve around issues of "collegiality," which may represent a veiled way of keeping out someone who is different (because of race, gender, political persuasion, or other reasons) or may entail not wanting to work for the next thirty years with someone who is unpleasant, unreasonable, and divisive. It is not uncommon for one reason to be given or alleged when the other is actually the case. How should a new professor negotiate this uncertain territory?

The etymology of *collegial* has both religious and educational roots. A *college,* according to the Oxford English Dictionary, is "An organized society of persons performing certain common functions and possessing special rights and privileges; a body of colleagues, a guild, fellowship, association," and the word's first associations were religious: it was used to refer to the body of Christ's apostles (by Wycliffe in 1380) and to the seventy cardinals of the Roman Catholic Church (by Shakespeare in 1593). In an educational context, *college* was first used to describe a community of clergy living together with the special task of study. When these religious colleges (such as New College, Oxford) were introduced into the university system, the name spread to the older, non-clerical foundations (such as Merton and Balliol). By the time of the Renaissance, *college* referred more generally to any society incorporated within a university or constituted for purposes of study or instruction. In the British system today, a *college* refers to scholars sharing a common lodging and academic supervision during their program of study at a university. In the United States, *college* initially was a general term, applied to a small degree-giving institution with a single curriculum. The rise of the university system in nineteenth-century America resulted in larger institutions becoming organized by various faculties, or courses of study, rather than by lodging, as was the case in Great Britain. Today, most four-year institutions of higher education in the United States define themselves as universities, and *university* and *college* have essentially become synonymous, with the few exceptions of a handful of liberal-arts institutions who cleave to *college* nomenclature. Being *collegial,* then, first referred to belonging to one of these colleges and then expanded to include belonging to a body of persons associated as equals in the performance of any function. In referring to the equal sharing of power among colleagues (people holding the same status), *collegial* contrasts with *bureaucratic* and implies cooperating for a common end by working jointly with cordiality and companionship. The historical roots of the term demonstrate its long-standing importance for an academic community.

Collegiality involves both written and unwritten rules, and naturally the unwritten ones are the most difficult to decipher. Here are a few common unwritten rules. Always work through channels to voice a complaint or request — that is, don't start with your dean when you could start with your chair. Don't go to the president before you've talked about an issue with your provost. Don't meet with a trustee without the president's knowledge. This may seem counter to what I've been saying about collegiality, but the truth of the matter is that even if chairs, deans, provosts, and presidents define themselves as colleagues, which they are to a certain extent, power is not shared equally in these cases, and you must follow hierarchies to avoid a reputation as a troublemaker. Another important rule is to attend department and faculty meetings faithfully during your first year, even if your senior colleagues are nowhere in sight. Although it may be tempting to hole up in your office and emerge only to teach your courses, make an attempt to mingle with your colleagues over coffee or lunch occasionally. Don't always have your door closed; you'll miss out on the important but unofficial "hall meetings," at which many departmental issues may be discussed and even resolved. Try to join at least one cross-campus faculty group during your first year — whether it be a faculty seminar, a book discussion group, a nursing mothers group, or pickleball players united. Take your family or friends to an occasional campus sports event, musical performance, or poetry reading.

In heated faculty discussions, don't be afraid to speak up, but couch your comments in non-threatening terms, asking for elaborations, background, or examples. You can play the newcomer's card for a while, pleading ignorance and requesting information. Perhaps the worst course of action is repeatedly citing another institution as doing something better: "Back at Perfect University, where I did my degree, the department always supplied proctors for final exams." Instead, share such information when asked, or propose that a list be made of ways that other institutions handle a problem. Another prime strategy for cultivating collegiality is to inquire about your colleague's work rather than only talking about your own. Request advice on dealing with a troublesome student; ask someone to share lecture notes, film suggestions, or paper assignments with you. But don't turn into a Needy Nellie, having to have your hand held by your mentor or chair before you accomplish anything. It's a fine line.

When I think of faculty members renowned for their lack of collegiality, the same few descriptors emerge: egotistical, rude, not a team player. The non-collegial colleague won't be in her office during scheduled office hours, so other professors will have to answer questions and even advise her students. The non-collegial colleague will constantly talk about the various papers that he has had published and conspicuously drop the names of academic superstars into his conversation. The non-collegial colleague will never be available to serve on a committee, advise a student group, lead a small-group chapel, or help students who are applying to graduate school. The non-collegial colleague will not volunteer to teach a class for you when you are ill or attending a conference, will not pass on the opportunity to do a book review to you, will not speak highly of you to your other colleagues. The non-collegial colleague will let his classes out early, cancel her assigned term papers at the last minute, and allow students to take final exams at a different time than the university-wide schedule states.

Some problems with collegiality may arise from the fact that college faculties today include both Baby Boomers, born between 1943 and 1960, and subsequent generations, made up of those born after 1960. Richard Chait and Cathy Trower, from the Harvard Graduate School of Education, have conducted research on the different values held by what they term "embedded" faculty and "emerging" faculty. Chait states, "Senior faculty and junior faculty live in vastly different assumptive worlds. What the former take for granted, the latter seek to reform. The changes championed by a new generation challenge the commitments and convictions of an older generation."[32] Based on repeated surveys of college faculty and graduate students, Chait identifies four values with significant generational differences:

1. Embedded faculty hold that "secrecy assures quality and collegiality" with respect to promotion and tenure, which results in emerging faculty not understanding clearly the way to tenure. Emerging faculty prefer greater transparency and articulated expectations, which they believe assure equity.
2. Embedded faculty employ an objective epistemology: "For each discipline, there are — and, indeed, must be — absolute standards of quality uniformly applied." Emerging faculty are more sensitive to the social construction of knowledge: "Quality and merit are relative, and

32. Richard P. Chait, "The Academic Keyboard," paper presented at the annual meeting of the Chief Academic Officers of the Council of Independent Colleges, San Antonio, Texas, 5 November 2005.

inevitably conditioned by personal experience and tacit bias as demonstrated, for example, by studies which indicate that peer assessments of identical resumes and identical research differ markedly as a
function of the gender-specific name assigned to the material under
review."

3. Embedded faculty embrace individualism and competition: "The promotion and tenure process, as a slightly kinder and gentler version of
Darwinism, assures that only the very best earn lifelong appointments." Emerging faculty believe that collaboration and cooperation
are superior to competition.

4. Embedded faculty view work and family as two distinct entities that
should remain separate. Personal circumstances are irrelevant and
should be kept out of the workplace. Emerging faculty believe "that
personal life matters and that a balanced life should not be incompati-
ble with an academic career. If success requires 80-hour workweeks,
then we have misconceptualized what should constitute success."[33]

Again, one would hope that at a mission-driven institution, success is
not understood in terms of sacrificing personal life and family in order to
put in an eighty-hour workweek. None of the mission-driven institutions I
know would overtly endorse such a view, but I've known faculty who pursued such a shape to their lives — whether because of their own ambitions
or because their institutional reward structures required it, despite the
rhetoric. Nonetheless, all four of the different values that Chait identifies
reflect a certain ethos and way of thinking that are prevalent. Understanding the differences between the assumptions of younger faculty like yourself and embedded senior faculty may help both in your efforts to work for
reform, if necessary, and in your efforts to be collegial in the process.

Although collegiality usually refers to relationships among faculty, I
define it as referring to how one works with institutional staff members as
well. Some faculty are respectful and considerate of their fellow professors,
but subject the departmental administrative assistant, the academic services staff member in charge of classroom assignments, or the manager of
the campus copy shop to scornful condescension and unrelenting demands. Such behavior, while rude in any setting, violates the norms of

33. Chait, "The Academic Keyboard." Also see Sarah Gibbard Cook, "A Perfect Storm:
Gen X and Today's Academic Culture," *Women in Higher Education,* http://www.wihe.com/
printBlog.jsp?id=16593.

Christian community endorsed by many mission-driven institutions. Besides, such people have the ability to make your academic life run more smoothly, and their essential contributions to the mission should be acknowledged and appreciated. Academic novels provide an interesting perspective on this fact. In *Moo* (1995), a satirical view of life at a Midwestern agricultural university (MU) which contains some of the most accurate descriptions of American academic folly that I have read, Jane Smiley reveals something that many of us have long secretly suspected — the university is actually run by the provost's secretary, Mrs. Walker. Whenever the institution appears to be losing sight of its academic mission, Mrs. Walker (who naturally understands everything about campus computers and accounting procedures — areas of deep mystery to many faculty) surreptitiously transfers funds from the athletic department to the library budget. Your own institution no doubt has its own version of Mrs. Walker.

Most of us thoroughly enjoy our colleagues and believe that one of the unparalleled joys of our vocation is the opportunity to work with so many fascinating, unique, intelligent people. College professors enjoy their jobs: the 2007 survey on the American College Teacher by the Higher Education Research Institute indicates that 74.8 percent of the faculty (77.2 percent at private four-year colleges) are satisfied overall with their jobs and that 88.4 percent (90.5 percent at private four-year colleges) would definitely or probably choose an academic career again, although women show less satisfaction than men. Collegiality ranks high as a reason for job satisfaction at private institutions.[34] Although academic citizenship is sometimes a struggle for embedded faculty, the new priorities of the emerging generation, your generation, bodes well for the future of collegiality, community, and collaboration.

---

34. De Angelo et al., *The American College Teacher*, pp. 37, 99.

CHAPTER 8

Composing a Life:
Balance and Improvisation

One of the most pressing concerns I regularly hear from emerging faculty is how they can lead a balanced life. By this point, you may be feeling overwhelmed, thinking that the previous chapters have painted an unachievable portrait of an Amazing Super-Professor. How can you be a superb teacher, a productive scholar, and an involved academic citizen, and maintain your sanity? How can you balance your personal and your professional life — an increasingly complex and pressing question with the influx of women and minorities into the professoriate, the rise of two-career families, and changing life expectations for both men and women. How does your personal call to be a teacher-scholar complement the pleasures and obligations of your vocational life? Such questions plague most faculty, not only newcomers. The 2007-2008 HERI Faculty Survey reveals that only 34.2 percent of faculty believe that they have established a healthy balance between their personal and professional lives, and women report more difficulty in striking a balance (27.3 percent report succeeding versus 38.7 percent of the men).[1]

A 2009 study by the American Association of University Professors (AAUP) found that the emerging generation of doctoral students "has different expectations and values from previous ones, primary among them the desire for flexibility and balance between career and other life goals." Although 45 percent of the men and 39 percent of the women surveyed be-

1. Linda De Angelo et al., *The American College Teacher: National Norms for the 2007-2008 HERI Faculty Survey* (Los Angeles: Higher Education Research Institute of UCLA, 2009), pp. 38, 68, 99.

gan their graduate study intending to pursue a research-university position, after a few years of witnessing the lives of their graduate professors, only 36 percent of men and 27 percent of women kept this career goal, and many were planning to leave the academy entirely: "In the eyes of many doctoral students, the academic fast track has a bad reputation — one of unrelenting work hours that allow little or no room for a satisfying family life."[2] However, the same survey reports that the total percentage of doctoral students intending to pursue teaching-oriented careers has remained the same. The emerging generation's priorities may pose future difficulties for research institutions but bode well for mission-driven institutions that emphasize teaching and affirm a different sense of vocation than the academic fast track. Our institutions value family life, parish or church involvement, and community service. Nonetheless, the pressures of competing priorities remain real issues with which most new faculty struggle. I believe that the metaphors we use to think about and wrestle with these issues are formative, shaping our lives in vital ways. Although a common way to discuss what David F. Ford calls "the multiple overwhelmings" of our lives is in terms of balance, let's consider what happens when we think in terms of rhythm instead.[3] Within the sometimes mysterious and unpredictable rhythm of our lives, practical skills in time-management, taking a periodic vocational inventory, and annual re-affirming of one's vocation are valuable ways to compose a faithful and joyful life.

Embracing the Constantly Changing Balance of Rhythm

The familiar metaphor of a balanced life does not adequately account for the complex reality of what it means to be a human being enmeshed in a social and physical world that does not always neatly separate the private and the professional. One might neatly balance a robot's activities or a spreadsheet, but the messy reality of our lives is not so neatly corraled. One's life in July is never exactly like one's life in September, for reasons as different as the state of the garden, school calendars, whether you are pregnant, or if your father is dying. Rather than using the metaphor of

2. Mary Ann Mason, Marc Goulden, and Karie Frasch, "Why Graduate Students Reject the Fast Track," *Academe*, January/February 2009, http://www.aaup.org/AAUP/pubsres/academe/2009/JF/Feat/maso.htm.

3. David F. Ford, *The Shape of Living: Spiritual Directions for Everyday Life* (Grand Rapids: Baker Books, 1998), p. 20.

balance, we might think about the shape of our lives with the metaphor of a dance, in which there is constant movement and variations in position, weight, and direction, but in which there is also harmony and teamwork.[4] Another metaphor with rich resonances for the apportionment of responsibilities and delights is that of jazz improvisation: a constant movement between soloing and supporting among a group of musicians intently listening to and responding to each other in pursuit of a shared goal: magnificent music. Sometimes the sax will soar, and other times the piano will whisper. A distinctive individual voice and tight group interactions are both vital components. In the ebb and flow of a jazz improvisation, when the pianist takes the lead, the bass subsides into the background, providing supporting notes and chords. Jazz performances are open, spontaneous, and responsive — to the composer, one's own mood, one's fellow performers, and the audience — without disintegrating into chaos. The fourth improvisation might sound radically different from the second, but remnants of melody or motif will linger, enough for listeners to recognize the song.

In *Composing a Life,* Mary Catherine Bateson uses both the metaphors of jazz and cooking to talk about the unexpected ways a number of different fragments can be put together into an innovative whole. She writes that her interest in improvisation

> started from a disgruntled reflection on my own life as a sort of desperate improvisation in which I was constantly trying to make something coherent from conflicting elements to fit rapidly changing settings. At times, I pictured myself frantically rummaging through the refrigerator and the kitchen cabinets, convinced that somewhere I would find the odds and ends that could be combined at the last minute to make a meal for unexpected guests, hoping to be rescued by serendipity. . . . The improvised meal will be different from the planned meal, and certainly riskier, but rich with the possibility of delicious surprise. Improvisation can be either a last resort or an established way of evoking creativity.[5]

The idea of improvising or composing a life brings us full circle to the question of vocation with which we began this book; within our lives, the

---

4. I'm indebted to Professor Susan Felch at Calvin College for the metaphor of faculty life as a dance.

5. Mary Catherine Bateson, *Composing a Life* (New York: Plume, 1989), pp. 3-4.

shape of our vocation will change. The metaphor of the journey is often used to describe vocational progress: one receives a call and then follows a distinct path to a specified end. But my initial call to be a professor did not include my current destination. I stand here in surprise, and that surprise has not all been prompted by joy. I'm not so sure the journey image is the best picture for me, for it makes me feel as if I have taken many a wrong turn, gone down too many dead ends, zigged and zagged erratically.

None of us follow the ideal life-schedule because none of us lives as *isolatos*, a favorite word of Herman Melville. Those of us who have been professors for many years have followed a long and winding road between entering the profession and our current reality. If we understand vocation as encompassing more than our careers, we will not be surprised to find that the work part of our life constantly alters: it grows, shrinks, refocuses, expands, and contracts. You will experience numerous developmental stages as a professor, and I am referring to something much more profound than working your way up from an assistant professor to a tenured chair. Ford wisely says, "Given the complexity of any life, it is probable that each of us will need to imagine our lives in many images, or will find at different stages that we need to identify with new ones."[6] When I began my professorial life, I was more of a teacher than a scholar; I primarily taught composition and American literature; I was married but had no children; I would never have described myself as a feminist; and I had never been seriously ill. Today I juggle teaching and scholarship and administration; I work with faculty development and write about African literature; I have a son who has transformed my life; I am definitely a feminist; and I am a cancer survivor. All of these experiences have affected and changed the way I read and write and think and teach. Some of these changes were chosen; others were not. The blessed reality of life at a mission-driven institution is a greater flexibility to make these kinds of adjustments; your path does not have to follow the kind of lockstep career ladder found at most research universities. Our institutions value and support family life, church involvement, and community service. That's not to imply that improvising a life, living harmoniously, is easy; you will need to deliberately work on developing coping strategies for the rhythms of your life.

6. Ford, *The Shape of Living*, pp. 72-73.

Managing Yourself

The shelves of your local bookstore are full of insightful books about time management, which most of us seldom find the time to pursue. And if we do find a spare hour or two to skim such a book, even fewer of us will actually implement its recommendations or act on its insights. The truth of the matter is that we don't need to manage time; we need to manage ourselves. There are numerous simple strategies that truly work, although some approaches will work well for one person and not for another. Some experimentation will be necessary. However, you also need to realize that you have not really tried a strategy unless you have implemented it for at least a couple of weeks. Intending to implement it and failing to do so does not count as a real trial! The suggestions that follow are not radically original; similar ideas can be found in a number of places, but they are described in terms of an academic setting in the mission-driven institution and are methods that I have witnessed as particularly beneficial for new faculty. Many follow logically from earlier parts of this book.

The first and most essential means of keeping your life together is to make and keep a Sabbath. Growing up in a small Dutch Reformed community, I experienced the observance of the Sabbath as a set of prohibitions: many of my friends could not play baseball, no one ever did yard work (the grass was never mown), and nary a single store or restaurant in our small town was open on Sunday. It is only recently that I have adopted a different understanding of the Sabbath as a time of refreshment and delight. Dorothy Bass writes,

> The practice of Sabbath keeping may be a gift just waiting to be unwrapped. . . . For many of us, receiving this gift will require first discarding our image of Sabbath as a time of negative rules and restrictions, as a day of obligation (for Catholics) or a day without play (in memories of strict Protestant childhoods). Relocating our understanding of this day in the biblical stories of creation, exodus, and resurrection will be essential if we are to discover the gifts it offers.[7]

In my first ten years as a professor, I did a poor job of keeping the Sabbath, but I gradually was able to unwrap the gift of the Sabbath as I

---

7. Dorothy C. Bass, "Keeping Sabbath," in *Practicing Our Faith: A Way of Life for a Searching People,* ed. Dorothy C. Bass (San Francisco: Jossey-Bass, 1997), p. 76.

learned more about this ancient practice. Human beings are patterned, cyclical creatures who organize time in basic blocks. Anthropologists have determined that many ancient societies had rest days after a certain lunar phase, and early Roman society had an eight-day calendar. For those who follow the Abrahamic faiths — Jews, Christians, and Muslims — time is arranged in seven-day cycles: six days of work, followed by one of rest. One scientific study even suggests that there is a biological need for rest every seventh day.[8]

In the Jewish and Christian traditions, the direction to keep a Sabbath is one of the longest of the Ten Commandments, appearing in two slightly different forms in the Old Testament, both of which include extensive detail. Both versions call for work on six days and rest on one day, but each gives a different reason for the command.[9] In Exodus 20:8-11, we are told to observe the Sabbath because "in six days the LORD made heaven and earth, the sea, and all that is in them, but rested the seventh day; therefore the LORD blessed the sabbath day and consecrated it" (NRSV). We keep the Sabbath because it is a pattern established and grounded in the story of creation. God worked for six days, and then he rested. We should follow God's pattern, as we are made in God's image. Deuteronomy 5:12-15 provides a second reason:

> Observe the sabbath day and keep it holy, as the LORD your God commanded you. Six days you shall labor and do all your work. But the seventh day is a sabbath to the LORD your God; you shall not do any work — you, or your son or your daughter, or your male or female slave, or your ox or your donkey, or any of your livestock, or the resident alien in your towns, so that your male and female slave may rest as well as you. Remember that you were a slave in the land of Egypt, and the LORD your God brought you out from there with a mighty hand and an outstretched arm; therefore the LORD your God commanded you to keep the sabbath day.

As Egyptian slaves, the Israelites were not able to take a day off, but as free people, they can. God's deliverance from Egyptian bondage pro-

---

8. This study was done by Juan-Carlos Lerman at the University of Arizona; see Marva J. Dawn, *Keeping the Sabbath Wholly: Ceasing, Resting, Embracing, Feasting* (Grand Rapids: Wm. B. Eerdmans, 1989), p. 69.

9. Bass, "Keeping Sabbath," pp. 78-81.

vided the Israelites with freedom. By stopping work every seventh day, the people will remember this release from slavery, and they will not allow anyone else (even animals) to work. The establishment of the Sabbath thus testifies against slavery, bondage, and sin. Christians share with Jews these reasons for observing the Sabbath, but they have another reason to keep the Sabbath. Early Christians celebrated the first day of the week as an Easter day, because it was the day on which the disciples first encountered the risen Christ. They honored it by gathering together, feasting, and rejoicing. The pattern of God's creative work, the routine memory and celebration of God's redeeming and sustaining acts of liberation — creation, exodus, resurrection — these are the reasons why Christians keep the Sabbath.

Marva Dawn advises that the rhythm of six/one is more important than the precise day.[10] You probably know pastors or priests who dedicate their Mondays to quiet time, walking, reading novels, listening to music, going to movies, and so on. Many college professors have found that observing a Sabbath from sundown Saturday to sundown Sunday allows for a time of Sunday morning worship, the space for feasting and rest, but also the necessary period to prepare for a Monday-morning class. It's extremely hard at certain points in the academic year to keep from grading papers, writing exams, or revising lectures during a Sabbath period, but without exception, everyone that I know who has attempted to honor a twenty-four-hour hiatus in their professorial life has never found it detrimental to his or her job performance. Our natural tendency, however, is to work at a manic pace for five days, engage in a whirl of family and housekeeping activities on Saturday, attend church on Sunday morning, and then dive back into academic work Sunday afternoon. We need to make a conscious commitment to keep a twenty-four-hour Sabbath and plan our weekend activities around that commitment. I've heard many new faculty say, "I can't possibly take that much time off; I'm too busy." But you will be surprised how much more you can accomplish by taking time off, and I believe you will also discover God's faithfulness in equipping you for the remainder of your week.

A true Sabbath observance, however, incorporates more than ceasing work; it includes purposeful resting and celebrating. Sleeping in, taking a Sunday-afternoon nap, or going to bed early are obvious ways to rest; my grandfather, who worked hard physically five days a week in a factory and

10. Dawn, *Keeping the Sabbath Wholly*, p. xi.

one day a week on home improvement and maintenance, regularly took a Sunday-afternoon nap. But for someone who leads an academic life requiring constant reading, thinking, analyzing, and critiquing, resting the mind by engaging the body may prove more beneficial. For me, the physical labor of digging up dandelions and deadheading dahlias in my garden is supremely restful. This might not be the case if I were a flower grower, like my father. A Sabbath rest, whatever form it takes, provides fresh perspectives, creative insights, and extra energy for the coming six days. The Sabbath is also made for celebrating — participating in the sacrament in worship, or having friends over for soup after mass or church. Although the community in which I grew up emphasized prohibitions, my immediate family celebrated each Sunday morning with hard-boiled eggs and freshly made cinnamon rolls, and we eagerly anticipated watching "Walt Disney's Wonderful World of Color" — on our small black-and-white television set — each Sunday evening. One professor I know celebrates Sunday evenings with her three sons by indulging in an unconventional dinner of popcorn and soda. The boys look forward all week to the cessation of vegetable consumption and healthy drinks. As these examples suggest, discovering and selecting your own best ways to rest and celebrate, creating rituals for your family and yourself, is a key part of keeping the Sabbath.

I've spent a lot of time on the importance of Sabbath-keeping because I believe it is one of the most important ways for the mission-driven professor to flourish and keep his or her life in tune. A second guiding principle for shaping a flourishing academic life involves basic time management to defeat the constant tyranny of the urgent. The unique demands of academic life, Kenneth E. Foote explains, "mean that time management is not simply a process of making a work list and ranking the items in priority order. Such a list would imply that teaching, research, and service tasks are commensurate and can be readily compared and linearly ranked when, in fact, they are usually very difficult to judge side by side."[11] Foote has developed a visual aid for professors derived from Stephen Covey's *Seven Habits of Highly Effective People* (1989), in which tasks are classified in a two-dimensional matrix rather than in a one-dimensional list. Using a matrix of *Important–Non-important* and *Urgent–Not Urgent*, you can or-

---

11. Kenneth E. Foote, "Time Management," in *Aspiring Academics: A Resource Book for Graduate Students and Early Career Faculty*, ed. Michael Solem, Kenneth Foote, and Janice Monk (Upper Saddle River, N.J.: Pearson, 2009), p. 6.

ganize your academic tasks in a more useful fashion. (See figure below.) Foote comments, "If we spend all of our time addressing work tasks in the upper-left quadrant, we can quickly become exhausted without ever getting to some of our important, but not urgent work."[12] Many faculty with whom I've worked have found it useful to sort their tasks with this matrix and then to organize their workweek in order to spend some time on Important, Not Urgent tasks.

Time Management for Faculty

	Urgent	*Not Urgent*
Important	Teaching a class	Working on your current writing project
	Grading	Researching grant sources and ideas
	Meeting a publication deadline	Improving your teaching
	Mentoring a student in crisis	Advising a student club
Non-important	Social interruptions	Web discussion groups
	Some calls	Some calls
	Some mail and email	Some mail and email
	Some reports	Some reports
	Some meetings	Some meetings

Kenneth E. Foote, "Time Management," in *Aspiring Academics: A Resource Book for Graduate Students and Early Career Faculty,* ed. Michael Solem, Kenneth Foote, and Janice Monk (Upper Saddle River, N.J.: Pearson, 2009), p. 5 [slightly revised].

Both Sabbath-keeping and resisting the tyranny of the urgent provide an indispensable structure within which discrete decisions can be made and unexpected adjustments can be calibrated. Here are a few additional pieces of advice for this fine-tuning:

1. Don't overprepare. The number-one mistake made by new faculty, as we have discussed in Chapter 4, is spending too much time getting ready to teach. Set and enforce strict time limits on your preparation.
2. Just say no occasionally. You do not have to agree to do everything that your students or chair or dean or provost requests. When someone asks you to do something, always ask for at least a few days to think

12. Foote, "Time Management," pp. 6-7.

about the impact of saying yes on your life. Some of us (and it is often women, for some reason or other) have a tendency to say yes to every request: we're flattered that someone thinks we can help; we don't want to hurt the asker's feelings; the request involves an exciting or stimulating opportunity; we think we need to say yes in order to get tenure — the poor reasons for saying yes are manifold. Some academics, especially younger ones, exhibit a White Knight complex, feeling compelled to swoop to the rescue in order to get things done right or help a student in trouble. If someone comes to you with a sob story about needing a certain class in order to graduate, don't agree to supervise an independent study until you have checked with your department chair and the student's advisor. Perhaps that student ignored advice to take this class earlier, or didn't like the professor who was offering it. You don't have to save everyone. Sometimes the only circumstance in which one should say yes is when one says no to something else. A "no buddy" can help in processing and discerning your response to requests.

3. Learn e-mail discipline: turn off any mechanical signal that new e-mail has arrived, and limit your reading and responding to e-mail to once or maybe twice a day. I tell my students and colleagues that I read my e-mail first thing in the morning, but then I might not read it again the rest of the day. If someone is sick and going to miss class, needs a recommendation (immediately!), or can't make a committee meeting, that person needs to notify me before 9 A.M., or I might not get the message until the next day. As you read your e-mail, sort it immediately: put it in the trash, put it in a folder with a flag for the appropriate follow-up date, or deal with the issue then and there. It takes an immense amount of ruthless self-discipline to follow this rule, and it is one that I regularly violate, but when I do follow it, I find myself to be more efficient and productive. But I too often find it easier to read the latest discussion on facnet or answer a minor, non-urgent question than to tackle more complex and sensitive issues. I temporarily feel that I have accomplished more by zipping through fifty e-mails, but more often than not I've only done a lot of Urgent–Not Important work.

4. Don't completely neglect a social life during your first years of teaching. Try to tear yourself away from your desk and computer at least once a week to have lunch with another human being, whether that be a mentor or a fellow green professor.

5. Exercise at least three times a week. This can be combined with socializing; one friend of mine walks around Seattle's spectacular Green Lake at six A.M. every morning with a different person, using this time to make and maintain friendships that would otherwise be difficult in her life as a professor, associate dean, and mother of four. I feel privileged to join her once a week, even though I am not a morning person and would never get out of bed and walk around a lake by myself. Other faculty play basketball or racquetball once a week with colleagues or students. Neuroscience research — often ironically ignored by research-obsessed professors — demonstrates the intellectual as well as the physical benefits of exercise.

6. Realize that teaching is your priority, but during the course of a typical semester or quarter, make sure that you devote some time, no matter how minimal, to scholarship and community life. You don't need to balance these areas, but you do need some movement in each.

Taking a Vocational Inventory

Beyond these day-to-day and semester-to-semester strategies, conducting an annual vocational inventory is also a vital part of flourishing as an academic at a mission-driven institution. I recommend that you step back to reflect on the larger shape of your life annually. Either at the conclusion or the beginning of each academic year, take a few hours alone — on a beach or in a cabin or at a retreat center — to examine the past year and think about the upcoming one. Begin by naming and remembering your context: you are not on an academic fast-track and should not have fast-track R1 expectations. It's likely that your professional socialization, chance meetings at conferences with friends from graduate school, or conversations with graduate-school mentors have created a subconscious conditioning and set of professional expectations that may not be appropriate for your context. That's why it's important to articulate and embrace your situation honestly, to remind yourself of the cathedral which you are building, the particular garden plot that you have chosen to tend.

A vocational inventory should also involve identifying the unexpected improvisations that have occurred in the previous year. Typically your academic life will be concentrated on teaching, but there may also be other seasons in which you spend the majority of your time on research or writing, perhaps during a sabbatical or study leave, or doing university service by directing a self-study, chairing a department, or writing a major report. I've spoken before about the necessary period of adjustment that takes place during one's first two or three years as a professor at a mission-driven institution, during which time it is probably not realistic to think about doing much research or scholarship. And these seasons of professional life will also ebb and flow in relationship to what is happening in your family life (births, illnesses, deaths), church or parish life, and community life. Some faculty give less of themselves to their teaching and research for a period in order to serve on their local school board, reorganize a community food bank, or hold office in a national professional organization.

You also will need to consider what new improvisations need to be made in response in the upcoming year to changing circumstances. We and our institutions and supervisors must be careful that we don't just keep adding more and more to our plate without removing something else. Once I worked with a young female professor who loved teaching and advising students, who wanted to analyze and publish on the large pool of data she had gathered but had not touched in her dissertation, and who played a major leadership role in her church's refugee resettlement program. When she had her first child, she also began to develop a vision for the growth of her department, but she was having great difficulty in giving up some parts of her life in order to cope with the major new addition of a baby, much less beginning a leadership role in the department. It's simply impossible to just keep adding to an academic life without subtracting something. I advised her to give up her work in the refugee center, scale back her publication ambitions, and wait a few years before taking on major departmental responsibilities. There will be other seasons in her life. Once she has learned the ropes of a new institution, become a more proficient and efficient teacher, and her baby starts sleeping through the night, she will gradually be able to take up other activities.

A vocational inventory is a time to identify the shape of your dance. Use it to examine how the shape of your life is unfolding, how your balance and rhythm are shifting. Consider what new vocational metaphors might be appropriate at this point in your life. Re-ground yourself in the God-centered part of your vocation. Readjust, if necessary, your vocational focus to encompass your academic work without being confined to that work, and prayerfully decide what new improvisations you may need to make in the coming year.

Remembering the Beginning

One last ritual to assist in composing a flourishing academic life is to remember the beginning of your vocation. As a fan of the academic novel, I
especially appreciate Richard Russo's *Straight Man* (1997), a hilarious yet
poignant account of William Henry Devereaux Jr., the forty-nine-year-old
chair of the English department at West Central Pennsylvania University,
an undistinguished state school under constant threat of budget cuts. Unable to determine how many sections of freshman composition he can offer in the fall because he still has no budget in April, Devereaux resorts to
the unlikely tactic of announcing on television that he will kill a duck from
the campus pond every week until he gets his budget. (He does this while
holding a goose, but English professors are not well-known for their proficiency in the identification of fauna.) Devereaux has other problems. After
he unwittingly insults a feminist poet at a meeting, she hits him with a
spiral-bound notebook, snagging a nostril with the wire and inflicting a
seeping and tender wound that he nurses throughout the rest of the novel.
His father, William Henry Devereaux Sr., is a retired academic superstar,
the acclaimed Father of American Literary Criticism (with capital letters),
creating a Bloomian "anxiety of influence" beyond anything that the Romantic poets ever faced. Devereaux Jr. had always assumed that he would
stay at West Central for a few years and then move on to the Shangri-la of a
Carnegie 1 research institution, with graduate assistants, pie-in-the-sky
teaching loads, and unrestricted travel funds that wouldn't require five signatures to be released. Instead, he has written one book, received tenure,
built a big house, and sunk into the morass of campus politics.

Like all good satire, *Straight Man* provides us with a cautionary tale.
Devereaux's humorous adventures remind us never to lose sight of our vocation in the midst of the mundane grind of irresponsible students, cranky
colleagues, detail-obsessed administrators, boring meetings, and the
depths of contemporary critical jargon. And it also speaks volumes about
the unhappiness and sense of failure that will ensue when one is always
wishing that one is elsewhere — at another kind of institution, in another
part of the country, in the city, in the country, and so on. If we concentrate
our vision and energy on the green pastures beyond our domain, we will
inevitably fail to recognize the beauty and opportunities right before us.
Your life will never be in harmony if you always wish you were elsewhere.
That's why serious vocational reflection is mandatory during your first
professorial years. Either you must realize that you are unable to join the

institution's mission enthusiastically and so leave, or you must commit to pursuing that mission with diligence and devotion. Believing in the essentials of the mission, however, does not mean that you will agree with every current practice or idea; rather, it means that you are committed to helping the mission to be implemented in increasingly better ways, working to improve and develop the mission faithfully.

Occasionally we need to step back from the pragmatic details of teaching, scholarship, and service, or educational philosophy and politics, to consider our work within the context of our Christian vocation, as part of the ongoing creative activity of the Triune God. This book has attempted to give you some preliminary starting points, some ways into this reflection, whether through agreement or disagreement, but these issues can be fruitfully pondered for the rest of your professorial life. College professors traditionally have been understood as those who pursue truth and search for knowledge, and who then share or spread that truth through their teaching and scholarship. In today's academy, there is much discussion about whether we *discover* or *create* truth (modernism versus postmodernism). But I think about our quest for truth as one that involves *exploring* and *developing*. All truth and knowledge have been created by God and are continually sustained by God, so as human beings we are developing and elaborating upon God's created possibilities. We explore and develop the physical, social, and cultural world. Think about your particular field of endeavor within this context. We have been called to discover things about X and their contexts, to help them unfold in ways that honor God and help others.

For me, as a professor of English, that X represents the various historical, cultural, and aesthetic texts that human beings and communities have developed in response to God and God's creation. I look closely at these texts and their contexts to help the world continue to unfold in ways that lead to shalom. As a teacher, I then help others to explore, discover, develop, and create. I contribute to the formation of students and help them understand vocation in the full-bodied sense. In this act of helping students to develop, I too participate in God's ongoing creative activity. Identifying, exploring, interpreting, judging — gaining in knowledge and truth and love.

But we are also called to wonder, and I want to conclude by thinking about the calling of the professor in light of our calling to wonder, as it is an act so often overlooked in the contemporary academic world represented by William Devereaux. And the sense of wonder is integral to our efforts to remember and live out of vocation in flourishing ways.

In a brief essay called "A Sense of Wonder," the Greek Orthodox bishop Kallistos Ware describes an Orthodox ceremony known as the Great Blessing of the Waters, which is always performed on January 6, the Feast of Theophany or Epiphany. On this day, the Orthodox Church commemorates the baptism of Christ in the Jordan (not the three wise men). The blessing is often held outdoors, by a river or a spring, or on an ocean beach. Water is placed in a large bowl, prayers are said over it, the grace and power of the Holy Spirit are invoked, and ultimately a cross is plunged into the water. Ware says, "In an unexpected way this ceremony of the Great Blessing of the Waters helps us to understand the purpose, from a Christian standpoint, of a college or university."[13] In the Orthodox tradition, our baptism is seen as a purification from sin. But Christ is sinless. Why, then, should he be baptized, as John the Baptist himself inquires. The imagery of washing explains the Orthodox answer very simply and effectively. We are dirty, and we go down into clean water and come out cleansed and sanctified. But Christ is clean. At his baptism he goes down into the dirty water and cleans *the waters,* making them pure. The liturgical text for the Feast of Epiphany reads, "Today the Master has come to sanctify the nature of the waters." It isn't the waters that sanctify Christ, but Christ who imparts holiness to the waters, and by extension to the entire material creation. The world is fallen, broken and shattered by the effects of sin, but God himself enters this world in the Incarnation, cleaning and healing the brokenness through his crucifixion and resurrection. Ware explains, "What we are doing, then, at every celebration of Epiphany, at every Blessing of the Waters, is to reaffirm our sense of wonder before the essential goodness and beauty of the world, as originally created by God and as now recreated in Christ."[14]

How does this help us understand the vocation of the college professor? The word *education* comes from the Latin *educere,* "to evoke," and a college or university is precisely a place in which, with rigor and discipline, we evoke and cultivate a sense of wonder. For me, studying literature is one way we develop our sense of wonder before the universe that God has made — a universe with intricate languages and linguistic resources, a universe that makes sense to us only through narrative and metaphor, a universe in which ideas and emotions and actions are all embodied in words, a universe in which human beings are makers and discoverers of meaning

---

13. Kallistos Ware, "A Sense of Wonder," in *The Inner Kingdom,* vol. 1 of *The Collected Works* (New York: St. Vladimir's Seminary Press, 2001), pp. 69-74.

14. Ware, "A Sense of Wonder," p. 71.

through their use of words. For others, that sense of wonder is developed in other disciplines, with other methods and other material.

The Great Blessing of the Waters is performed not only at Epiphany, however, but also at the start of any major task or period, such as on the first day of the month, at the blessing of a foundation stone, or at the commencement of an academic year. At Seattle Pacific we begin every year with a formal convocation at which faculty, staff, and students repeat words taken from a Wesleyan service of dedication, as a communal reminder of the bigger picture. Many institutions similarly mark the beginning of their year. This sense of wonder, of potential, of the possibility of a fresh start is one of my favorite aspects of academic life. As college professors, we have a continual chance to begin over; when it seems as if a class is a complete failure, I always can look forward to the end of the quarter or the end of the year. *Next time I'll get it right!* I tell myself. *Next year I'll teach better, I'll have my life more in balance, and my students will actually participate in class discussions.*

One key to leading a balanced life is to periodically remember your own call, thus putting the daily grind or current crisis into a larger perspective. For some of us that call came as a sudden revelation; for others it was a gradual unfolding or growing in understanding. But no matter how our call occurred, we had a sense of excitement, a feeling of possibility, of hope. Can you remember your own initial call to be a professor? My call came when I was twenty; some of you heard this call earlier in life; others, later. Do you remember the sense of discovery, potential, and excitement that you felt? Part of our challenge is to keep this sense of calling alive, even as growth, change, and adjustments occur. We can renew our calling by remembering our initial calling. We do this with other important events in life, such as anniversaries and birthdays. On my son's birthday every year, I tell the story of his birth-day — his prompt arrival on his due date, my waking up to find my water broken, the driving to the hospital through the icy streets of Grand Rapids, my request about six hours into labor to just call the entire thing off.

Perhaps we need liturgies or rituals in which we remember how we came to be professors. Remembering our calling, we can experience renewal. Remembering and rehearsing: we need to share these memories of the discernment of our task with others, to tell our own stories of discovery. Ask your new colleagues about how they entered this unusual profession and talk with others about your call. I dare say that you will find an astonishingly varied number of stories. Wonder at and celebrate that variety.

Sample Syllabus Template

[Regular print is sample text; italic print is advice.]

XXXX 1234: Name of Class

Term 201X

Professor:	Emily Dickinson
Office:	The Homestead, Amherst
Phone:	What?
E-mail:	Huh?
Office hours:	Oh, no!

Mission:

Include the University's mission statement and then any particular mission statement or goals of your school/department/program. The course description that follows should connect to these mission statements.

Seattle Pacific University seeks to change the world and engage the culture by graduating students of competence and character, cultivating people of wisdom, and modeling a grace-filled community.

Course Description:

Start with a provocative question that the course will address: Why would a Christian be a scholar? *(Christianity and Scholarship).* What is an American? *(American Literature Survey). Next, provide a statement that briefly describes the course, its main goal, and why it is important. Finally, sum up how the course is connected to the mission statements above, and how it fits into the overall University curriculum: Is it part of the major? The exploratory curriculum? Does it have prerequisites? What might a student take after this course?*

Required Texts:

I usually give these with full bibliographic citations, following the correct style manual for my discipline. I can then point to them as examples later.

Marsden, George. *The Outrageous Idea of Christian Scholarship.* Oxford: Oxford University Press, 1997.

Learning Objectives:

Learning objectives should be phrased in terms of what students are able to do when they've completed the course. Using verbs from Bloom's taxonomy of education objectives is helpful. Remember, the goal is not to "cover" material, but to help students learn.

By the end of this quarter, students will be able to

- Describe . . .
- Analyze . . .
- Evaluate . . .

Learning Activities:

This section describes what students need to do to successfully complete the course and achieve the learning objectives listed in the previous section. The message you are sending is that students are responsible for learning to take place. Here are a few examples of the kinds of things that can be included:

1. Read assigned work by the date indicated.
2. Attend class faithfully, arrive promptly, listen courteously, and participate actively in class presentations, writing, and discussions.
3. Write and revise one short essay.
4. Take two exams.
5. Complete a group research project.

Some faculty include something like this: In addition, we will all attempt to
model a grace-filled community by respecting the opinions and work of
others and by coming to class prepared to participate.

Policy Notes:

*This is a crucial section that spells out all the rules and regulations for the
course. Some of these policies, indicated with an asterisk, address issues that
should be covered in every syllabus in some way or other. Other policies are
samples of matters on which different faculty may have different preferences.
It's useful during the first week of class to discuss with your students your reasons for having policies, some of which might be to better facilitate learning,
to minimalize distractions, to help students learn to be responsible enough to
enter the workforce, to keep you organized, and so on.*

1. *Academic Integrity: The current edition of the SPU's Undergraduate
   Catalog describes the University's commitment to academic integrity,
   which is breached by academic dishonesty of various kinds. Among
   these is turning in another's work as your own and committing plagiarism, which is the copying of portions of another's words from a published or electronic source without acknowledgment of that source.
   The penalty for a breach of academic integrity is a failing grade for the
   work in question on the first offense and a failing grade for the course
   as a whole with repeated offenses.
2. *Exam Policy: Note when the final exam is scheduled and avoid making conflicting travel plans. I will not re-schedule final exams.
3. *Disability Statement: In accordance with Section 504 of the Rehabil-
   itation Act of 1973 and the Americans with Disabilities Act of 1990,
   students with specific disabilities that qualify for academic accommodations should contact Disabled Student Services (DSS) in the
   Center for Learning. DSS in turn will send a Disability Verification

Letter to the course instructor indicating what accommodations have been approved.

4. *Emergency Procedure: Note the emergency procedures posted in the classroom or laboratory, and note the emergency exits. In case of an emergency (fire, earthquake, hazardous material spillage, bomb threat, etc.), the class will evacuate the building and gather in the [location]. Please try to stay together so that we can check that everyone has made it safely out of the building.

5. Course Evaluation: I hope that you will participate in an online evaluation of this course and its instructor in a thoughtful and constructive manner. The evaluation data is used to make improvements in the course, and your feedback is considered when selecting textbooks, designing teaching methods, and preparing assignments. Courses are evaluated using the Banner Course Evaluation System. All answers are completely confidential — your name is not stored with your answers in any way. In addition, I will not see any results of the evaluation until after final grades are submitted to the University.

6. Inclement Weather: The University maintains an Emergency Closure Hotline (206-281-2800). In the event of inclement weather or an emergency that might close the university, please call the Hotline for the most up-to-date closure information or check the SPU Web site. Both will be updated before six A.M. Information on evening classes, events, and athletic games will also be updated.

7. In order to receive a final grade above an E, you must complete both essays and take both exams.

8. Due dates are firm; exceptions will be made only for dire illness or emergencies, not poor planning or lots of work.

9. *Late work will be lowered one grade (from A to A-) for each 24-hour period, including weekends.

10. Please turn off your cell phones at the beginning of class, or set them to silent mode, so that you don't disturb our time together.

11. You are welcome to bring food and drinks to class, but try not to be too distracting when consuming them. Also, please take care of other personal needs (i.e., bathroom visits) before class begins.

Evaluation:

It is important to indicate to the students how they will be assessed; how much various activities weigh. Some faculty members use percentages, like those below; others will assign points and provide a point/grade chart.

Attendance, participation, and in-class writing	20
Essay	20
Poster presentation	10
Prospectus	50
	100

Syllabus and due dates:

Include a list of days that the class will meet, the topics to be covered, and any major assignments that will be due. Try to stick to these dates as much as possible, with obvious latitude when it comes to snow days, instructor illness, and so on.

Acknowledgments

My initial foray into faculty development began many years ago when Karen Longman, then at the Council for Christian Colleges and Universities, invited me to join a team made up of Arthur Holmes, Stan Gaede, and Harold Heie. Together, we led a week-long summer workshop for new CCCU faculty for many years. I'm grateful for that initial invitation and for the wisdom, grace, and friendship of that working group. Movies and ice cream cemented our bond.

This book could never have been written without all that I learned, as well, from the hundreds of new faculty I met during those CCCU workshops, over fifteen years of leading the New Faculty Seminar at Seattle Pacific University, and through many workshops and talks given at numerous faith-based institutions. In addition, I've learned much about the joys, perils, and challenges of faculty life through working with the Lilly National Network, the Lilly Endowment–sponsored Programs for Theological Exploration of Vocation, and the Pew-sponsored Preparing Future Faculty Program. Consequently, these pages contain much communal wisdom.

Finally, special thanks to SPU for providing me with a sabbatical during which I completed this project; to Steve Perisho, from the SPU library, for research assistance; to SPU Academic Vice President Les Steele for his unflagging support for faculty development; and to all the kind folks at Eerdmans who have exercised great patience during this book's extended gestation.